NATURAL RESOURCE ECONOMICS

Recent Economic Thought Series

Warren J. Samuels, Editor
Michigan State University
East Lansing, Michigan, U.S.A.

Other titles in the series:
Feiwel, G. R., *Samuelson and Neoclassical Economics*
Wade, L. L., *Political Economy: Modern Views*
Zimbalist, A., *Comparative Economic Systems: Recent Views*
Darity, W., *Labor Economics: Modern Views*
Jarsulic, M., *Money and Macro Policy*
Samuelson, L., *Microeconomic Theory*

This series is devoted to works that present divergent views or the development, prospects, and tensions within some important research areas of international economic thought. Among the fields covered are macromonetary policy public finance , labor and political economy. The emphasis of the series is on providing a critical, constructive view of each of these fields as well as a forum through which leading scholars of international reputation may voice their perspectives on important related issues. Each volume in the series will be self-contained together these volumes will provide dramatic evidence of the variety of economic thought within the scholarly community.

NATURAL RESOURCE ECONOMICS

Policy Problems and Contemporary Analysis

edited by
Daniel W. Bromley
University of Wisconsin

Kluwer Nijhoff Publishing
a member of the Kluwer Academic Publishers Group
Boston/Dordrecht/Lancaster

Distributors

for the United States and Canada: Kluwer Academic Publishers, 190 Old Derby Street, Hingham, MA, 02043, USA

for the UK and Ireland: Kluwer Academic Publishers, MTP Press Limited, Falcon House, Queen Square, Lancaster LA1 1RN, UK

for all other countries: Kluwer Academic Publishers Group, Distribution Centre, P.O. Box 322, 3300 AH Dordrecht, The Netherlands

Library of Congress Cataloging-in-Publication Data
Main entry under title:

Natural resource economics.
(Recent economic thought series)
Includes index.
1. Natural resources—Addresses, essays, lectures.
2. Economic policy—Addresses, essays, lecturers.
3. Externalities (Economics)—Addresses, essays, lectures.
I. Bromley, Daniel W., 1940- . II. Series: Recent economic thought.
HC59.N318 1985 333.7 85-24215
ISBN 0-89838-203-3

PRINTED IN THE UNITED STATES.

Contents

Contributing Authors

Glen D. Anderson
Economic Analysis Division
U.S. Environmental Protection Agency
401 M Street, SW
Washington, DC 20460

Richard C. Bishop
Department of Agricultural Economics
University of Wisconsin
Taylor Hall, 427 Lorch Street
Madison, WI 53706

Daniel W. Bromley
Department of Agricultural Economics
University of Wisconsin
Taylor Hall, 427 Lorch Street
Madison, WI 53706

Ronald G. Cummings
Department of Economics
University of New Mexico
1915 Roma, NE
Albuquerque, NM 87131

Ann Fisher
Economic Analysis Division
U. S. Environmental Protection Agency
401 M Street, SW
Washington, DC 20460

A. Myrick Freeman, III
Department of Economics
Bowdoin College
Brunswick, ME 04011

Geoffrey Heal
Graduate School of Business
Columbia University
New York, NY 10027

Kenneth E. McConnell
Department of Agricultural and Resource Economics
University of Maryland
College Park, MD 20742

Wallace E. Oates
Department of Economics
University of Maryland
College Park, MD 20742

Spencer R. Pearse
Department of Economics
University of New Mexico
1915 Roma, NE
Albuquerque, NM 87131

James P. Quirk
Division of the Humanities and Social Sciences 228–77
California Institute of Technology
Pasadena, CA 91125

Alan Randall
Department of Agricultural Economics
Ohio State University
Columbus, OH 43210

V. Kerry Smith
Department of Economics and Business Administration
Vanderbilt University
Nashville, TN 37235

Tom Tietenberg
Department of Economics
Colby College
Waterville, ME 04901

PREFACE

When approached by Warren Samuels, the series editor, about organizing a volume on natural resource economics, I was at a loss as to how one might possibly capture in "several major essays plus several shorter comments thereon" all of the diverse activities that fall within this exciting discipline. I was further asked to have the book take an "affirmative but constructively critical look at its subject." The volume was to be interpretative, it was to be reasonably comprehensive, and yet it was to attempt to present divergent views on the "development, tensions, present status, and, especially, possible lines of development of each field."

Upon reflection, I decided to have the book focus on natural resource economics as a distinctly applied policy science.

Hence the title: *Natural Resource Economics: Policy Problems and Contemporary Analysis*.

While this allowed clarification of a particular sort, it did little to narrow the range of policy issues that ought to be considered candidates for inclusion. But it did seem, after some thought, that three broad issues persist at center stage in natural resource policy. These are: (1) the proper regard for future generations; (2) the ubiquity and persistence of unwanted joint costs (externalities) among citizens of an increasingly crowded and technologically threatening world; and (3) the policy conflict between goods and services that pass through recognized markets and hence carry prices (some would say values), and those that are not marketed—or are non-marketable—and so cannot be easily reckoned vis-a-vis those with accepted prices attached.

It should be clear at the outset that these three classes of natural resource policy problems provide an arena for exploring the tensions that exist within the sub-discipline. While the chapters and comments that follow are not overly contentious, the reader will detect a broad sense of uneasiness among all of the contributors as regards the conventional wisdom, as well as the suitability of dissenting views.

In his chapter "The Intertemporal Problem" Geoff Heal notes that much of the early work on efficiency of resource use was concerned with either capital or labor—rarely with natural resources, particularly of the non-renewable type. Heal turns to the problem of non-renewable (or, as he calls them, exhaustible) resources by addressing the issues of choosing among depletion rates, and then selecting the optimal rate. Heal goes on to discuss the characteristics of an efficient allocation over time, and the matter of intergenerational equity.

Heal concludes by noting that there are, in general, infinitely many efficient resource-depletion programs. One of these will conform to a concept of intertemporal equity, and it is this one that becomes the optimal depletion program.

Spencer Pearse and Ron Cummings take rather quick issue with Heal, particularly regarding his assertion that few economists were interested in the intertemporal problems surrounding natural resources. They go on to challenge, and with some vigor, the discussions about discounting and utilitarian approaches to depletion. Here the main disagreement concerns the assumption that the time of extinction is independent of our intertemporal consumption patterns.

In the companion comment on Heal's chapter, James Quirk approvingly notes that Heal has elucidated some of the basic ethical dilemmas of the intergenerational problem, as well as commented on the logical and computational problems therein. Quirk's most interesting observation concerns the mechanism for aggregating preferences across members of society—the social welfare function. Following Hansson, he notes that while the Arrow Impossibility Theorem holds when dealing with a finite population, the intertemporal problem introduces an expanding population in which case there are infinitely many aggregating mechanisms that will satisfy the Arrow axioms. This happy result is overshadowed, however, by the realization that any particular finite population is immediately outweighted (outvoted) by the large mass of the yet unborn. Hence, the Arrow axioms require bare subsistence for all populations in the "foreseeable future" in order to provide for the masses yet to come.

Quirk reminds us that an actual Pareto improvement is impossible in an intergenerational sense owing to the infeasibility of intergenerational compensation of losers (us) by gainers (them). Quirk closes with an illustration of an important problem for natural resource economists. Specifically, he points out that a solution to the intertemporal problem is made difficult by the ethical issues raised by Heal, but also by the measurement issues facing the applied economist who attempts to conduct benefit-cost analysis of a program with intertemporal implications.

Turning to the problems of joint costs, my chapter is concerned with matters of externalities—their definition and their resolution. My primary intent in the chapter is to remind the reader that externality problems are nothing more than entitlement problems. That is, since joint costs are those that transcend the nominal boundary of decision-making units, externalities can only be understood by understanding how those boundaries are defined, how it is possible that certain decision units are free to ignore trans-boundary impacts, and how the structure of entitlements—that is institutional arrangements—will influence the incentives of the various parties voluntarily to resolve joint-cost situations.

It is my contention that economists are too innocent of the legal foundations of capitalism, and that this lack of knowledge is manifest in numerous debates about the efficiency of taxes and subsidies while little interest is shown in the larger institutional environment that defines joint-cost situations.

Wallace Oates extends my small-numbers examples to the more realistic large-numbers case, and suggests that for these more prevalent situations the naive Coasian argument is pure fiction. In each a world, where there are many polluters and/or many recipients, Oates believes that there are compelling arguments in favor of quantity-directed policies rather than the price-directed policies so long favored by economists (viz. effluent taxes). He elaborates by citing several studies that support the relative efficiency of a marketable permit system as opposed to the classic pollution tax scheme.

Tom Tietenberg considers my prognosis to be far too bleak, but seems pleased with the extensions into the legal dimension which offer, at least in his view, great promise for future scholarship. He quite properly points out that my general concern for the victims of "unwanted costs" can be carried to the extreme. I was remiss for not paying more attention to the general problem of ascertaining the "cheapest cost avoider." Of course. "cheapest" is a loaded term since existing institutions determine the costs for the various parties to an externality; and there remains the problem of the larger moral question attending the conflict. While his point is a good one, the sunglasses example is hardly the stuff of contemporary environmental disputes.

Tietenberg goes on to talk of the role of presumptive rights and the status quo in the implementation of air-quality improvements. He has been an important participant in the theoretical as well as practical dimensions of emissions trading and his insights into this process are valuable.

Moving from the domains of time and joint costs to that of resource valuation, we have two chapters, the first concerned with valuation studies, and the second with the role of such studies in the policy process. The first chapter, by Glen Anderson and Richard Bishop, is primarily concerned with methodological issues that attend efforts to assign monetary values to amenities. They survey three general approaches to this valuation problem—two that are "related-market approaches" and one that refers to the contingency that a market for amenities exists. The related-market approaches are the familiar *travel-cost* method, and the *hedonic-price* technique. The *contingent-valuation* method calls for personal interviews in search of indications of value if markets did exist.

In a synthesis of the three approaches, Anderson and Bishop note that researchers will most often be faced with a choice of the contingent-valuation method or one of the two related-market approaches. In making this choice, Anderson and Bishop caution against several problems with the related-market approaches, and come out—on balance—favoring the contingent-valuation method in many circumstances.

In his comment on the chapter, Rick Freeman addresses several valuation issues that were not addressed by Anderson and Bishop; he then offers comments on the chapter, and concludes with some observations on the comparative assessment offered by Anderson and Bishop. In his elaboration, Freeman reminds us that the three approaches covered by Anderson and Bishop do not exhaust the possible methods for imputing amenity values. He goes on to explore "production or market values" and the ways in which one might estimate them. Another approach is within the household production framework, where individuals make expenditures to avoid environmental disamenities.

Freeman addresses, in a brief section, the problems associated with an automatic acceptance of the neoclassical paradigm upon which the three approaches of Anderson and Bishop rest. He concludes with a challenge to economists to undertake a systematic discussion of the criteria and appropriate framework for choosing among techniques.

Ted McConnell raises the very obvious point that the results of empirical work are interjected into the public-decision-making arena under a variety of circumstances; in some settings those results will only be noted in passing; in other cases those results—as well as the methods employed to obtain those results—will be the subject of careful inquiry. He reminds us that the methods of evaluation must be convincing outside of the narrow scientific arena in which they were produced. He notes two ways in which the measurement of amenity values will differ from the idealized scientific process: (1) the techniques must be understood by nonspecialists; and (2) goodness-of-fit criteria cannot be used to compare competing approaches.

He goes on to offer a nice summary of the strengths and weaknesses of the three valuation approaches.

In the final chapter Alan Randall does—as we have come to expect of him—an interesting and compelling job of discussing the valuation problem in a more explicit policy context. He reminds us of the philosophical antecedents of political economy; and he challenges those who would deny the validity of benefit-cost analysis in general, and the valuing of environmental amenities in particular. The benefit-cost test is rejected as an attempt to impose on governmental choice the alien values of the market. Rather, it is a test of the potential for Pareto improvements, and this he regards as the ultimate utilitarian criterion derived from an explicit theory of government.

He concludes with the observation that the fundamental role of nonmarket valuation of amenities is to alter the terms of the public debate over environmental policy. By providing seemingly commensurate indications of potential benefits and costs, both sides—environmentalists and developers—are forced to consider dimensions of the choice problem that they might rather disregard.

Ann Fisher brings to her task the important perspective of a government official daily involved in environmental policy. She reminds us that differences in data availability (and quality) hold important implications for the level of sophistication with which resource valuation work can proceed. And this, in turn, is critical for the degree of sophistication of the ultimate benefit-cost analysis. Her view warrants careful consideration by researchers and students of environmental policy.

In the final comment, Kerry Smith questions Randall's assault on a "straw man," and proceeds to offer an instructive inquiry into benefit-cost analysis employing literature that may not be familiar to many readers. This is followed with the reminder that benefit-cost analysis is never the sole information set on which public decisions are based.

Smith disagrees with Randall's position that Executive Order 12291 was an attempt to make it more difficult for government regulation of the private economy. He offers the possibility that the call for a benefit-cost analysis contained in EO 12291 came precisely because of the multiple objectives of public decisions. The more complete evaluation called for by the Order offers the chance to evaluate more systematically the opportunity costs of meeting these several objectives in terms of their implications for net national income.

Smith believes that for all of the problems with benefit-cost analysis, large national income gains can be realized from only incremental modifications in public choices. And, developing a point made by Ted McConnell in his earlier comment, Smith argues that progress in the development of valuation methods requires that more attention be given to procedures for assessing that authenticity of the various approaches used in benefit estimation.

It is my hope that this collection will stimulate and encourage new perspectives on the problems of natural resource policy and analysis.

NATURAL RESOURCE ECONOMICS

1 THE INTERTEMPORAL PROBLEM

Geoffrey Heal

Economists have traditionally been much concerned with defining what is meant by the efficient, or indeed optimal, use of resources, and with questioning whether the unhampered play of market forces will achieve such a state; if not, why not, and what forms of government intervention are in consequence most necessary and appropriate.

Though much intellectual energy has been devoted to the issue of how society uses its resources, in the extended sense of the word, and how those use patterns can be altered, it is fair to say that those involved in this work, at least this century, have always had at the back of their minds an interpretation of the word "resources" that more or less restricts it to capital and labor: certainly most of the concrete examples they have chosen to study have involved capital, or labor, or both. Of course, this is not surprising when one considers the conditions under which this theory evolved: during the 1930s the dominant economic problem was clearly the appalling misuse of society's labor resources, and during and immediately after the war it was generally seen as a shortage of, or the existence of an outdated stock of, capital equipment. To find examples of resource-allocation theorists explicitly concerned with the use of the earth's nonrenewable resources as exemplars of their problems, one has, bar one notable exception (Harold Hotelling) in the 1930s, to go back to the nineteenth century. Again, this is not surprising: in the eighteenth and nineteenth centuries, the ownership and productivity of land were clearly of great importance in determining the distribution of income, and the timing and location of the industrial revolution in the United Kingdom were greatly influenced by the exhaustion of traditional resource supplies and the availability of others. So to nineteenth-century man, it would have seemed unthinkable that one could explain the dynamics of an economy, or analyze the process of production and exchange, without giving special attention to the role of natural resources. Yet, amazing though this would seem to nineteenth-century man, this is just the procedure adopted by most twentieth-century economists—presumably reflecting the fact that for the first two-thirds of this century, exhaustible resource constraints have not been important for industrialized countries: these countries either possessed their own supplies of resources, which they felt to be adequate, or felt confident of importing them in unlimited amounts from developing countries, initially in many cases because they controlled these as parts of the colonial system, and subsequently because though independent, the supplying countries remained politically quiescent, with foreign exchange needs so great that they could be relied on to export unlimited amounts of their principal (often only) exports.

One of the points that emerges from this brief review is that though economists have traditionally been very concerned with the allocation of a society's resources, the particular category of resource on which they have chosen to focus attention has varied in response to the economic and social conditions of the times—from natural resources in the nineteenth century, to labor in the 1930s and capital subsequently. Naturally the wheel has now turned full circle: increasing intellectual effort has recently been focussed on issues raised by the existence of exhaustible resources.

When one is discussing the use of exhaustible resources, one basic issue dominates all others, at least in the long view. And that is, quite simply, *how fast should we use them up*? For something that is important, is destroyed in use, and is available only in limited amounts, we *have* to take a position on this question. Clearly some groups, notably conservationists, feel that we are using resources "too fast." On the other hand, it is more-or-less explicit in much political and press discussion of these matters that the sooner we can use the resources the better. Who is right here?

I shall begin to tackle this issue with a brief review of factors relevant in (1) choosing between depletion rates and (2) selecting an optimal depletion rate. Fundamental are considerations of efficiency and of equity—not of equity between those currently alive, but of equity between present and future, between current and subsequent generations. Clearly, the faster we consume exhaustible resources, the less is left for our children and our childrens' children; and so, other things being equal, the lower will be the living standard they can achieve. Thus over the long run, we must strike a balance between our own wishes and those of our successors. This clearly involves some analysis of what might seem equitable in this field. Note that there is an important difference between this problem of intergenerational economic equity and the problem of achieving economic equity among those currently alive, who are members of the current generation. The poor of the present generation are alive and can press their case; obviously, although the rich may choose not to act in response to this pressure, they cannot be entirely unaware of the problem. But future generations, whose well-being is at stake in the intergenerational problem, have no way of presenting their case. And if the rich of today can largely neglect the present poor, who are here to press their case, then the future will need very articulate spokesmen if they are to obtain a fair hearing.

My plan is to devote the next two sections to analyzing and characterizing the concepts of efficiency and of equity in an intertemporal context, and then in a final section to pull these together into an analysis of how one formulates the problem of choosing a depletion rate. In the process I shall highlight the similarities and differences between the atemporal and intertemporal cases. This will give us an insight into the importance and distinctiveness of the time dimension in resource-use problems.

Characterizing an Efficient Allocation

In this section I shall be more formal and address myself to the question of how to characterize an efficient intertemporal allocation of exhaustible resources?[1] By what signals can we test whether a particular pattern of allocation is efficient?

Consider an economy where output Y is given by

$$Y_t = G(K_t, R_t, t)$$

where K_t is the capital stock at time t, and R_t is the rate of use of an exhaustible resource.[2] G is assumed increasing, concave, and twice continuously differentiable in K and R—the presence of t as an argument reflects the possibility of technical progress. Output may be consumed (C_t) or invested ($dK_t/dt = \dot{K}_t$) and S_t is the resource stock remaining at t:

$$S_t = S_0 - \int_0^t R_t d_t \qquad \text{so} \qquad \dot{S}_t = -R_t$$

We shall describe an evolution $\{K_t, S_t, R_t, C_t\}_0^\infty$ of this economy as *intertemporally inefficient* if there exists another feasible program $\{\bar{K}_t, \bar{S}_t, \bar{R}_t, \bar{C}_t\}_0^\infty$ such that $\bar{C}_t \geq C_t$ for all t, and $\bar{C}_t > C_t$ for some t. If a feasible program is not intertemporally inefficient, then it is *intertemporally efficient*. This criterion of efficiency defines a partial ordering over feasible programs. In general, there are infinitely many efficient programs. In figure 1-1, α and β are efficient, and γ is inefficient.

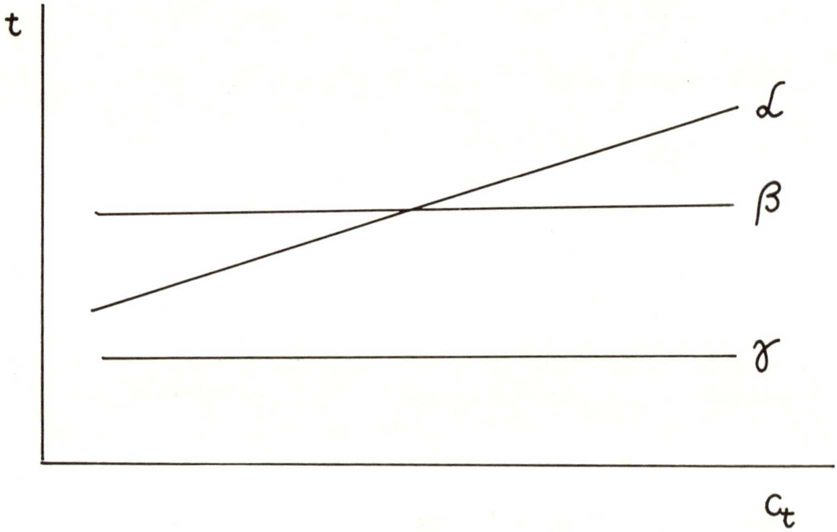

Figure 1-1. Three possible allocation programs.

As by assumption the marginal productivity of the resource, $\partial G/\partial R$, is positive, it is necessary for efficiency that over the relevant time horizon (assumed infinite here) all of the resource should be used up, i.e., it is necessary that

$$\lim_{t\to\infty} S_t = 0$$

However, this condition is clearly not sufficient: one could have $K_t = Y_t$ for all t, so $C = 0$ for all t, and

$$\lim_{t\to\infty} S_t = 0$$

In order to characterize efficiency more fully, we suppose

$$\lim_{K\to 0} \partial G/\partial K = \lim_{R\to 0} \partial G/\partial R = \infty$$

and restrict our attention to programs where K_t, R_t, $C_t > 0$ for all $t > 0$.

Imagine to begin with that time is measured in discrete intervals of length θ. Subsequently we shall take the limit as $\theta \to 0$. Along a program $(K_t, S_t, R_t, C_t)_0^\infty$, $C_t\theta$ and $R_t\theta$ by convention represent the levels of consumption and resource utilization during the interval $(t, t+\theta)$. Let $(\bar{K}_t, \bar{S}_t, \bar{R}_t, \bar{C}_t)_0^\infty$ denote a feasible program where $\bar{K}_t, \bar{R}_t, \bar{C}_t > 0$ for all $t \geqslant 0$. Consider two adjacent intervals of time, $(t, t+\theta)$ and $(t+\theta, t+2\theta)$. The idea now is to see if, by keeping the program entirely unchanged at all intervals other than these two, one cannot reap a higher level of consumption during $(t, t+\theta)$ without reducing the level of consumption during $(t+\theta, t+2\theta)$. If one can, the original program must be inefficient. In the two intervals concerned, we have

$$\begin{aligned} C_t\theta + K_{t+\theta} - K_t &= G(K_t, R_t, t)\theta \\ C_{t+\theta}\theta + K_{t+2\theta} - K_{t+\theta} &= G(K_{t+\theta}R_{t+\theta}, t+\theta)\theta \end{aligned} \tag{1.1}$$

Write $I_t\theta = K_{t+\theta} - K_t$ and $I_{t+\theta}\theta = K_{t+2\theta} - K_{t+\theta}$ for investment carried out during the two adjacent intervals. If $(\bar{K}_t, \bar{S}_t, \bar{R}_t, \bar{C}_t)_0^\infty$ is intertemporally efficient it will not be possible to increase C_t while holding $\bar{C}_{t+\theta}, \bar{K}_t, \bar{K}_{t+2\theta}, \bar{S}_t$, and $\bar{S}_{t+2\theta}$ fixed in equation 1.1. Thus, conducting a variation on the first equation in 1.1 gives

$$\Delta C_t + \Delta I_t = G_{R_t}\Delta R_t \tag{1.2}$$

Similarly conducting a variation on the second equation in 1.1 yields

$$\Delta I_{t+\theta} = G_{K_{t+\theta}}\Delta K_{t+\theta} + G_{R_{t+\theta}}\Delta R_{t+\theta} \tag{1.3}$$

Since $\bar{K}_t$ and $\bar{K}_{t+2\theta}$ are held fixed in this variation, $\Delta I_t + \Delta I_{t+\theta} = 0$. Likewise, since $\bar{S}_t$ and $\bar{S}_{t+2\theta}$ are held fixed, $\Delta R_t + \Delta R_{t+\theta} = \theta$. Adding equations 1.2 and 1.3 then yields

$$\Delta C_t = (G_{R_t} - G_{R_{t+\theta}})\Delta R_t + G_{K_{t+\theta}}\Delta K_{t+\theta} \tag{1.4}$$

Since by assumption $(\bar{K}_t, \bar{S}_t, \bar{R}_t, \bar{C}_t)_0^\infty$ is efficient, the proposed variation can yield no extra consumption during $(t, t+\theta)$. Hence $\Delta C_t = 0$. Since $\bar{K}_t$ is given, one has $\theta\Delta I_t = \Delta K_{t+\theta}$. Using these two facts and equation 1.2 in equation 1.4 then implies

$$G_{K_{t+0}} = \frac{(G_{R_{t+\theta}} - G_{R_t})}{G_{R_t}\theta} \tag{1.5}$$

Now if $(K_t, S_t, R_t, C_t)_0^\infty$ is to be intertemporally efficient it is necessary that it satisfies equation 1.5 for every adjacent pair of intervals. The foregoing argument has shown that if $(K_t, S_t, R_t, C_t)_0^\infty$ fails to satisfy the condition at any adjacent pair of intervals, it is possible to alter the rates of capital accumulation and resource depletion in such a manner that consumption is increased at one of the intervals, leaving unchanged the level of consumption at all the other intervals. If we now take the limit as $\theta \rightarrow 0$, equation 1.5 reduces to the form

$$G_{K_t} = \frac{(d/dt)(G_{Rt})}{G_{Rt}} \quad \text{for all} \quad t \geqslant 0 \tag{1.6}$$

Even though this equation has been arrived at from purely technological considerations it can be given a ready interpretation. Let the stock of the composite commodity serve as the numeraire. Under competitive conditions G_{K_t} denotes the spot rental rate earned by owners of the capital stock. Since by assumption the composite good does not deteriorate, G_{K_t} is also the own rate of return on this good. Furthermore, under competitive conditions G_{R_t} is the spot price of the exhaustible resource. Consequently under such conditions 1.6 is the familiar arbitrage equation or Hotelling Rule requiring that the rate of capital appreciation of the resource equal the rate of return on the other asset in the model. This goes a long way toward establishing the manner in which an efficient program can be decentralized.

It has been established that for a program to be intertemporally efficient it must satisfy the Hotelling Rule. It is not a sufficient condition though, for one problem is that it is possible for 1.6 to be satisfied along a program that does not exhaust the entire stock of the resource, and we have already argued that this would be inefficient.

It is worthwhile discussing more formally how this can come about despite the implicit optimization undertaken in arriving at equation 1.6. The critical point to note is that the condition has been arrived at by making a local perturbation on the base program $(\bar{K}_t, \bar{S}_t, \bar{R}_t, \bar{C}_t)_0^\infty$; in particular, perturbing only two adjacent intervals at a time. But for each pair of intervals $(t, t+\theta)$ and $(t+\theta, t+2\theta)$ and t no matter how large, there is an infinity of future to come. Given this, one cannot tell from the fact that 1.6 holds whether all the resource stock will be utilized in infinite time. To put it more vividly, suppose a fraction of the initial stock, S_0, is thrown away. Now consider an intertemporally efficient program with the reduced initial stock. It will satisfy equation 1.6. But in terms of the original stock, S_0, the program is not intertemporally efficient. Consequently equation 1.6 does not represent a condition sufficient for efficiency. The argument that has been used demonstrates that a feasible program satisfying it is not dominated by any feasible program that is identical to it for large enough t. In other words, a feasible program satisfying equation 1.6 is efficient with respect to the set of all feasible programs that are eventually identical to it. We shall refer to such a program as locally efficient; "local," because the comparison is being made among programs that are eventually identical to one another. Equation 1.6

is necessary and sufficient for local efficiency. Plainly, an efficient program is locally efficient. Moreover, we have argued that a locally efficient program can be intertemporally inefficient since, for example, it is consistent with a fraction of the resource stock never being utilized.

Therefore we need something in addition to condition 1.6 to guarantee intertemporal efficiency. We have labored these points at some length here because it suggests that at least for some simple economies this "something" is the condition

$$\lim_{t \to \infty} S_t = 0 \tag{1.7}$$

This, in fact, can be shown to be the case for a Cobb-Douglas economy. If the production function is of this form then a necessary and sufficient set of conditions for a program to be intertemporally efficient is that it satisfies conditions 1.6 and 1.7.

This is an extremely convenient characterization of efficient programs. It is intuitively appealing and easy to use. It differs somewhat from the characterization of efficient programs for economies with durable capital goods and no exhaustible resources. For such economies it is legitimate to identify intertemporal inefficiency with a systematic overaccumulation of capital assets. Roughly speaking, inefficiency in such economies is due to too high a rate of investment in the long run, in the sense that the high rates of consumption made possible by such accumulation are never utilized. For the Cobb-Douglas economy the story can be told in the following manner: if a feasible program satisfying equation 1.6 is intertemporally inefficient, it is due to an underutilization of the exhaustible resource. If a program satisfying 1.6 in addition fully utilizes the resource, it is intertemporally efficient. Capital overaccumulation cannot take place along a program satisfying conditions 1.6 and 1.7.

In characterizing an efficient allocation, there is one further issue that repays careful examination, and that is the relationship between price and marginal extraction cost. The above results were derived on the assumption that the resource could be extracted costlessly. If, more generally, there is a nonzero marginal extraction cost $C(S_t, R_t)$, which depends on both the remaining stock and on the current rate of extraction, then efficiency requires that the net marginal product of the resource, that is, its marginal product minus its marginal extraction cost, should change at a rate given by the rate of return on capital:

$$G_K = \frac{d}{dt} \ln (G_R - C) \tag{1.8}$$

Letting $G_K = r$ and $G_R = P$, this can be rewritten as

$$\frac{\dot{p}}{p} = r\left[\frac{p-c}{p}\right] = \left[\frac{\partial c}{\partial R}\frac{\dot{R}}{c} + \frac{\partial c}{\partial s}\frac{R}{c}\right]\frac{c}{p}$$

which of course reduces to equation 1.6, and $\dot{p}/p = r$ if $C = 0$.

This more general form shows that the rate of price change of the resource will, along an efficient competitive program, be equal to a weighted average of the return on capital, r, and rate of change of extraction costs, which is the bracketed expression in the second term. The weights are respectively the proportions of price made up by rent (p – c) and marginal cost. One simple but important point to emerge from this analysis is that the price of the resource need not under competitive conditions be equal to, or even be near, its extraction cost. This is of course very clear from 1.6, which shows that the price may eventually become very large even if extraction costs are zero on the margin. Equation 1.8 elaborates on the precise relationship between price and marginal extraction cost.

Intergenerational Equity

The next topic to be considered is that of intergenerational equity or, more generally, the determination of the weights to be placed on consumption at different points in time. Any optimal intertemporal allocation presumably embodies a balance between equity and efficiency, and in the case of nonrenewable resources the equity issue appears to be of particular concern.

Intertemporal equity is no easier to define than cross-sectional equity. Indeed I am not proposing to give a definition, merely to look at the assumptions implicit in the approaches that economists usually take. There are two such approaches, the *utilitarian*, which defines intertemporal optimality as the maximization of a discounted sum of utilities, and the *maxi-min*, where optimality is defined as choosing the highest sustainable consumption level.

The traditional justification for the utilitarian approach is of course to be found in the doctrines of classical utilitarianism, the essence of which probably cannot be better expounded than by one of the last of the great classical utilitarians:

"By Utilitarianism is . . . meant the ethical theory, that the conduct which, under any given circumstances, is objectively right, is that which will produce the greatest amount of happiness on the whole; that is, taking into account all whose happiness is affected by the conduct." [Sidgwick 1890, 409]

Two pages later Sidgwick expounds on the theory in unambiguous terms:

> We shall understand, then that by Greatest Happiness is meant the greatest possible surplus of pleasure over pain, the pain being conceived as balanced against an equal amount of pleasure, so that the two contrasted amounts annihilate each other for purposes of ethical calculation. And of course, here as before, the assumption is involved that all pleasures included in our calculation are capable of being compared quantitatively with one another and with all pains: that every such feeling a certain intensive quantity, positive or negative (or, perhaps, zero) in respect of its desirableness, and that this quantity may be to some extent known: so that each may be at least roughly weighted in ideal scales against an other.
>
> [Sidgwick 1890, 411]

Let u_t^i be the utility level of individual i in generation t. Total utility, from the present ($t = 0$) to the indefinite future, is then given by the expression

$$W = \sum_{t=0}^{\infty} \sum_{i=1}^{L} u_t^i \tag{1.9}$$

A central feature of the formulation, as will be seen in equation 1.12, is that future utilities are not being discounted at positive rates. Indeed, several utilitarians have judged the discounting of future utilities morally objectionable. Thus, for example, Ramsey regarded the practice, "ethically indefensible" and thought it "arises merely from the weakness of the imagination" [Ramsey 1928]. More recently Harrod has judged it as "a polite expression for rapacity and the conquest of reason by passion" [Harrod 1948, 40].

There is at least one major defect with *ex cathedra* pronouncements such as Harrod's. It is injudicious to comment on a moral doctrine without having, as a first step, undertaken an analysis of its implications under various plausible circumstance. Explorations in the theory of optimum economic growth with positive utility discounting have suggested that in many circumstances positive utility discounting implies consumption rates in the early years that are not remotely rapacious.

But quite apart from this, the Ramsey-Harrod position overlooks an important point: that there is a positive chance that life on earth will cease to exist at some future date. As physical theories stand, if nothing else, the gradual cooling of the sun will eventually spell doom for us all. There is of course the chance, however remote the chance may be, that this eventual extinction date will be farther away than any date that we care to mention. This, as we noted earlier, is precisely the reason why morally we are compelled to take all future generations into account. But this is not to say that it carries with it the moral implication that the *utilities* of all generations be given the same weight. The point then is that one might find it ethically reasonable to discount future utilities at positive rates, not because one is myopic, but because there is a positive chance that future generations will not exist. Sidgwick, as usual, is unambiguous on what the utilitarian stand is:

> It seems . . . clear that the time at which a man exists cannot affect the value of his happiness from a universal point of view; and that the interests of posterity must concern a Utilitarian as much as those of his contemporaries, except in so far as the effect of his actions on posterity—*and even* the *existence of human beings to be affected*—must necessarily be more uncertain." [Sidgwick 1890, 412]

Let $y_t(>0)$ denote the utility discount factor applied to generation t. Discounting future utilities at positive rates implies that $y_t < y_{t-1}$ for all $t \geqslant 0$. Total discounted utility is then

$$W = \sum_{t=0}^{\infty} y_t \left(\sum_{i=1}^{L} u_t^i \right) \qquad (1.10)$$

In what follows we shall abstract from all items other than consumption that affect an individual's utility level, and as well normalize and suppose $L = 1$. Presumably the utility level of a given generation is influenced by the postulated future consumption level.

Using this in equation 1.11 yields total (discounted) utility as

$$\sum_{t=0}^{\infty} y_t u(C_t) \qquad y_t > y_{t+1} > \cdots > 0 \qquad (1.11)$$

and $u(\cdot)$ is a continuous and increasing function of C_t.

Since y_t is the utility discount factor, one can now define the *utility discount rate* between t and $t+1$ as $(y_t - y_{t+1})/y_{t+1}$. It is also occasionally referred to as the *rate of pure time preference* and sometimes as the *rate of impatience*. A simple form of the discount factor that has been much used in recent years is the one for which $y_t = 1/(1+\delta)^t$, with $\delta \geqslant 0$. The discount rate is then a constant δ. This would seem an appropriate procedure if it is felt that the probability of extinction in the next T years is approximately the same as the probability of extinction during the interval t to $t+T$ should the world survive till t and that this is true no matter what t and T are (i.e., the stochastic process generating the possibility of extinction is a Poisson one). In this case we have

$$W = \sum_{t=0}^{\infty} \frac{u(C_t)}{(1+\delta)^t}, \qquad \delta \geqslant 0 \qquad (1.12)$$

The utilitarian would wish to select the feasible consumption profile $[C_t]$ that maximizes W. But note that if $[C_t^*]$ is an optimum consumption program when $u(\cdot)$ is the utility function, it remains an optimum consumption program if instead the utility function is $au(\cdot)$, where $a > 0$. One does not require an absolute scale in which to measure utility. A utilitarian prescription is invariant to the *same* positive homogeneous transformation applied to all utility functions. This restriction—that, if such a transformation is used on one individual's utility function then the same transformation must be used on all other utility functions—defines the sense in which interpersonal comparisons of welfare are made by utilitarianism for our particular problem.

All very well, one might say. But how is this interpersonal comparison to be made in principle? One strand of utilitarianism, as exemplified in the writings of Sidgwick, has faced the question in a remarkably interesting manner. The idea lies in postulating a rational and impartial spectator who in effect empathizes with the needs and aspirations of all individuals. The moral calculation is then done on the basis of this empathy. This particular utilitarian exercise has been described eloquently by today's leading antiutilitarian.

> A rational and impartial sympathetic spectator is a person who takes up a general perspective: he assumes a position where his own interests are not at stake and he possesses all the requisite information and powers of reasoning. So situated he is equally responsive and sympathetic to the desires and satisfactions of everyone affected by the social system. His own interests do not thwart his natural sympathy for the aspirations of others and he has perfect knowledge of these endeavors and what they mean for those who have them. Responding to the interests of each person in the same way, an impartial spectator gives free reign to his capacity for sympathetic identification by viewing each person's situation as it affects that person. *Thus he imagines himself in the place of each person in turn, and when he has done this for everyone, the strength of his approval is determined by the balance of satisfaction to which he has sympathetically responded.* When he has made the round of all the affected parties, so to speak, his approval expresses the total result. Sympathetically imagined pains cancel out sympathetically imagined pleasures, and the final intensity of approval corresponds to the net sum of positive feeling." [Rawls 1971, 186–187]

The moral exercise seems clear enough. Each one of us, or so the argument goes, should assume the mantle of this rational and impartial sympathetic spectator. Having conducted this introspective utility comparison, each of us will then be led to seek the happiness of all.

Although the utilitarian prescription may seem clear, there is in fact a problem that is deep and far from self-evident: this is that an optimum in the utilitarian sense may not exist. For example, even the very simple problem

$$\text{maximize} \sum_{t=0}^{\infty} \frac{u(C)_t}{(1+\delta)^t} \quad \text{subject to} \quad \sum_{t=0}^{\infty} C_t \leq S$$

will have no solution if $\delta = 0$ and $u(C)$ is strictly concave. This is the famous "cake-eating problem" (see for example Heal [1973]), and it recurs in a particularly acute form in resource-depletion problems. Conditions sufficient to ensure the existence of an optimum are discussed in Dasgupta and Heal [1974]. The issues underlying this problem, some of which are unique to the resource-depletion problem as posed here, are explored in the next section.

I now turn to a rather different ethical approach to the construction of an intertemporal welfare function, that of *choice behind a veil of ignorance*.

We have noted that at least one variant of classical utilitarianism envisages interpersonal comparison of utilities as being arrived at through pure introspection. Postulating a rational and impartial spectator that makes the rounds, so to speak, is merely an articulation of the idea that an assertion such as "the gain to one person due to a policy exceeds the loss suffered by another" is a statement of fact: a statement that can be confirmed by introspection. The utilitarian prescription that these gains and losses be *added* is given coherence by supposing these spectators to respond sympathetically to each such gain and loss.

A recently advanced alternative conception of distributive justice is founded on the social contract doctrine [Rawls 1971]. The idea here consists in the claim that the principles of justice are to be conceived as those principles that free and rational persons concerned to further their own interests would agree should govern their social life and institutions if they had to choose such principles from behind a "veil of ignorance"; that is, in ignorance of their own abilities, of their psychological propensities, and of their status and position in society as well as the level of development of the society of which they are to be members. This position of primordial equality of the choosing parties has been named by Rawls *the original position*. The veil of ignorance is designed to "ensure(s) that no one is advantaged or disadvantaged in the choice of principles by the outcome of natural chance or the contingency of social circumstances. Since all are similarly situated and no one is able to design principles to form his particular condition, the principles of justice are the result of a fair agreement or bargain" [Rawls 1971, 12]

Rawls supposed that

> The (choosing) parties do not know which generation they belong to.... They have no way of telling whether it is poor or relatively wealthy, largely agricultural or already industrialized.... The veil of ignorance is complete in these re-

spects.... Since *no one knows to which generation he belongs, the question is viewed from the standpoint of each* and a fair accommodation is expressed by the principle adopted. All generations are virtually represented in the original position, since the same principle would always be represented" [Rawls 1971, 287]

The critical point to note is that the conception of justice advanced above, when stripped down to its bones, is built on the problem of individual choice under uncertainty. But merely noting this does not get us very far; we still have to provide an account of how an individual will choose under uncertainty. In fact there is some ambiguity about the manner in which Rawls envisages the parties in the original position to choose among *intertemporal* consumption programs. Here we take a route that is an extension of the one advanced originally by Harsanyi [1955].

Intertemporal allocation and intergenerational equity

For simplicity of exposition we continue to normalize and suppose that each generation consists of precisely one individual (i.e., $L = 1$), and again, to make the moral calculation simple, suppose that generations are all identical in terms of their preferences. A party in the original position has to choose from among the set of feasible consumption programs. Suppose for simplicity that the chooser is concerned with ordering the set of all consumption sequences bounded between zero and (some) $\tilde{C}(>0)$. Thus $0 \leq C_t \leq \tilde{C}$, for all $t \geq 0$. We have already supposed that each generation prefers more consumption to less. Thus each generation's preference can be represented by *any* increasing function, $w_t(C_t)$. But in the Harsanyi framework each generation is invited to present its preference ordering over *lotteries* defined on its own consumption; (i.e., it is invited to present its preference ordering over probability measures defined on $[0,\tilde{C}]$). But, by hypothesis, generations have identical preferences. This means that their preferences over such lotteries are identical. We now suppose that the choosing party knows this preference ordering. Moreover we suppose that the representative generation's preference ranking over these lotteries satisfies the von Neumann-Morgenstern axioms. Then we know that generation t's preference ordering over *sure* consumption levels can be represented by a function that is unique up to a positive linear transformation. Thus we have

$$w_t(C_t) = a_t u(C_t) + b_t, \qquad a_t > 0 \tag{1.13}$$

where $u(\cdot)$ is an increasing and continous function, and a_t and b_t are arbitrary constants. We note as well that $u(\cdot)$ defines the representative generation's attitude to risk. Thus, for example, if it is risk-averse, then $u(\cdot)$ is strictly concave. By hypothesis, the choosing party in the original position knows $u(\cdot)$; but we have already noted that a knowledge of $u(\cdot)$ merely restricts the admissible set of utility functions for generation t to the (infinite) family defined by equation 1.13. In ranking alternative consumption sequences, therefore, it is not enough for the choosing party in the original position to know $u(\cdot)$. This is so because in order to aggregate intergenerational welfares, the choosing party needs to have a rule by which to select a member from each set in 1.13. We are therefore back with the problem of intergenerational welfare comparisons, a problem we noted earlier in our discussion of classical utilitarianism. Now, the manner in which intergenerational welfare comparisons is conducted in the Harsanyi-Rawls framework is similar to the one discussed earlier. The choosing party is assumed to make the rounds from generation to generation, so to speak, and having empathized with the needs and aspirations of each and every generation it arrives at a normalization, one for each generation's utility function $w_t(\cdot)$ (i.e., it chooses a_t and b_t for 1.16—one pair for each generation.) Again, for expository simplicity suppose that generations are identical in every respect. Then the choosing party will use the same normalization for all generations, and we shall have, for example, $w_t(C_t) = w(C_t) = u(C_t)$. Given this normalization the choosing party can associate with each consumption sequence $[C_t]$ a corresponding utility sequence $[w(C_t)]$. Since behind a veil of ignorance the choosing party does not know which generation it belongs to, it would regard each $[C_t]$ as an unknown lottery. The original ethical problem with which we began is thereby reduced, in the Harsanyi-Rawls framework, to a classical decision problem under uncertainty. But the point to reiterate is that the choice problem is given its moral dimension by the assumption that the party is behind the veil of ignorance and therefore does not know to which generation it belongs. Its vested interests are removed by this device. It will rank consumption programs in an impartial manner, taking into account the interests of all generations, since it may end up as a member of any generation. Moreover, as we have been supposing that more consumption is preferred to less by all generations, $w(\cdot)$ is an increasing function. Indeed, this framework provides one with one of the most powerful defenses of the demand that we should be interested in intertemporally efficient programs. If more consumption is preferred to less by all generations and the chooser does not know to which generation he or she belongs he/she will not choose an intertemporally inefficient consumption program.

The question becomes: what decision rule should be followed by the choosing party behind the veil of ignorance. Harsanyi supposed that the choosing party's preference over hypothetical lotteries satisfies the von Neumann-Morgenstern axioms. Assume now that behind the veil of ignorance the party faces a (subjective) probability π_t of being a member of generation t. It will follow then that as between two programs $[C_t]$ and $[C_t^1]$ it will choose on the basis of the expected utility associated with the programs; i.e., according to whether

$$V([C_t]) \equiv \sum_{t=0}^{\infty} \pi_t w(C_t) < V([C_t^1]) \equiv \sum_{t=0}^{\infty} \pi_t w(C_t^1) \tag{1.14}$$

It is important to recognize that despite the *formal* similarity between the functions 1.14 and 1.11, their interpretations are different. While $w(\cdot)$ in 1.14 is usually called the utility function of generation t it is not a utility function in the sense of classical utilitarianism. Generation t's attitude to risk determines the form of $w(\cdot)$, whereas $u(\cdot)$ in 1.14 is a measure of the quantity of happiness of a given generation. $t(\cdot)$ and $w(\cdot)$ have different geneses.

Expression 1.14 is still not a decision rule, because there arises the question of what probability distribution the choosing party ought to base its decision on. If the number of generations is finite one route is to have the party assume an equal chance of being a member of any generation. This may be justified by an appeal to the principle of insufficient reason. Alternatively, as in the Harsanyi framework, the assumption of equiprobability could be intrinsic to the meaning of "impersonal choice" for the choosing party.

> ... an individual's preferences satisfy this requirement of impersonality if they indicate what social situation he would choose if he did not know what his personal position would be in the new situation chosen (and in any of t's alternatives) but rather had an equal *chance* of obtaining any of the positions." [Harsanyi 1955]

But for our problem matters are different. One cannot have a uniform probability distribution defined over the integers (i.e., $t = 0, 1, 2, \ldots$). But presumably there is a chance that the world will be extinct at some date. Let λ_t denote the (subjective) probability on the part of the choosing party at $t = 0$ that the world will terminate at a date *beyond* t. Then the natural analogue of the principle of insufficient reason, or indeed Harsanyi's condition characterizing impersonal choice, is one that leads the choosing society to maximize

$$V[(C_t)] = \sum_{t=0}^{\infty} \lambda_t w(C_t), \qquad \lambda_t > 0 \tag{1.15}$$

Since by definition $\lambda_t > \lambda_{t+1}$ for all t, λ_t is formally akin to the discount factor introduced in our discussion of classical utilitarianism. For example, if it is thought that the probability of extinction is generated by a Poisson process, then

$$\lambda_t = (1+\delta) - t, \qquad \delta > 0$$

The Harsanyi framework postulates that the choosing party's preferences over lotteries satisfy the von Neumann-Morgenstern axioms and, in particular that behind the veil of ignorance it chooses on the supposition that it has an equal chance of being a member of any generation. In developing the contract doctrine Rawls conceived of the veil of ignorance as complete, in the sense that the choosing party has no basis for imputing any probability distribution to the uncertainty it faces. In particular, it is supposed that the decision rule that the choosing party obeys is the maxi-min criterion. Using this criterion for the problem at hand the party ranks two programs $[C_t]$ and $[C_t^1]$ according as

$$\inf [w(C_t)] \gtreqless \inf [w(C_t^1)]$$

(That is, we rank as higher that program on which the lowest consumption level is highest.) Since by our hypothesis generations are identical and $w(\cdot)$ is increasing, the party ranks the two programs $[C_t]$ and $[C_t^1]$ according as

$$\inf [C_t] \gtreqless \inf [C_t^1] \tag{1.16}$$

In fact the criterion embodied in 1.16 would emerge from the Harsanyi framework as well if it were the case that each *generation* is infinitely risk averse. To see this, suppose by way of illustration that

$$w(C_t) = -\frac{C_t^{-(\eta-1)}}{\eta - 1}, \qquad \eta > 0$$

One can show that the larger is the value of the parameter η the greater is the extent to which the representative generation is risk averse. But using this utility function in 1.18 we have

$$V([C_t]) = -\sum_{t+0}^{\infty} \frac{\lambda_t C_t^{-(\eta-1)}}{\eta - 1}, \qquad \eta > 0, \lambda_t > 0 \tag{1.17}$$

What happens when $\eta \to \infty$? To answer this consider two consumption sequences $[C_t]$ and $[C_t^1]$. Suppose that each sequence has a minimum term. It can then be shown that if the choosing party ranks $[C_t]$ and $[C_t^1]$ according to the function 1.17, then in the limit as $\eta \to \infty$ it chooses that program whose minimum term is the larger.

This should not be overly surprising. The larger is η the more risk averse is the representative generation. Therefore, with larger and larger values of η those dates at which consumption is relatively low loom larger and larger in the choosing party's eye. In the limit it is obsessed with the dates at which consumption is lowest. Its choice conforms to the maxi-min strategy.

Our interest in this criterion is not because Rawls, in his well-known work, has argued that the choosing party will obey it when choosing an intergenerational consumption sequence. In fact he has not. But it is eminently worth considering such extreme cases. They enable one to see sharply the implications of different hypothesis.

It is clear from this that the usual formulation of the intertemporal objective, $\Sigma_t U(C_t)\lambda^t$, can be derived either from the utilitarian basis with which it is usually associated, or from the ethically rather distinct axioms that associate fairness with choice behind a veil of ignorance. And it is interesting that this latter approach is capable of providing a justification either of what is normally thought of as the utilitarian approach, or of the apparently very different maxi-min definition of intertemporal equity.

Optimal Depletion Policies

In choosing a resource depletion policy, we should certainly select one that is efficient. Otherwise we would, in an obvious sense, be wasting the economy's potential. There are two aspects to the characterization of efficiency—a local characterization via the Hotelling rule, and a global characterization in terms of the asymptotic behavior of stocks. The former is relatively easy to check. The latter, of course, is not—checking it requires information about a path's behavior over unbounded intervals of time.

In general there are infinitely many efficient resource-depletion programs—efficiency guarantees that a program is on the boundary of the set of intertemporally possible consumption profiles. Of the many efficient programs, we should choose that which best conforms to our conception of intertemporal equity: call this one the optimal depletion program (see figure 1-2).

This optimal depletion program is the solution to the problem of maximizing social welfare, as measured by the objective function, equation 1.11 or 1.14 depending on ethical viewpoint, subject to constraints imposed by technologies and by resource availability.

Neglecting production constraints, which actually add little to the intrinsic structure of the problem, this can be formalized as

$$\text{maximize } \sum_t \lambda_t U(C_t) \quad \text{subject to} \quad \sum_t C_t \leq S \tag{1.18}$$

(This is just the cake-eating problem referred to above.) Unfortunately this

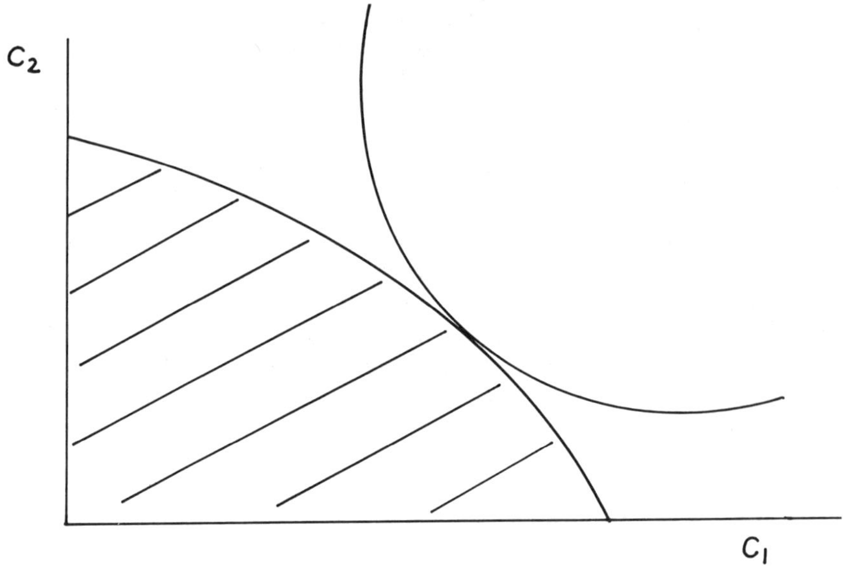

Figure 1-2. This illustrates the set of possible consumption programs (shaded) in a two-period model, and the set of efficient programs (the upper frontier of the shaded set). The optimal program is a point on this efficient frontier where it is tangent to a contour of the objective function.

problem, simple though it appears, has one tricky characteristic: it may have no solution, and the need to ensure that it does have a solution may place constraints on our choices of λ_t and the function U. This if course limits the ethical judgements that we can express in the objective of the problem. Some ethical judgements turn out to be in a basic sense incompatible with the fact of limited resource availability.

To understand this problem, consider for a moment problem 1.18 with $\lambda_t = 1$ for all t—all generations are given equal weight. Also truncate the time horizon to a finite number of years, T, giving

$$\text{maximize } \sum_{t=1}^{T} U(C_t) \quad \text{subject to} \quad \sum_{t=1}^{T} C_t \leq S$$

In this case, if U is strictly concave (shows diminishing marginal utility), it is easy to show that the solution is

$$C_t^* = S/T \quad \text{for all } t$$

So on an optimal path consumption is spread evenly over time, and all the stock is used.

Now ask what happens as the time horizon T becomes larger. Clearly C_t^* tends to zero, but for any finite T, however large, the solution will involve a constant strictly positive consumption level. However, for infinite horizons ($T = \infty$), this solution sets C_t^* equal to zero—obviously not an optimal policy. And in fact one can show that for this case, there is no optimal policy; it is always possible to improve upon any feasible depletion program.

Why is this? Intuitively, the problem is as follows. For $\lambda_t = 1$ for all t, and U strictly concave, a necessary condition for the optimality of a program is that the marginal utility of consumption, and thus the level of consumption, be the same at all dates. So the same amount must be consumed at every date. This is fine for finite horizons, but the only constant consumption level that can be maintained over an infinite horizon, given the finiteness of the initial stock, is zero. So the only path satisfying the necessary conditions for optimality is clearly not optimal.

Analytically, the problem is one of discontinuity. For $\lambda_t = 1$ for all t, the maximand $\Sigma_{t=1}^{\infty} U(C_t)$ turns out not to be a continuous function of its argument, which is the sequence $(C_1, C_2, \ldots, C_t, \ldots)$. It is this discontinuity that causes the nonexistence of an optimum (see Heal [1984] for details). One can show that provided that $\Sigma_{t=1}^{\infty} U(C_t)\lambda_t$ is continuous in an appropriate sense, an optimal depletion policy always exists. For a single-period payoff function that does not change over time, this continuity occurs if and only if utilities are discounted. For time-varying payoff functions $U_t(C_t)$, continuity can occur without discounting if there is appropriate limiting behavior of the payoff function $U_t(C_t)$ for very large t. Basically this function has to become very flat, which is a form of discounting (see Chichilnisky [1977] and Heal [1984] for exact characterizations).

Ultimately, then, the logic of the finiteness of the resource constraint, taken together with an unbounded time horizon, limits the ethical judgements about intertemporal equity that can be incorporated consistently in the analysis of optimal depletion programs. In particular it rules out complete evenhandedness. Note that this difficulty arises not because it is intertemporal rather than atemporal equity being considered—at the level of abstraction with which we are concerned here, there is really not much difference. The problem arises from the conjunction of a finite stock (the essence of a resource-depletion problem) with an infinite horizon. An emphasis on the long run is also a very natural and indeed important component of the analysis of resource-use problems.

Notes

[1] For a more exhaustive development of these and related ideas, see Dasgupta and Heal [1979].

[2] I shall assume the labor supply to be constant and fully employed, and its availability and use subsumed into the properties of the function $G(\ )$.

References

Chichilnisky, G. 1977. "Nonlinear functional analysis and optimal growth." *Journal of Mathematical Analysis and Applications* 61:504–520.

Dasgupta, P. S., and G. M. Heal. 1974. "The optimal depletion of exhaustible resources." *Review of Economics*, Symposium on the Economics of Exhaustible Resources.

Dasgupta, P. S., and G. M. Heal. 1979. *Economic Theory and Exhaustible Resources*. Cambridge: Cambridge University Press.

Harrod, R. A. 1948. *Towards a Dynamic Economics*. London: St. Martin.

Harsanyi, J. 1955. "Cardinal welfare, individualistic ethics and interpersonal comparisons of utility." *Journal of Political Economy* 63.

Heal, G. M. 1973. *The Theory of Economic Planning*. Amsterdam: North Holland Publishing.

Heal, G. M. 1984. "Depletion and discounting: A classical issue in the economics of exhaustible resources." In *Natural Resource Mathematics*. Ed. R. McKelvey. Providence, RI: American Mathematical Society.

Ramsey, F. 1928. "A mathematical theory of saving." *Economic Journal* 38.

Rawls, J. 1971. *A Theory of Justice*. Cambridge: Harvard University Press.

Sidgwick, H. 1890. *The Methods of Ethics*. London: Macmillan.

COMMENT 1

Ronald G. Cummings and Spencer R. Pearse

Professor Heal's discussion of some of the issues relevant to the intertemporal use question serves to highlight two central facts: (1) The issues are extraordinarily complex and their solutions, in many instances, seemingly defy resolution—there is clearly no unique answer for questions raised by these issues. (2) Economists are anything *but* unanimous in terms of the efficacy of alternative analytical frameworks used in studying these issues. Particularly relevant in this respect are Quirk's comments on the Heal paper, which conclude this chapter. Indeed, an appreciation for the range of controversy among economists concerning major topics in resource economics is a primary goal sought in this book. In that spirit, the comments that follow will highlight those views by other writers that contrast with many of Heal's arguments.

As a brief aside, Heal's efforts to motivate the substance of his later discussions, and his overview of historical interest in exhaustible resources, convey an unwarranted suggestion of barrenness. He asserts that one must look to writings in the nineteenth century to find theorists explicitly concerned with exhaustible resources (excepting H. Hotelling), reflecting, it would seem, "the fact that for the first two-thirds of this (the twentieth) century, exhaustible resource constraints have not been important for industrialized countries" (Heal, p. 2). This view ignores substantial literature in both the economics of conservation—the "home" for concern with exhaustible and other resources problems through the 1960s—and in agricultural economics, a distrinct subdiscipline in economics since the early 1900s with whose literature Heal is seemingly unfamiliar. Classic examples of the former literature include works by Ciriacy-Wantrup [1942, 1944, 1952], Gray [1914], Hess [1917], Renner [1942], Hammar [1942], Scott [1955], O'Neill [1940], and Van Hise [1910]. An historical overview of conservation economics in 1937 is given in Pinchot [1937]. Earlier twentieth century interests in valuing/managing mineral and other exhaustible resources are seen, e.g., in Ise [1925] and in Tyron and Berquist [1932]. Economists in agricultural economics have long been concerned with soil and water as exhaustible resources; as examples, see Gray [1914] and also Crabbe's [1983] assessment of Gray's contribution to the theory of exhaustible resources, Ciriacy-Wantrup [1938], Bunce [1942], Shepard [1945], Bartz [1949], Milliman [1956], and Weitzell [1943].[1] We might also note concern with exhaustible resources in the late 1940s reflected in the Paley [1952] report which provided the impetus for the later formation of Resources For The Future, Inc. (See Howe [1979, 48–49]). Finally, we might acknowledge earlier twentieth century concern with minerals—Logan [1930], Osgood [1930], Watkins [1937], Wallace and Edminster [1930], Barnett [1950], Harberger [1955], Herfindahl [1955], Scott [1953], Tyron and Berquist [1932], O'Neill [1940]; with water development—see particularly, Maass, et al. [1962] and Eckstein [1958]; and the fishery—e.g., Scott [1955] and Gordon [1954].

Professor Heal's paper essentially examines a subset of problems of concern to resource economists, specifically problems related to the determination of optimal user rates for exhaustible resources over time. Heal frames the intertemporal use issue as "how fast should we use them (exhaustible resources) up ..."; he then contrasts views by conservationists, who feel that resources are used too fast, with asserted, uncited "political and press discussion" that generally argues "the sooner we can use the resource the better." Heal then argues that we *have* to take "a position" on this "too fast–faster the better" question. As one might expect, following his consideration of but a few of the equity/efficiency issues relevant for assessment of the intertemporal use question, Heal's earlier-noted "need" to take a position on the question is dissipated. If an objective method exists for responding to the question "who is right here (in terms of the too fast–faster the better debate)" that seemingly motivated Heal's inquiry, he either fails to find it or chooses not to share it with the reader.

We would do well to recall again the opening sentence of Harold

Hotelling's 1931 article:

> Contemplation of the world's disappearing supplies of minerals, forests, and other exhaustible assets has led to demands for regulation of their exploitation. The feeling that these products are now too cheap for the good of future generations, that they are being selfishly exploited at too rapid a rate, and that in consequence of their excessive cheapness they are being produced and consumed wastefully has given rise to the conservation movement. [Hotelling 1931, 151]

Hotelling clearly was motivated by the optimal intertemporal resource-use debate emerging from the conservation movement. The original conclusions—that the competitive resource owner would deplete the resource at a socially optimum rate (assuming no divergence between the private and social discount rate) has been strengthened and extended, not weakened as implied by Heal, during the last half century. The heart of the current debate on optimum use rates focuses upon issues of equity rather than economic efficiency.

Within the context of efficiency, however, there are those in the profession who might well challenge the claim, implicit in Heal's inquiry, that the costs associated with the extremely simplified, competitive model used in these discussions are out weighted by interesting, *relevant* insights that result from the analysis. Such claims may be viewed as specious given the implications of the counter-factual structure of the competitive assumptions. Thus, Fisher, in discussing the "standard," competitive equilibrium approach to analyzing the intertemporal use question, notes the many types of imperfections that *are known* to interfere with "the tendency of a system of competitive markets to allocate resources efficiently" [Fisher 1981, 10]. Sources for such well-known imperfections include monopoly, environmental disruptions, and uncertainties peculiar to resources industries [Fisher, 10, 11, 45–48; Herfindahl and Kneese 1974, 47–53; and Howe 1979, 103–107]. Just as economic analyses have failed to recognize changes in economic organizations, still further analyses of optimal competitive behavior for industries typified by *non*competitive structures may, as suggested by Howe [1979, 151], justify Schumacher's charge that "much of economics is concerned with optimizing the arrangement of deck chairs on the Titanic."

The core of Professor Heal's paper addresses "the determination of the weights to be placed on consumption at different points in time," as applied to either consumption or utility arguments in a presumed social welfare objective function. Two lines of argument developed by Heal in this section are of particular interest given our concern with contrasting views with other writers. First, noting that some utilitarians judge the discounting of future utilities as morally objectionable, Heal finds a compelling rationale for discounting, in the possible future extinction of life on earth, as might result, for example, from the cooling of the sun": "one might find it ethically reasonable to discount future utilities at positive rates, not because one is myopic, but because there is a positive chance that future generations will not exist." It is interesting to note that other writers turn this argument on its head. Arguing that it is not the sun's finite stock of energy that sets a limit on human survival—rather, it is the meager stock of the earth's resources. Georgescu-Roegen [1971, 1979] (see also Burness et al. [1980]) essentially argues that such potential extinction implies the need for low or zero discounting of future utilities. In this regard, it should be acknowledged that Georgescu-Roegen's intergenerational equity argument is qualitative in nature: He says "[given the earth's finite stock of energy] if we stampede over details, we can say that every baby born now means one human life less in the future [however, at issue in terms of intergenerational equity is that] . . . every Cadillac produced [now] . . . means fewer lives in the future" [Georgescu-Roegen 1971, 304]. His view of the moral implications of discounting is seen in his observation about man's nature: "man's nature being what it is, the destiny of the human species is to choose a truly great but brief, not a long and dull, career." [304]. Also, "confronted in the distant future, with the impending exhaustion of mineral resources . . . mankind, one might try to assure us, will retrace its steps . . . [a thought that] ignores that, evolution being irrevocable, steps cannot be retraced in history" [chap. x, *passim*].

Thus, if the time of extinction is independent of man's intertemporal consumption patterns *a la* Heal, it makes little sense to "save" resources for generations that will not exist and Heal's rationale for discounting follows. If, *a la* Georgescu-Roegen, the time of extinction is determined by man's intertemporal consumption patterns, the argument for equal weighting of each generations' consumption may have greater force.

Secondly, Heal's discussions of ethical theories and their economic implications invite the reader to conclude that economists' concern with the intergenerational equity issue is limited to two approaches: utilitarian and maxi–min. Moreover, utilitarians, at least some (Ramsey, Sidgwick, and Harrod) utilitarians, reject discounting not on economic grounds but seemingly (*a la* Heal) strictly on the grounds that discounting is ethically indefensible. In this latter regard, the reader should be advised that the economics/ethics interface has more substance: the implications of the utilitarian ethic for discounting depends upon one's assumptions regarding utility functions/measures.[2]

But economists' concern with the ethical and/or equity dimensions of intergenerational allocative issues extend *well* beyond the utilitarian and maxi–min issues described by Heal. The implications for discounting of *eight* different ethical systems/conditions are examined by Schulze and Brookshire [1982]. Paralleling Quirk's remarks concerning Heal's paper, Schulze, Brookshire, and Sandler [1981] demonstrate the consistency of the libertarian ethic with the economists' Pareto criteria, *given* actual compensation by gainers to losers. Finally, there exists an enormous literature that centers on what Schulze et al. refer to as the "Democratic Ethic" [1981, 820–823]. Economists writing in this area have long been concerned with the consistency of discounting with ethical systems implied by democratic institutions (voting, committees, etc.); examples include works by Nozick [1974], Black [1958], Hammond [1976], and Neher [1976].

Efficient and equitable resource use over time is indeed complex and controversial—both the context and the issues relevant for the considerations are dynamic and changing. Heal's discussions of those considerations are most useful in pointing to the challenges facing economists concerned with intertemporal resource use questions. The breadth of these contemporary challenges reflects, in many ways, the long strides made in resource economics vis-a-vis earlier, more limited, concerns with "conservation."

Notes

[1] Issues of purely theoretical interest enjoy a distant legacy, such as optimal forest rotation paths [Faustmann, 1849] and common pool problems [Warming 1911].

[2] See Kneese, et al. [1983a, b], and, particularly, Schulze et al. [1981].

References

Barnett, H. J. 1950. "Energy use and supplies 1939, 1947 and 1965," Bureau of Mines Circular 7582. Washington, DC: Department of the Interior.

Bartz, P. M. 1949. *Groundwater in California, the Present State of Our Knowledge*. CA: Giannini Foundation Groundwater Studies No. 1. Berkeley.

Black, Duncan. 1958. *The Theory of Committees and Elections*. London: Cambridge University Press.

Bunce, A. C. 1942. *The Economics of Soil Conservation*. Ames: Iowa State College Press.

Burness, S., Ronald Cummings, Glenn Morris, and I. Paik. 1980. "Thermodynamic and economic concepts as related to resource use politicies." *Land Economics* 56 (February):1–9.

Ciriacy-Wantrup, S. V. 1942. "Private enterprise and conservation." *Journal of Farm Economics* 24 (February).

Ciriacy-Wantrup, S. V. 1938. "Soil conservation in European farm management" *Journal of Farm Economics* 20 (February).

Ciriacy-Wantrup, S. V. 1944. "Taxation and the conservation of resources." *Quarterly Journal of Economics* 58 (February).

Ciriacy-Wantrup, S. V. 1952. *Resource Conservation: Economics and Policies* Berkeley: University of California Press. (1963).

Crabbe, P. J. 1983. "The contribution of L. C. Gray to the economic theory of exhaustible resources." *Journal of Environmental Economics and Management* 10:195–220.

Downs, Anthony. 1957. *An Economic Theory of Democracy*. New York: Harper & Row.

Eckstein, Otto. 1958. *Water Resources Development: The Economics of Project Evaluation*. Cambridge, MA: *Harvard University Press*.

Faustmann, M. 1849. "On the determination of the value which forest land and immature stands possess for forestry. English ed. in M. Gane, "M. Faustmann and the evolution of discounted cash flow." Oxford Institute paper 42, 1968.

Fisher, Anthony C. 1981. *Resource and Environmental Economics*. Cambridge: Cambridge University Press.

Georgescu-Roegen, Nicholas. 1971. *The Entropy Law and the Economic Process*. Cambridge, MA: Harvard University Press.

Gordon, H. Scott, 1954. "The economic theory of a common property resource: The fishery." *Journal of Political Economy* 62 (April):124–142.

Gray, L. C. 1914. "The economic possibilites of conservation." *Quarterly Journal of Economics* 28:466–489.

Hammar, C. H. 1942. "Society and conservation." *Journal of Farm Economics* 24 (February):109–123.

Hammond, P. J. 1976. "Changing tastes and coherent dynamic choice." *Review of Economic Studies* 43(1):159–174.

Harberger, A. C. 1955. "The taxation of mineral industries." In *Federal Taxation Policy for Growth and Stability*, Washington, DC.: GPO. Pp. 439–449.

Herfindahl, O. C., and A. V. Kneese 1974. *Economic Theory of Natural Resources*. Columbus, Ohio: Merrill.

Herfindahl, O. C., and A. V. Kneese. 1955. "Some fundamentals of mineral economics." *Land Economics* 31 May:131–138.

Hess, Ralph H. 1917. "Conservation and economic evolution." In *The Foundations of Natural Prosperity*. Ed. Ely et al. New York: Macmillan.

Hotelling, H. 1931. "Economics of natural resources." *Journal of Political Economy* 39 (April):137–175.

Howe, Charles W. 1979. *Natural Resource Economics*. New York: Wiley.

Ise, J. 1925. "The theory of value as applied to natural resources." *American Economic Review* 15:284–291.

Kneese, Allen V., et al. 1983a. "Economic issues in the legacy problem." Chapter 9 in *Equity Issues in Radioactive Waste Management*, Roger E. Kasperson (ed.). Cambridge, MA: Oelgeschlager, Gunn and Hain.

Kneese, Allen V., Saul Ben-David, and William D. Schulze 1983b. "The ethical foundations of benefit-cost analysis." Chapter 4 in *Energy and the Future*, D. MacLean and Pier G. Brown (eds.) Totowa, NJ: Rowman and Gallauheld.

Logan, Leonard M. 1930. *Stabilization of the Petroleum Industry*. Norman: University of Oklahoma Press.

Maass, A., et al. 1962. *Design of Water Resources Systems*. Cambridge, MA: Harvard University Press.

Milliman, J. 1956. "Commonality, the price system and use of water systems." *Southern Economic Journal* 22:426–437.

Neher, P. A. 1976. "Democratic exploitation of a replenishable resource." *Journal of Public Economics* 5:361.

Nozick, Robert. 1974. *Anarchy, State and Utopia*. New York: Basic Books.

O'Neill, John. J. 1940. "The exploitation and conservation of mineral resources in a balanced development of Canada." *Transactions of the Royal Society of Canada* ser. III, 34 (May).

Osgood, William. 1930. *Increasing the Recovery of Petroleum*. New York: McGraw-Hill.

Paley, W. S., et al. 1952. "Resources for freedom: Report of the President's Materials Policy Commission." Washington, DC.: GPO. (5 vols).

Pinchot, G. 1937. "How conservation began in the U. S. "*Agricultural History* (October).

Renner, George T. 1942. *Conservation of Natural Resources*. New York: Wiley.

Schulze, William D., and David S. Brookshire. 1982. "International ethics and the depletion of fossil fuels." Chapter 10, in *Coal Models and Their Use in Government Planning*, Jame Quirk et al. (eds.). New York: Praeger.

Schultz, William D., David S. Brookshire, and Todd Sandler. 1981. "The social rate of discount for nuclear waste storage: Economics of ethics." *Natural Resource Journal* 21 (October):811–832.

Scott, Anthony, 1953. "Notes on user costs." *Economic Journal* 63:368–384.

Scott, Anthony, 1955. *Natural Resources: The Economics of Conservation*, Toronto University Press. McClelland & Stewart (Carleton Library 1973).

Scott, Anthony. 1955. "The fishery: The objectives of sole ownership." *Journal of Political Economy* 63 (April):116–124.

Shepard, Ward. 1945. *Food of famine: The Challenge of Erosion*. New York: Macmillan.

Tryon, Frederick G., and F. E. Berquist, 1932. "Mineral economics—An outline of the field." In *Mineral Economics*. Ed. F. G. Tryon. New York: McGraw-Hill.

U. S. Commission on Organization of the Executive Branch of the Government. 1949. *The Hoover Commission Report on Organization of the Executive Branch of the Government*. New York: McGraw-Hill.

Van Hise, Charles R. 1910. *The Conservation of Natural Resources in the U. S.*, New York: Macmillan.

Wales, Henry B., and H. U. Lathrop 1944. *Conservation of Natural Resources*. Chicago: Laurel Book.

Wallace, Benjamin, and L. R. Edminster 1930. *International Control of Raw Materials*. Washington DC: Brookings Institute.

Warming, Jens. 1911. In Anderson P. "On rent of fishing grounds." *History of Political Economy* 15(13):391–96, 1983.

Watkins, Myron W. 1937 *Oil: Stabilization of Conservation*. New York: Harper & Row.

Weitzell. E. C. 1943. "Economics of soil conservation." *Land Economics* 19 (August):339–353.

COMMENT 2

James Quirk

Of all the contentious issues associated with resource economics, certainly the most controversial is that examined in some detail by Professor Heal, the issue of intergenerational equity and the role it plays in arriving at a notion of intertemporal optimality. Welfare economics is on shaky enough grounds when dealing with resource allocation questions involving a population of presently living individuals with known preferences and with a known technology, but the appeal of its utilitarian foundations erodes sharply once intergenerational aspects enter the picture. One of the main contributions of the Heal paper is to bring some of the basic ethical dilemmas and logical and computational difficulties of the intergenerational problem to the fore.

The particular view of intergenerational equity espoused in the Heal paper is certainly still quite speculative from the point of view of the economics profession, but the lack of agreement among economists as to how intergenerational equity questions should be posed and answered really should come as no surprise. Fifty odd years ago, when Lionel Robbins [1935] presented his pathbreaking analysis of the appropriate role for economic science in policy matters, he concluded that interpersonal comparisons of utility were beyond the scope of economics. Certainly the history of economics since the 1930s affords rather convincing evidence that concentrating on efficiency (Pareto optimality) issues has been a much more productive enterprise for economists interested in policy matters than was the earlier pursuit by the utilitarians of the *optima optimorum*. For that reason, those portions of Professor Heal's paper dealing with intertemporal efficiency appear to me to be of more fundamental importance and relevance to policy makers and economists than do those dealing with intergenerational equity.

However, having said that, it certainly is understandable that intergenerational equity is given so much attention in the Heal paper, because the ethical questions and paradoxes associated with it are so intriguing and so debatable. Even though the main thrust of these comments is directed toward more applied matters, I can't resist adding a few more comments on a somewhat different approach to the intergenerational equity issue, one that has produced a rather lively literature of its own. Thus one can look at the problem of intergenerational equity as one of deriving a social welfare function (a mechanism for aggregating preferences) for a sequence of populations extending into the indefinite future. Putting things in this context then raises the question as to whether or not the Arrow impossibility result [Arrow 1951] holds in this setting as it does in the case of a finite population of presently existing individuals.

Making the heroic assumption that the Arrow axioms are as *reasonable* a specification of an aggregating mechanism in the intergenerational case as they are in the case of a finite population, then any *acceptable* welfare function for the intergenerational case should satisfy the axioms. But in contrast to the impossibility theorem, which holds in the case of a finite population (any mechanism satisfying all of the other Arrow axioms turns out to be dictatorial), in the intergenerational case there are infinitely many mechanisms that satisfy all of the axioms. (See Hansson [1976].) However, the disturbing feature common to all these acceptable mechanisms is that populations extending from the present to any finite time in the future are outweighed in the welfare function (outvoted) by those populations arising in the years beyond. Thus, in the intergenerational case, the Arrow axioms imply that any *optimal* allocation of exhaustible and other resources over time (one arising from an acceptable social welfare function) is one that in effect consigns all populations into the foreseeable future to subsistence levels, in order to benefit those coming later.

If that result sounds paradoxical enough, things become even more confusing when we turn to the case of a welfare function of the type employed in the Heal paper. Ferejohn and Page [1978] have examined the use of welfare functions that take the form of the sum of discounted utilities, in the intergenerational case, from an axiomatic point of view. They have appended the Koopmans [1960] axioms for the existence of a welfare function of this form (with constant discount rate) to the Arrow axioms. Because there is convergence under the Koopmans axioms, the Koopmans axioms are not consistent with the Arrow axioms in the infinite case, due to the Hansson result. In fact, what Ferejohn and Page show is that if the Koopmans axioms are satisfied, and all other Arrow axioms are satisfied, then the resulting social welfare function is dictatorial, with the first generation being the dictator! This provides us with a reverse-English switch on the Hansson result, and has only slightly more in the way of intuitive appeal in addressing the problem of intertemporal allocation of an exhaustible resource.

Turning from intergenerational equity and intertemporal optimality to somewhat more mundane matters, one might ask about the policy implications of the Heal notion of intertemporal optimality. What needs to be emphasized is that the standard application of welfare economics to policy questions does not involve the recommendation of a policy simply because it generates an optimal outcome, however optimality might be defined. Instead, a policy is recommended for adoption when it can be shown that the policy leads to a Pareto superior allocation, namely one in which every individual is at least as well off, and some individuals are better off. As the debates in the 1930s concerning the Hicks–Kaldor (see Quirk and Saposnik [1968]) "compensation principle" made clear, what is required for an allocation under policy A to be deemed unambiguously better than one under policy B is not only that it is possible for the gainers in the move from B to A to more than compensate the losers, but the compensation must actually be paid. There's the rub, of course, in the intergenerational case. There are no obvious devices available for insuring that future generations will adopt the compensation provisions that might be needed to implement a Pareto superior policy. There is a one-way street about this, since the current generation can only impose penalties (or rewards) on itself (or on future generations in the aggregate), but cannot fine tune the intertemporal allocation on a generation-by-generation basis when this is needed to insure a Pareto superior allocation.

Moreover, even if it were possible to devise binding contracts to insure that future generations would make those decisions needed to attain intertemporal optimality or even efficiency, any such contract would have to be of the contingent claim variety. Contingent claim contracts are required because it is almost of the essence of the intergenerational problem that it is one of decision making under major uncertainties. Professor Heal has indicated one source of uncertainty, that is, uncertainty as to survivability, or the existence of a future generation. (Presumably this uncertainty is endogenous to the problem, depending in part on the levels and patterns of consumption adopted by earlier generations, although this added complication is not dealt with in the Heal treatment.) But there is also uncertainty as to the progress of technology over time, uncertainty as to the preferences of future generations, and uncertainty as to the evolution of institutions. Thus from a policy-oriented point of view, the intergenerational problem is subject to all of the trials and tribulations associated with attaining optimality under uncertainty, but raised to a much higher power.

Even in the case of intertemporal allocations among an existing population, the presence of uncertainty causes major difficulties for the two basic theorems of classical welfare economics: Theorem 1—Every competitive equilibrium is a Pareto optimum; Theorem 2—Every Pareto optimum can be achieved as a competitive equilibrium. To attain optimality under uncertainty through a market mechanism, a complete set of contingent claim markets (or a spanning set of such markets) is needed. Given that spot markets for goods and for contingent claims are open not only in the present but at future points in time, this means that markets for contingent claims over future spot market price vectors must exist, which implies in turn that there must be a continuum of contingent claim markets for optimality. Even if this could be achieved, there still would be the problem of maintaining a competitive environment in such markets due to problems of market thinness.

Given that we live in a world with an extremely limited number of futures markets, and with nothing approaching the idealized Arrow–Debreu contingent claim market economy, policy makers considering projects with intertemporal aspects as reduced to such expedients as cost-benefit studies, using measures such as expected (discounted) benefits less expected (discounted) costs, to determine the desirability of proposed policies. This represents the modern-day implementation of the utilitarians' goal of "the greatest good for the greatest number" or Sidgwick version of this as cited by Professor Heal. Needless to say, the problems posed by intergenerational equity are not handled very well in the usual cost-benefit study. But even ignoring the intergenerational aspects of the problem, cost-benefit analysis under uncertainty poses some inherent difficulties for the economist interested in intertemporal problems. It is to such matters that I wish to direct the rest of my remarks.

The particular example we will work with involves the construction of a dam-reservoir complex to control the flow of water to users, but the argument holds for any resource, exhaustible or not, for which future output is subject to uncertainty, which in turn affects prices in future spot markets. The point of the example is to show that there are some pitfalls in the construction of a measure of benefits under uncertainty, once we leave the idealized case of a world of a complete set of contingent claim markets.

Consider then the following highly stylized example. The economy produces two goods: x, water; and y, "all other good." There is a two-period horizon. p_t is the price of water in period t, and q_t is the price of the composite good, for $t = 0.1$. We wish to calculate a consumer's surplus measure for an individual in this economy, in order to determine the benefits from building a dam-reservoir complex with capacity S^*, to control water flows. Let x_t denote the consumption of water by the individual in period t, and let y_t denote his consumption of the composite good. We take income M_t in period t for the consumer to be known with certainty. We also assume a perfect capital market with a known interest rate of i percent.

It is assumed that the flow of water in period 1 is regarded as a random variable in period 0. Constructing the dam-reservoir complex changes the individual's probability density function over period 1 water availability.

This is a spot market economy, so that in addition to uncertainty concerning availability of water, there is also uncertainty on the part of the consumer at time 0 as to the spot market prices that will prevail at time 1. We will simply aggregate both kinds of uncertainty into a single *pdf* over time 1 prices, of the form $f(p_1, q_1, S^*)$. The capacity of the dam-reservoir complex thus shows up as a parameter of the consumer's *pdf* over spot market prices at time 1.

We adopt the usual separability assumptions. The consumer solves his maximization problem as a dynamic programming problem. To keep the notation simple, suppose that the utility associated with zero or negative consumption of either good is minus infinity so that bankruptcy problems don't arise. Then, at time 1, when p_1, q_1 are known, as well as the choices x_0, y_0 that were made at time 0, the consumer solves the problem:

$$\underset{x_1, y_1}{\text{maximize}}\ u_1(x_1, y_1) \quad \text{subject to} \quad p_1x_1 + q_1y_1 = M_1^*(1 + i)$$

where $M_1^* = DPV - (p_0x_0 + q_0y_0)$, $DPV = M_0 + [M_1/(1 + i)]$

This generates the demand functions

$$x_1 = x_1(p_1, q_1, M_1^*)$$
$$y_1 = y_1(p_1, q_1, M_1^*)$$

Reverting to time 0, the decision problem is

$$\max Eu = u_0(x_0, y_0) + \delta \int_0^\infty \int_0^\infty u_1[x_1(p_1, q_1, M_1^*), y_1(p_1, q_1, M_1^*)] f(p_1, q_1, S^*) dp_1 dq_1$$

where δ is the consumer's personal rate of time preference.

Note that this is an unconstrained maximum, since M_1^* already incorporates the budget constraint.

First-order conditions are given by

$$\frac{\partial Eu}{\partial x_0} = \frac{\partial u_0}{\partial x_0} + \delta\,\frac{\partial Eu_1}{\partial x_0} = 0, \qquad \frac{\partial Eu}{\partial y_0} = \frac{\partial u_0}{\partial y_0} + \delta\,\frac{Eu_1}{\partial y_0} = 0$$

where

$$\frac{\partial Eu_1}{\partial x_0} = (-p_0)\int_0^\infty\int_0^\infty \left[\left(\frac{\partial u_1}{\partial x_1}\right)\left(\frac{\partial x_1}{\partial M_1^*}\right) + \left(\frac{\partial u_1}{\partial y_1}\right)\left(\frac{\partial y_1}{\partial M_1^*}\right)\right] f(\cdot)dp_1\,dq_1$$

and

$$\frac{\partial Eu_1}{\partial y_0} = \frac{q_0}{p_0}\frac{\partial Eu_1}{\partial x_0}$$

Consider a measure of the benefits from constructing the dam-reservoir complex. We wish to calculate the change in DPV that will just compensate the consumer for the benefits received due to a change in the dam-reservoir capacity from 0 to S^*.

Note that implicitly, $Eu = Eu(p_0, q_0, x_0, y_0, DPV, S)$, hence we have

$$dEu = \left(\frac{\partial Eu}{\partial p_0}\frac{dp_0}{dS} + \frac{\partial Eu}{\partial q_0}\frac{dq_0}{dS} + \frac{\partial Eu}{\partial x_0}\frac{dx_0}{dS} + \frac{\partial Eu}{\partial y_0}\frac{dy_0}{dS} + \frac{\partial Eu}{\partial S}\right)dS$$
$$+ \frac{\partial Eu}{\partial DPV}dDPV = 0$$

Using the first-order conditions and the usual partial-equilibrium assumption ($dq_0/dS = 0$), we can simplify the above to

$$dDPV = (-)\left(\frac{\partial Eu}{\partial p_0}\frac{dp_0}{dS} + \frac{\partial Eu}{\partial S}\right)\frac{dS}{\dfrac{\partial Eu}{\partial DPV}}$$

Moreover, note that

$$\frac{\partial Eu}{\partial p_0} = \delta\frac{\partial Eu_2}{\partial M_1^*}(-x_0), \qquad \text{while} \qquad \frac{\partial Eu}{\partial DPV} = \delta\,\frac{\partial Eu_2}{\partial M_1^*}$$

Hence we obtain

$$dDPV = x_0\left(\frac{dp_0}{dS}\right)dS - \frac{1}{\delta}\left[\frac{\dfrac{\partial Eu}{\partial S}}{\dfrac{\partial Eu}{\partial M_1^*}}\right]dS$$

where

$$\frac{\partial Eu}{\partial S} = \int_0^\infty \int_0^\infty u(x_1, y_1) \frac{\partial f}{\partial S} dp_1 \, dq_1$$

Given a change from an uncontrolled river ($S = 0$) to a river with a dam-reservoir complex of storage capacity S^*, the relevant consumer surplus (CS) measure is then given by

$$CS = -\int_0^{S^*} x_0 \left(\frac{dp_0}{dS}\right) dS + \frac{1}{\delta} \int_0^{S^*} \left[\frac{\frac{\partial Eu}{\partial S}}{\frac{\partial Eu}{\partial M_1^*}}\right] dS$$

The interesting thing about this consumer surplus measure is that the second term is not observable from price-quantity data. The second term incorporates the benefit to the consumer from reducing the variability of $f(\cdot)$, even when the first-period consumption of water remains unchanged. Since $\partial Eu/\partial M_1^* > 0$ and $\partial Eu/\partial S > 0$, this means that the usual cost-benefit analysis based only on the area under the compensated demand curve (the first term in CS above) understates the benefits from building the dam.

We might note that this problem of an unobservable component of CS does not arise when there is a complete set of contingent claim markets and either no spot markets or spot markets with no uncertainty about prices in those markets. (These are the two cases considered in Arrow's seminal work on optimality under uncertainty.)

The point of this exercise was to indicate that there are basic problems in the intertemporal allocation of resources at all levels, from the abstract ethical problems highlighted by Professor Heal in his treatment of intergenerational equity, to the measurement problems faced by the applied economist attempting to perform a defensible cost-benefit study. There is a fertile field here for the resource economist to explore, since it is clear that what has been done thus far amounts mainly to identifying problems, without arriving at much in the way of acceptable solution. Perhaps this might be regarded as one more instance of lack of intergenerational equity, with the next generation of economists being left to solve the problems uncovered by this generation.

References

Arrow, K. 1951. *Social Choice and Individual Values*. Cowles Foundation Monograph. New York: Wiley.

Ferejohn, J., and T. Page. 1978. "On the foundations of intertemporal choice."

American Journal of Agricultural Economics 68:15–21.

Hansson, B. 1976. "The existence of group preference functions." *Public Choice* (Winter):89–98.

Koopmans, T. 1960. "Stationary ordinal utility and impatience." Econometrica 28: 287–309.

Quirk, J., and R. Saposnik. 1968. *Introduction to General Equilibrium Theory and Welfare Economics*. New York: McGraw Hill.

Robbins, L. 1935. *An Essay on the Nature and Significance of Economic Science*. 2d ed. London: Macmillan.

2 MARKETS AND EXTERNALITIES

Daniel W. Bromley

The Issues

The general recognition of a divergence between private costs and social costs can be attributed to Adam Smith in the *Wealth of Nations*, although it was A. C. Pigou and Alfred Marshall who gave the concept specificity. In essence we are interested in instances where the actions of one party (A) result in unwanted costs being visited on another party (B). In this context, *social* costs are those falling beyond the boundary of the decision-making unit that is responsible for those costs (Bromley 1982). This notion of costs, going *beyond* the decision unit that creates them, explains the origin of the term *externalities*. There is clear agreement among economists up to this point.

In a world where a multitude of decision units go about their business of producing or consuming, it hardly requires elaboration to understand that there are a multitude of ways in which these units make decisions that hold implications for others. It is the very nature of human interaction that what

I am indebted to Benoit Blarel, John Braden, and Kathleen Segerson for comments on an earlier draft.

we do influences the actions that others might take—and the costs that they must bear. The theory of externalities is concerned with this immense domain in which unwanted costs are visited on others. When the economist attempts to employ externality theory in the service of public policy a number of very critical issues intervene. And it is here that economists begin to quibble.

Before turning to these matters it would seem appropriate to discuss, in an introductory manner, the policy problems and the current issues in contemporary analysis. These brief remarks are intended to alert the reader to the theoretical turf we intend to cover, and to the relevance of those conceptual issues for the role that economists might play in the policy formulation process.

Although such problems are not listed in order of importance, I want to start with an implicit problem in externality theory and policy that may be one of the most troubling. Economic theory and conventional folk wisdom are in agreement—at least in the West—that the world works best when individuals possess the widest possible range of choice in their daily task of making a living. Again going back to Adam Smith, who was formulating his conceptual model at a time in history when the crown and the state held inordinate control over the individual, we see the celebration of individual initiative, individual choice, individual control of economic resources, and individual responsibility for actions taken. Economic theory and political thought are melded into a tribute to the individual—voting in the polling booth and in the market place.

This individualization of the world—its atomization—is argued to be the very best means for individuals to be made better off and, by simple aggregation, for the collection of all individuals (society) to be better off. Now, if *externalities* arise at the boundary of decision units, and if theory and policy celebrate and sanctify atomization, then theory and policy would seem to advocate the maximization of decision units and, ipso facto, the number of boundaries across which costs might travel. That is, atomization ensures externalities.

The interesting question in this regard then has to do with the policy response to these ubiquitous external costs. One obvious response is that all of the atomistic decision units should begin to bargain over those costs that now transcend their respective borders. A whole new domain of commodity relations is opened up—only now in terms of discommodities rather than in terms of commodities. But how is this new market to arise? Will it not require an infrastructure not unlike that now in place for commodities? Will not some entity be required to define and protect property rights? Will there not be a need for information and research when two bargainers in dispute cannot reach agreement? And will not third parties have some interest in the bargained outcome even though they are not present at the bargaining table? What sort of entity might be called upon to establish this new market in discommodities?

The dilemma is seen to be that the very result of extreme atomization is to seek assistance from that force in society that is often viewed as the enemy—the state.

And if this weren't bad enough, another dilemma appears if a different externality solution is offered. While this solution does not raise the specter of the state, there are anticompetitive implications that would seem to be uncomfortable for those who advocate atomization. Essentially, one of the preferred solutions to externalities is to *internalize* them by combining the number of decisions units over which unwanted costs are visited. If the pulp mill discharges liquors that impose costs on the downstream brewery and cheese factory, then the proffered solution is simply to unify their ownership and management so that the quantity of liquors being dumped by the pulp mill subsidiary will be what is best for the aggregate of the three. Ignoring, for the moment, the fact that there may be fishermen who would not be part of this new unified firm and thus who may continue to have unwanted costs visited on them, the idea of one or two firms in major river basins, each with several hundred subsidiaries, is not a thought to be considered favorably by those who believe in atomistic competition.

So, perhaps *the* fundamental theoretical and policy issue in the domain of externalities is one of how to reconcile these seeming contradictions between the idea (in both theory and popular political wisdom) of extreme atomization and the abundance of opportunities that creates for the rise of externalities, and the need to address those externalities with collective action (the state) or with anticompetitive firm consolidation.

A second issue in externality theory and policy concerns the matter of the liability for unwanted costs. Since Coase's article [1960] on social costs, economists have disputed this issue incessantly. The issue as put by Coase was that property rights are as much a factor of production as labor and raw materials. Firms could buy and sell rights to visit external costs on others and if the market for rights were functioning well, the ultimate outcome in terms of goods and services would not differ regardless of who held the initial rights. In the classic case of A's cattle wandering into B's cornfield, if the rancher was liable for damages then B would be reimbursed for the corn eaten and would be indifferent as to whether the corn was sold on the market or eaten by A's cattle directly and then bought ex post by A for (presumably) the market price. If liability ran the other way, then B would pay the rancher to keep cattle away from B's corn and the rancher would take this new income and make other feeding arrangements. Lost in all of the interest in Coase's quaint examples is the fact that he mixed up quite different forms of legal entitlements, all under the name of "liability."

Subsequent literature has pointed out that the very assumptions necessary to render the Coase neutrality conclusion true are the same assumptions that would deny the existence of externalities in the first instance. That is, in the absence of transaction costs, and assuming away income (welfare) effects among disputants, the assignment of liability would not matter for resource allocation for the simple reason that there would be no externalities to bargain away. We will return to this matter in more detail later in this chapter.

A third major issue in externality theory and policy concerns the distinction among taxes, subsidies, and standards for dealing with environmental pollution. Early on, economists argued that either taxes or subsidies would result in the same level of pollution abatement. That was soon refuted [Kamien, Schwartz, and Dolbear 1966] and now there is widespread recognition of the important distinction between emissions per firm, and the number of emitting firms. Specifically, subsidies encourage more firms to enter an industry and while emissions per firm might be reduced compared to the status quo, there would be more firms and so total loadings may be greater than originally. Another aspect of subsidies is that the regulatory agency may leave itself open to extortion in the sense of firms threatening to pollute more, so as to collect a subsidy not to.

The other aspect of this issue concerns the role of standards. Essentially, economists are united in their preference for effluent charges as opposed to discharge quotas (or standards). In spite of this near unanimity in the profession, politicians and industry overwhelmingly prefer standards. We will explore the probable causes for this divergence below.

In a world without any transaction costs there could be no externalities. What do we mean by transaction costs, and how do they contribute to the presence of externalities? The acronym ICE is a convenient way to remember the three types of transaction costs—Information costs, Contracting costs, and Enforcement costs. Any transaction requires knowledge about the opportunities for exchange, the nature of the items to be exchanged, and the willingness of the participants to engage in a bargaining process. This information is not costless and the lack of information can prevent certain exchanges from ever occurring. Efforts to acquire information fall on individual decision units and the incidence of information costs is an important policy issue. Once willing bargainers locate one another they can get down to the serious business of striking a deal. However, this is a costly process—perhaps in terms of the time involved. Finally, once a bargain is struck, there are certain enforcement costs that must be incurred. Although these costs can be covered by the state, it is also possible that the individual participants pay these costs.

I earlier said that if there were no transaction costs there could be no externalities. How can this be? The answer requires two things: (1) a distinction between physical interference being transmitted from party A to B, and the existence of an externality; and (2) a careful definition of what exactly constitutes an externality. Most economists agree that an externality has two aspects. First, there is the fact that a decision unit's utility or production function contains real variables whose values are chosen by others. Second, the decision unit responsible for choosing the value of those real variables does not compensate the recipients an amount equal to the marginal cost of its actions. In the case of positive externalities the responsible decision unit does not receive compensation for the beneficial effects imposed on the recipient. We now must differentiate this situation from the case where physical interdependence exists but is *not* an externality.

The distinction is to be found in the fact that there is an economically efficient level of physical interference among atomistic decision units, and when those directly involved in this interference—as perpetrators and as victims—have bargained out the preferred level, we must conclude that the externality has been resolved; even though the physical interdependence is still present. Notice that the externality no longer exists—by definition. That is, the parties have gotten together and bargained away all possible gains from trade. We will encounter this matter again in the following section where we talk of Pareto-relevant and Pareto-irrelevant externalities.

Hence we see that the absence of transaction costs—the costs of information, the costs of contracting, and the costs of enforcement—implies that all interdependent decision units should have costlessly bargained away all relevant physical interactions and by definition there would be no externalities. This does not mean that some physical interdependencies would not remain; it simply means that our notion of an externality could not exist.

We see, therefore, that transaction costs are essential ingredients in any conception of externalities. As will be seen later, Dahlman considers externalities to be nothing other than transaction costs.

A fifth issue in the general area of externalities concerns the policy response to the presence of uncompensated costs falling on victims. Imagine a situation—not so far-fetched—in which the status quo structure of institutions allows decision unit A to discharge large quantities of smoke containing certain chemicals that, when combined with atmospheric moisture, produce acids that allegedly cause damage to crops, forests, and buildings owned by other decision units. Now the nature of scientific knowledge means that we cannot be absolutely certain that the emissions from A's factory are uniquely responsible for damaging B's crops. What to do? Decision unit A—and those in similar lines of work—will marshall political support for the position that we do not yet know enough about cause and effect to be absolutely certain about the alleged link between emissions and crop damage and so more research is required. This strategy ensures that B will continue to bear unwanted costs while the search for a definitive answer goes on.

Alternatively the policy response could be to force A to cease all emissions immediately, thereby imposing unwanted costs on that unit. This would surely be the preferred action on the part of the recipients of A's emissions since it would liberate them from the damages—or so they think. If the situation is truly one of pure uncertainty then both parties have a reason to be concerned about the policy outcome; fairness requires that costs not be imposed in a cavalier manner. Economic efficiency demands as much.

And yet the status quo means that one party (A) is able to continue to impose unwanted costs on another (B) while the (possibly) lengthy search proceeds for a definitive answer. Some would argue that this is as it should be—after all, they might submit, party A has the presumptive right to continue with its discharges until its fault is clearly established. The victims would likely respond that while the legal doctrine of presumed innocence is fine in the courtroom, it is positively pernicious when the "preponderance of the evidence" points to a link between A's emission and B's damages.

Many externalities in the environmental area are characterized by just this situation. New chemicals and new processes seem to hold some responsibility for environmental problems; DDT, 2,4,5-T, Kepone, Aldicarb, PCB, EDB come immediately to mind. Yet the status quo is permissive of continued use until causality is established. That this situation puts the burden of proof on the victims—and the bulk of the transactions costs as well—is not lost on those who seek relief. Externality theory has not yet developed a meaningful way of handling this matter of presumptive rights, uncertainty, and the incidence of costs. It is possible that the reason for this lacuna is the simple fact that these matters are not theoretical ones at all, but rather ethical. We will return to this theme later.

The sixth issue we intend to explore in the context of externalities concerns what we consider to be the marginal expenditure in production and consumption decisions. An example from the automobile industry will illustrate the general issue. A few years back we were told that the auto industry opposed putting stouter bumpers on cars because it would add something like $50 to the price of a $7000 automobile. There is general recognition that as much as $1000 of a car's purchase price is attributable to "model changes"—by which is meant styling modification. Now, it might be fair to reconsider stouter bumpers at $50 against the last $50 spent on model changes. Would consumers prefer cars with $950 of embodied model changes, and a stouter bumper, or would they choose cars with the present bumpers (evidently ineffective since they are said to collapse in a 5 mph collision)?

This issue finds policy relevance in the externalities associated with strip mining. Prior to the Reagan administration there was considerable interest in restoring land that had been strip mined for coal to its approximately original condition. The arguments offered against strip-mine reclamation were in terms of the high cost of doing so; a classic response that applies to any regulatory discussion. First we must recall that the presence of externalities means that certain costs beyond the boundary of the responsible firm are not being compensated for. In this instance, these costs are in the form of downstream sedimentation, altered natural vegetation, and the aesthetic aspects of large areas of stripped land.

Simply put, the consumers of coal are not paying for the full social costs of producing that particular commodity. And, if coal were priced correctly, it would be somewhat more expensive, the use of coal would fall somewhat as cheaper alternatives found more favor, and there would be less environmental damage (and fewer offsite costs). The real economic issue concerns how we consider the costs of producing coal. If restoring the land after the coal is removed is considered to be a legitimate cost of producing coal then there can be no concern that reclamation costs too much. With reclamation part of production costs, the marginal decision becomes one of whether or not to dig up another hectare of land so as to produce another unti of coal. And this is as it should be. It coincides with coal-mining policy in Europe for many years now. An important issue in externality theory and policy, then, is one of fashioning an institutional environment that recognizes the true nature of *marginality* of various actions by decision units.

Another central issue in externality theory and policy concerns the way in which existing institutional arrangements influence our concept of economic efficiency. Several times in the preceding discussion I have mentioned the status quo, and presumptive rights. The firm that emits sulphur dioxide is considered to have a presumptive right (or privilege as we will see later) to continue its discharges until enough evidence is accumulated to mobilize politicians to alter the institutional arrangements. And, as we just saw, as long as the institutional environment is permissive of coal mining without reclamation, it will appear that reclamation is not economically efficient.

Markets and market processes operate within an institutional structure that defines rights and duties, obligations and opportunities. Because of this, the prevailing institutional structure defines for the economist what it is that will be considered efficient. Recall that for every structure of resource endowments—and institutions define and specify resource endowments—there is a Pareto-efficient outcome. Change the institutional environment and there will be a new efficient solution. Since institutions define markets, and since markets indicate to the economist what is considered to be efficient, institutions define what we consider to be efficient outcomes. But economists usually prefer to consider institutions as exogenous parameters and to search for efficient outcomes within a fixed institutional environment.

However, the bulk of what happens in externality policy concerns the restructuring of institutional arrangements. This poses a unique analytical challenge to the economist. After all, welfare economics and its applied analogue benefit-cost analysis are analytical devices for considering gains and losses from *within* an existing institutional (resource endowments again) environment. These are tools for measuring gains and losses of actions within the prevailing rules of the game. But institutional change is to change the rules. We face some difficult questions in this regard.

The final issue to be introduced here concerns the precise nature of the external effects being transmitted beyond the boundaries of the decision unit. More specifically, some authors develop models that treat costs being imposed by firm A on firm B—always in a different industry. Coase employed this approach to attempt to prove his point that the corn farmer would be indifferent between selling his corn on the market and being reimbursed by the rancher for the (market) value of the corn consumed by the latter's errant cattle. In theory the farmer should, of course, be indifferent since she gets the same amount of revenue from the corn crop. But does anyone really believe that farmers are indifferent to cattle wandering through their cornfields? The central issue still remains that Coase was using examples of producer–producer externalities; a dentist and a noisy confectioner, a rancher and a spark-emitting railroad engine; the manufacturer of sulfate of ammonia and the maker of cocoa-nut fiber matting. Coase does discuss several other types of disputes, but for the most part his examples come from disputes between two different producers.

A second category of externalities concerns those that involve producers and consumers; a factory that fouls the air; aircraft noise in a residential area; homes invading an agricultural area and then the residents demanding an end to odor and dust. The economic and ethical issues are different here than when two firms are involved. For one thing, consumers—unlike firms—are unable to pass along higher costs to someone; the costs they incur must be fully absorbed by them. A second difference in producer-consumer externalities is that those adversely affected may be difficult to locate and to bargain with—transaction costs again. So, while producer-producer externalities provide analytically simple situations to model, the world of producer-consumer externalities is perhaps closer to reality.

The final category is that of consumer-consumer externalities. This has been modeled most carefully in the fence-height dispute of Buchanan and Stubblebine [1962]. In consumer-consumer externalities neither party is able to pass costs along to customers and so the matter reduces to one of who is able to shift cost to whom. Apartment noise from loud stereos would seem to be the quintessential example.

To summarize so far, externality theory and policy is defined by at least eight issues that make it still, after a number of years, one of the least coherent and most contentious areas of economic analysis. Theory and popular wisdom favor a large number of atomistic producers and consumers, yet this very atomization is itself responsible for many of the externalities we wish to resolve. The literature still contains a number of references to the refuted Coase conclusion about the allocative neutrality of rights assignments. There is puzzlement over why, in the face of near unanimity among economists in their preference for emission charges on pollutants, most policy is still one of mandated emission standards or quotas. Transaction costs are said by some to be the raison d'etre of externalities, and yet the literature is not of one voice with regards to the important role to be played by such costs, and to the differential incidence of transaction costs under different institutional structures.

Much of externality policy is dominated by uncertainty over cause and effect. In the face of that uncertainty, some suggest that policy responses are stifled so as to empower current emittors to continue to shift abatement costs to victims, while at the same time sounding high-minded by calling for more research and study of the matter. The policy response is further stifled by the failure of economists to illustrate the pernicious nature of how externality disputes get framed; this is the matter of marginality—do reclamation costs, for instance, become a recognized part of the costs of producing coal, or does the industry continue to oppose reclamation because it is too expensive? It is this institutional environment that defines what is a cost, who shall bear unwanted costs, and how we compute what we consider to be the efficient outcome. This dimension is not well understood by many economists. Finally, we must begin to pay more careful attention to the important analytical and ethical differences that exist among externalities that I have here classified as producer-producer, producer-consumer, consumer-consumer.

In the remainder of the chapter I hope to develop the theory of externalities in a way that will allow explicit recognition of these issues, and possibly some general agreement as to their importance.

Types of Externalities

The newcomer to the study of externalities is sure to be overwhelmed by the number of ways that we refer to them—technical, technological, political, pecuniary, ownership, potentially relevant, Pareto-irrelevant, depletable, undepletable, marginal, inframarginal, Pareto-relevant, positive, negative. Small wonder that there is confusion.

This situation can be improved by beginning to consider externalities in one of four distinct—but not mutally exclusive—categories. Before turning to that, let us say that there are two broad categories of externalities that can be clarified straightaway. The actions of decision unit A can either impose costs or benefits on decision unit B. While this visitation is usually considered to be unintentional on the part of A—in the sense that it is incidental to A's main activities—the ultimate impact on others (here characterized as "B") can be either beneficial or detrimental.

If I like flowers and decorate my yard in a bright profusion of colors I am visiting positive externalities on other garden lovers and they receive those benefits without paying me. These are positive externalities. If, on the other hand, I paint my house pink with purple polka dots I am quite probably imposing negative externalities on others. Hence, while externalities can be either harmful or beneficial, the bulk of the externalities that we deal with are of the harmful kind. Theory tells us that harmful externalities will be produced in excess from a social perspective, and that beneficial externalities will be underproduced. Given the pervasive nature of negative externalities in environmental affairs, it seems appropriate to concentrate here on that domain. Let us now consider the four general classifications of externalities.

Externalities as types of interdependence

Beginning with Viner's classic article on the nature of cost curves, economists have drawn a distinction between pecuniary externalities and technological externalities. Pecuniary externalities are transmitted through the pricing system (hence pecuniary), while technological externalities are real-valued physical effects transmitted from A to B—smoke, toxic chemicals, noise, odor, traffic congestion. When a large retailer moves into a small community and puts downward pressure on the prices of certain commodities that had heretofore been somewhat sheltered from intense competition, the economic environment of the old-line retailers has been substantially altered. These are pecuniary externalities. They are pecuniary because they are transmitted through the price system. They are external because another decision unit has altered the economic environment of the firms. However, the very fact that they are transmitted through the price system suggests that they should not be referred to as externalities. The term implies, after all, that there is a problem requiring a solution. With pecuniary externalities we conclude that the market is doing its job of promoting competitive behavior—therefore why even use the term externality?

It is the class of technological externalities that captures the interest of the economist and the politician. Here we are dealing with nonprice-transmitted (hence physical) interdependence among ostensibly independent economic decision units.

A third dimension of this distinction was added over twenty years ago by Buchanan in his "Politics, Policy, and the Pigovian Margins" [1962]. Buchanan, being a good Paretian *and* a good Wicksellian, pointed out that whenever we have political action with less than unanimous consent then the opportunity set of decision units has been altered without their agreement or compensation. Isn't this too an externality?

We therefore have three general classes of externalities based on their origin—pecuniary (which some dispute as externalities at all), technological, and political.

Externalities as types of market failures

In his seminal article "The Anatomy of Market Failure," Francis Bator [1958] introduced the profession to three conditions that would cause individualistic wealth-maximizing behavior to result in outcomes that were less than socially optimal. Because of the close association among economists between externalities and market failure, Bator's analysis warrants mention here. Specifically, Bator found three general reasons why normal market processes might not result in the best of all possible worlds; he classified these as ownership problems, technical problems, and public-goods problems. Let us consider them in turn.

An ownership problem arises when all of the relevant variables to a production or consumption outcome are not owned and traded in markets. The classic honey-bee–apple-orchard problem comes to mind. The apiarist benefits from pollen collected far and wide but the ownership of that pollen is too difficult to ascertain and so proper remuneration of the owners never occurs; the apiarist is free riding on apple orchardists and others. As another example, my neighbor invests in time and materials to construct purple-martin bird houses so that the bugs in his vegetable garden are controlled without the use of chemicals. My garden abuts his and I too benefit from the appetite of the bug killers that his investment attracted in the first place. Moreover, by eating some of my bugs, his birds may be satiated and do a less-than-satisfactory job on his bugs. These are ownership problems and they lead to a less than optimal investiment in bird houses, bee hives, apple orchards, and broccoli. These suboptimalities are surely not of the nature or magnitude that would induce the well-meaning economist to lie awake nights. But neither are they irrelevant.

In one of the celebrated ownership externality cases, apple trees were harmed by a rust infestation that used red cedar trees as an intermediate host [Buchanan 1972; Samuels 1971, 1972]. Apple orchardists succeeded in passing a Virginia law that would empower—on a petition of at least 10 affected orchardists—the state to destroy without compensation red cedar trees serving as hosts for the rust in the vicinity. Some landowners owned the red cedar trees, and other landowners owned the apple trees. But no one owned the spores that travelled from cedar trees to do their thing to the apple trees.

Bator's analysis would suggest that the bulk of classic externalities are indeed ownership failures—the difficulty or impossibility of establishing control over phenomena that affect other decision units.

A second class of market failure arises because of technical problems—by which Bator principally meant lumpiness. Theory is most adept at treating mobility and divisibilities; when things such as dams, electric lines, and highways come in discrete chunks then the infinite continuity that we like in theory does not exist. As a result, conventional theory as a prescriptive norm becomes less relevant. Since technical problems are not much present in externality matters we will have little more to say about this type of market failure.

The third type of market failure, and one of considerable significance to externality theory and policy, is what Bator called *publicness*—public goods, or bads in the case of negative externalities. The matter of publicness is well understood by economists and we need little elaboration here; particularly since it will appear again very shortly under another name.

Externalities as policy prescriptions

In a 1962 article, Buchanan and Stubblebine develop a classification scheme for externalities that emphasizes the policy prescriptions to be drawn from the nature of their existence. These authors presented three general categories of technological externalities: (1) marginal or inframarginal; (2) Pareto-relevant or Pareto-irrelevant; and (3) potentially relevant and irrelevant.

Buchanan and Stubblebine were concerned with externalities in consumption and I will continue that focus here. They represented an externality as existing when the utility of individual A is dependent not only on the activities chosen by A, but on an activity whose level is chosen by another individual (B). Formally, A's utility function would be represented by:

$$U^A = f^A(X_1, X_2, \ldots, X_n, Z) \tag{2.1}$$

A marginal externality is said to exist when the partial derivative of A's utility function with respect to B's activity is non-zero. That is:

$$f^A_Z \neq 0 \tag{2.2}$$

We assume that the variation in Z is evaluated with respect to a set of equilibrium values for the X's optimally adjusted to the given value of Z.

An inframarginal externality is said to exist when condition 2.1 is present, and

$$f^A_Z = 0 \tag{2.3}$$

and

$$\int_0^Z f^A_Z \, dZ < 0 \tag{2.4}$$

The essence of inframarginality is that while the incremental effects of B on A (through Z in the utility function) are zero (condition 2.3), the total effect is negative (condition 2.4). We can imagine a situation in which a high-rise building blocks a scenic vista; regardless of the height of the building, once it reaches, say three stories in height, the damage to A has been done.

We are concerned with the relevance of externalities since policy should be directed toward those interdependencies that cause economic inefficiencies. Buchanan and Stubblebine [1962] define an externality as potentially relevant when the activity generates any desire on the part of the externally affected party (A) to undertake actions vis-a-vis the imposing party (B) to halt the unwanted effects. Such actions may include payments, threats, agreements, or going to the legislature. When an externality exists (condition 2.1) yet there is no desire on the part A to correct it, then, by definition, it is irrelevant. Formally, a potentially relevant marginal externality is said to exist when

$$f_Z^A \Big|_{Z=\bar{Z}} \neq 0$$

where $\bar{Z}$ is an equilibrium level of Z.

Buchanan and Stubblebine suggest that the mere desire to alter the behavior of the imposing party (B) does not imply the ability to accomplish this change. They define a Pareto-relevant externality as one in which the extent of the activity can be altered by the parties so that the victim (A) can be made better off without the imposing party (B) being made worse off. That is, there are mutual gains from trade.

We see, therefore, that a marginal externality can be potentially relevant—since the victim may seek for it to be eliminated—but still be Pareto-irrelevant—since it is impossible for both parties to gain from an adjustment of the status quo. When the economy is at a Pareto-optimal point we can only conclude that all remaining external effects are Pareto-irrelevant, even though there are surely many that remain potentially relevant.

What this situation obviously implies is that the costs of the status quo fall on the victim. If those costs are insignificant then we have what Buchanan and Stubblebine would call an irrelevant externality. If, however, those costs are important to the victim then we have a potentially relevant externality. However, unless the party responsible for imposing those unwanted costs on A will be made no worse off by eliminating those costs, then theory dismisses the costs as Pareto-irrelevant. While as theorists we may find certain satisfaction in this elegance, the victims of externalities may be excused if they are somewhat less sanguine.

Externalities as experienced by the victims

The final way in which we find externalities grouped is in terms of how the unwanted costs ultimately affect the victims, and also how the bearing of those costs by one victim influences the costs *available* to injure others. In essence we are here dealing with the obverse of public goods; that is, our concern here is with the nature of the incidence of public "bads."

The pure case of a public bad is represented by smog or haze in which case the consumption by one victim does not reduce the quantity of the smog or haze available for others to consume. In this example the victims, in the course of experiencing the costs of not being able to see a scenic mountain range, do not really use-up any of the externality; they do not consume it. This type of externality has been labeled *undepletable* by Baumol and Oates [1975]. Consider the externalities associated with urban airport noise. A given number of landings and takeoffs will generate a total decible level for a 24-hour period. If no one is around to hear the racket there can be no externality. When one person comes within earshot of the airport, a potentially relevant externality can be said to exist, although we would probably suggest that it is Pareto-irrelevant.

However, when the second individual comes within earshot of the noise there is no reduction in the noise level remaining for the first individual; there is no rivalry in the consumption of the externality. Surely it is a pure public bad.

As against undepletable externalities there are depletable externalities wherein the very act of being victimized by unwanted costs reduces the amount available to harm others. Consider the situation in which a farmer contracts with an aerial spraying company to spread a certain insecticide on her fields. If the wind comes up and scatters that spray onto a neighbor's bee hives then the externality is depletable to the extent that insecticide on A's bees is unavailable to keep drifting and kill someone else's bees.

The distinction between depletable and undepletable externalities was used by Baumol and Oates to motivate a discussion about differences in policy as regards to the two classes of external costs. While that policy conclusion is now under question by Freeman [1984], the power of the distinction for heuristic purposes seems to remain intact.

Summary

The complexity of the literature on externalities is seen to lie, in part at least, in the plethora of overlapping conceptions, and in the different purposes for classifying the phenomena.

The remainder of our concerns with externalities will, for the most part, be confined to negative externalities of the technological variety. While we will return to the depletable-undepletable distinction, the bulk of our time will be devoted to the theory and policy of externalities as informed by the treatment of them as potentially relevant, irrelevant, inframarginal, Pareto-relevant, and Pareto-irrelevant.

An Externality Model

There have appeared over the years a very large number of externality models, each designed to illustrate different theoretical or policy conclusions. Some of the better known models are those developed by Baumol [1972], Baumol and Oates [1975], Marchand and Russell [1973], Buchanan and Stubblebine [1962], Randall [1971] and Freeman [1984]. It would be impossible in the space available to present each of these, nor is a simple synthesis possible.

To anticipate the treatment in the following sections we require a model that allows us to illustrate several issues—most importantly those related to transaction costs, to the effects of alternative status quo rights structures (institutional arrangements), and to the cost incidence of alternative outcomes to externality problems. While this could be done using mathematical techniques as in the above models, I would prefer here to present the matter in rather simple graphical analysis so that the story is accessible to those not agile in the calculus. The model used here follows the approach taken by Burrows [1980].

We will consider several cases, moving from the most abstract to the most realistic. Case I is characterized by the most severe assumptions in that transaction costs are nonexistent. Imagine an externality situation in which Alpha is a firm that imposes unwanted—and uncompensated—costs on Beta, a firm in a separate industry. Alpha has an opportunity to abate the pollutant rather than dumping it on Beta, but to do so would be quite expensive to Alpha; better just to dump it.

Alpha has, of course, a supply curve of abatement; this is a schedule that shows the level of abatement undertaken by Alpha at various prices. We label this MAC in figure 2-1. It should be noted that Alpha's supply curve for abatement is also a demand curve for discharging effluents into the waterway. Beta also has a schedule, but in terms of costs incurred by being downstream from Alpha. We call it the demand for abatement on the part of Beta; this is shown as *MPC* in figure 2-1. Note that *MPC* is also a supply curve for pollution.

If we start with an assumed institutional structure that is permissive of the discharges on the part of Alpha—that is a legal structure that gives Alpha presumptive rights—then Beta would initially be willing to pay as much as *R* to be spared the first unit of pollutants. As we move to the left toward increased abatement we see that at level E_1 Beta would be willing to pay as much as *MJ* to Alpha for reduced emissions, but that Alpha would only require *KJ* to be willing to supply that level of abatement.

If we move beyond E_2 to emissions level E_3 we see that here Beta would

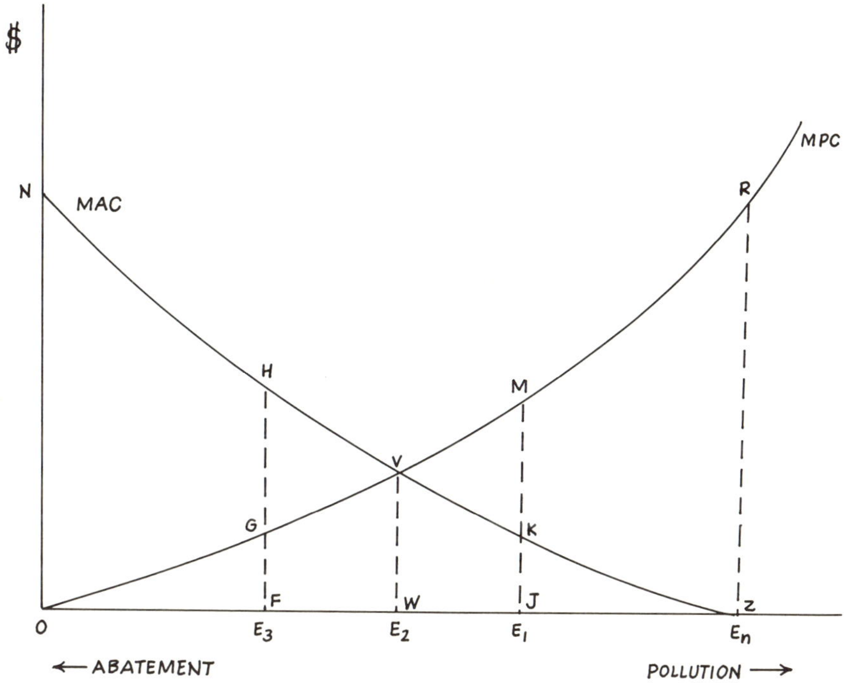

Figure 2-1. The efficient level of abatement.

be willing to pay only *GF* for Alpha to undertake that level of abatement, yet Alpha would require *HF*. Hence, omissions at E_2 would be the equilibrium outcome starting from E_n and the presumptive rights protecting Alpha. At this equilibrium level Alpha's willingness to undertake abatement for a payment of *VW* exactly matches Beta's willingness to pay for abatement.

Once we reach emissions level E_2 Beta may have paid as much as *WVRZ* to Alpha, of which *WVZ* has been spent by Alpha on abatement. The remainder, *VRZ*, represents rents accruing to Alpha because of Beta's ignorance of the exact amount necessary to bribe Alpha. Of course, in a world of zero transaction costs we know that perfect information is costless and so Beta would only pay Alpha the amount *VWZ*—which is the exact minimum that Alpha would require.

Now consider the alternative institutional structure in which it is Beta that is protected by presumptive rights. In this case we start at the origin with zero discharges (and full abatement by Alpha). Here, however, Alpha has a large incentive to convince Beta to permit some discharges. At the outset Alpha could afford to pay as much as *ON* to Beta to be permitted to discharge the first unit of effluent. Using the same logic as above the two parties would ultimately settle on an emissions level of E_2.

Notice that in a world of zero transaction costs the equilibrium level of emissions is indeed the same regardless of the status quo structure of rights. When Alpha is protected in the status quo it is Beta that must buy abatement at level E_2. When Beta is protected in the status quo it is Alpha that must buy discharges at level E_2. When Coase and others assume away income effects it should be clear what is being said. For here we see that the two different rights structure have different implications for the direction of payments as between the two parties. To assume away income effects is simply to assume that this movement of funds does not affect the respective demand and supply curves that define the bargaining space of the protagonists. Assuming away income effects does not mean that the ultimate income position of the two disputants is indifferent to the status quo legal structure.

We should also notice that in this world of zero transactions costs all Pareto-relevant externalities would have been bargained away. The ultimate level of emissions at E_2 has exhausted all gains from trade. Here Beta is still bearing unwanted pollution costs, and Alpha is bearing unwanted abatement costs. As indicated earlier, in a world of zero transaction costs there can be no Pareto-relevant externalities—by definition.

In Case II we now relax the assumption of zero transation costs. Under an assumed institutional structure where Alpha is protected by the status quo it is Beta that is harmed and so Beta will seek relief. Under the alternative legal structure it is Alpha that will desire to be allowed to discharge pollutants. Once transaction costs are no longer assumed to be zero, the efforts of either party will require time and financial resources. Recall that it is the party *not* protected by the extant legal structure that must initiate the action to deal with the other party. Information and contracting are expensive, and these costs are, for the most part, borne by the party that is vulnerable to unwanted costs in the status quo.

Under the status quo protection of Alpha it is Beta that must pay these costs. In terms of figure 2-1 we must then recognize that Beta's net willingness to offer payments to Alpha will be diminished to the extent that these transaction costs have fallen on Beta. This new net bid curve is labeled *BNB* (for Beta's Net Bid) in figure 2-2. If E_n again represents the status quo emissions level when Alpha is protected by presumptive rights, then Beta's new net bid is R' rather than R. Notice that this has the effect of shifting the ultimate equilibrium level of emissions to the right as compared to the solution with zero transaction costs (E_2). Beta must experience an increased pollution load. At this level Beta still has a willingness to pay along *MPC*,

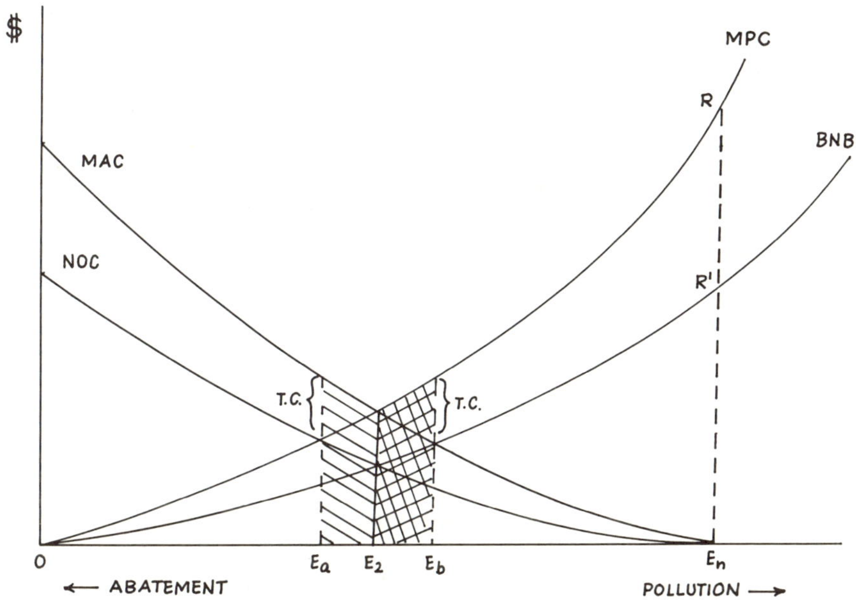

Figure 2-2. Efficient abatement with transaction costs.

but a reduced ability to buy out Alpha because of the transaction costs that must be incurred. The shaded area between E_2 and E_b represents the residual costs that Beta must bear because of the presence of transaction costs.

Now consider the opposite situation in which it is Beta that is protected by presumptive rights, and it is Alpha that must incur expenses to bargain with Beta over the possibility of emissions. Using the same logic, the incidence of these transaction costs on Alpha will reduce the ability to offer payments to Beta to be allowed to discharge affluents. We thus derive a new Net Offer Curve (*NOC*) in figure 2-2. The equilibrium level of pollution under this new assumed status quo (E_a) is seen to be restricted beyond the original equilibrium level when transaction costs were assumed not to exist. The shaded area between E_a and E_2 here indicates the excess costs borne by Alpha because of these bargaining costs.

The economically efficient level of an externality is seen to be dependent upon the status quo institutional set up, since it is this structure that both liberates and constrains decision units. Moreover, the structure is responsible for a different burden of transaction costs on the several parties to a dispute.

The real world is obviously much more complex than the simple two-party issue explored here. For one thing there may be many members of the two parties (Alpha and Beta) discussed here. With large numbers we encounter important third-party effects that merit consideration.

But the central conclusion to be drawn from these simple models is that the still-widespread notion that externalities are indifferent to the status quo property structure is untenable. Nor does it seem reasonable to hide behind an assumption of zero transaction costs, and no income effects. If transaction costs are zero there are no Pareto-relevant externalities to consider. But since transaction costs are obviously nonzero, and since income effects are surely important, externality theory and policy is dominated by the institutional realities of the world in which we live. Let us turn now to a discussion of that ignored—but critical—dimension.

The Institutional Issues

The essence of externalities is costs—costs imposed via a physical interdependence that links nominally independent decision units. I say "nominally" for the reason that as long as the two decision units are linked in this manner they are not really independent units. Not only are there unwanted costs visited on recipients of externalities, these costs are not compensated for by the emittor.

What is it that allows certain costs to transgress nominal boundaries of decision units and to persist in the face of opposition by the victim? It is the prevailing institutional structure of entitlements; it is the view that an emittor has a presumptive right to continue such activity since that is how things have always been. Factories have always spewed smoke and dumped their liquid garbage in rivers; farmers have been applying chemicals to control weeds and insects for the past 40 years; new buildings have been blocking the view from older buildings as long as there have been cities.

While we have elegant models with which to derive the optimal level of externalities, it remains obvious that any optimality we might derive is an artifact of the structure of entitlements taken for granted when the analysis is done. There is, after all, a Pareto-optimal allocation of resources for every possibly structure of resource endowments, which is another term for institutional structure.

To recognize this, and to discuss its implications, is not to abandon objectivity. Nor is it to be heretical against the neoclassical received doctrine. It is simply to attempt to make endogenous that which most economists have been taught to consider as exogenous. It is true that to raise the question of institutional arrangements is to raise some quite fundamental questions about the conventional wisdom of externality theory and policy.

To understand the incidence of unwanted costs, and the relationship to efficiency analysis, we must first understand the prevailing structure of entitlements (institutions), and we must be capable of viewing that structure in a conceptually useful way. This is necessary for the simple reason that it is the institutional structure that allows certain unwanted costs to remain uncompensated—and often unassailable. That is, this structure allows the perpetrator of unwanted costs to decline to enter into an exchange with the victim(s), at which time the true believer of neoclassical doctrine would place that particular externality in the category of Pareto-irrelevant. After that definitional coup de grace, the economist could announce, with some satisfaction, that at least for that particular interdependence, we had a Pareto-optimal outcome.

Policy makers, sad to say, are not much smitten by the notions of Pareto-optimality and Pareto-irrelevance. They see trees devasted by acid deposition, they see fish killed by Kepone, they see warnings not to eat whitefish, lake trout, and coho salmon from the Great Lakes and they ask—at the insistence of a subset of their constituents—why, if things are optimal to the economist, are these events going on? For the economists to hide behind Pareto-irrelevancy is to invite the most complete disbelief—not to mention scorn.

Let us, therefore, introduce into our discussion of externalities an understanding of the institutional arrangements that define the rights, privileges, duties, and exposures of the parties to a physical interdependence.

Any particular status quo can be defined in legal terms as consisting of a structure of actual rights, and presumptive rights. Actual rights have correlated with them a duty on the part of others to recognize those rights. Fee simple ownership of land bestows the right to construct certain types of buildings on that land, and for nonowners to exercise their duty to enter that land or building only at the prior agreement of the right holder. To have a right that is protected by a property rule is to be protected against unwanted (and proscribed) incursions of either a physical or an economic nature. To have a right that is protected by a liability rule is to rest assured that even if an untoward act occurs against your interests, the party committing that act is liable for damages. Fee simple ownership of land is a right protected by a property rule. In certain instances that same right is protected by a liability rule; this would be the case if errant pesticides ruined your garden and the guilty party was made to pay damages. The essence of actual rights is a correlated duty that is exercised ex ante (when a property rule is in place) or ex post (when a liability rule is in place). What we have then is a situation where the duty bearer is compelled to recognize a set of actual rights.

Instances of actual rights and correlated duties are best thought of as situations where the law is reasonably clear, although that does not imply that it deals adequately with new situations. The law can be clear about me not trespassing on your land, but quite unclear about my pesticides drifting to your land and causing harm; or about a nearby landfill ruining land values.

Externalities are found precisely in this gray area of the law, and instead of a clear institutional setting of rights and duties, we are more likely to find ourselves in the domain of presumptive rights on the part of the victim. The conventional legal terminology for this situation is "privilege" and "no rights."

What is meant by a situation of privilege and no rights? Privilege is the legal setting in which individual B is free to impose costs on individual A without any regard to A's feelings about those costs. Individual B has privilege, while A has no rights. If that sounds like the externality situations we have been discussing all along, do not be surprised. Externalities are precisely those instances in which the victim has no rights, and the party imposing the unwanted costs has privilege—or presumptive rights.

Of course not all externality situations are exactly this clear cut. Families that knowingly move into the immediate vicinity of a major airport cannot really be considered innocent and helpless victims of the airlines. For one thing, houses can be purchased in such neighborhoods at a discount over comparable housing in the absence of noise. And, as Coase reminded us, many externalities are reciprocal in the sense that stopping the unwanted costs to A will entail forcing unwanted costs on B.

But for the most part we can characterize externalities as situations in which one party has privilege, and the other party has no rights. In the case of acid rain the coal-burning utilities have privilege and those with forest or agricultural lands—or those who care about the quality of northern lakes—have no rights.

The nature of interdependence and interference among economic agents can be highlighted by drawing a more careful distinction among the various types of entitlements within the fundamental Hohfeldian legal relationships (table 2-1). There the concept of rights and duties was manifest both in practice and in the law. Consider two people—Alpha and Beta—who are represented by the rights-duties and privileges-no rights correlates. We say that Alpha has rights and Beta has duties. But what sorts of rights and duties are these? That is, how are these correlates given effect in everyday life? We can illuminate this further refinement in property relations by considering various way in which Alpha and Beta might interfere with one another. Such interference could take the form of allowing trees to block the other's access to the sun, building a high-rise apartment in the line of the

Table 2-1 The three types of entitlements under right-duty and privilege-no right[a]

Alpha	*Beta*
Right	*Duty*
Alpha has a right protected by a property rule.	Beta has duty against Alpha's protection by a property rule.
Alpha has a right protected by a liability rule.	Beta has duty against Alpha's protection by a liability rule.
Alpha has a right protected by an inalienability rule.	Beta has duty against Alpha's protection by an inalienability rule.
Privilege	*No Right*
Alpha has privilege protected by a property rule.	Beta has no right against Alpha's protection by a property rule.
Alpha has privilege protected by a liability rule.	Beta has no right against Alpha's protection by a liability rule.
Alpha has privilege protected by an inalienability rule.	Beta has no right against Alpha's protection by an inalienability rule.

[a] We here consider only two of the four legal relations advanced by Hohfeld; "power" and "liability", and "immunity" and "no power" are not discussed.

other's view of the lake, or dumping industrial wastes into a river which then kill the fish sought by the other party.

Consider first the rights-duties correlate. The rights that Alpha has are of several possible varieties. The first type is the right that says Beta may not interfere with Alpha without the latter's consent. This is the purest type of right-duty correlate, and the one most obvious when we mention the concept of a right and a duty. An example of this type of relationship would be the situation in which Beta could not harvest broccoli from Alpha's garden without the latter's permission. We will classify this type of right as the protection of Alpha by a *property rule*, or we will say that Alpha's *rights are protected by a property rule*. Similarly, Beta's *duties are proscribed by a property rule protecting Alpha* [Calabresi and Melamed 1972].

The essence of rights protected by property rules is that the party wishing to contravene those rights must initiate the bargaining process, and must bear the bulk of the transaction costs related to that process. In this instance it is Beta who must approach Alpha prior to any interference with the latter's rights. This is what the protection by a property rule requires.

Now consider a second way in which Alpha might have rights protected.

Assume it is possible for Beta to proceed to interfere with the rights of Alpha, but such interference is done with the knowledge that compensation will be required ex post—the exact magnitude to be determined by a (presumably) neutral third party. An example is found here with respect to certain types of damages that are difficult to anticipate before the fact; oil spills from tankers on the high seas are a classic case. A coastal nation is protected from oil spills by a liability rule that requires compensation from the ship owner after the fact. It would make little sense to have these rights protected by a property rule since this would require ex ante bargaining, when the full magnitude of the interference—that is the full magnitude of the damages from the spill—will never be known until *after* a spill. The ship owner (Beta) has duties while the coastal nation (Alpha) has rights. These rights are protected by a liability rule.

Another example of protection for Alpha by a liability rule is that of compensation for wildlife damage on a farmer's fields. In this instance the state agency responsible for wildlife management acts as agent for hunters, and pays damages to farmers who make claims for crop losses by, say, deer. Here, the farmers (Alpha) are protected by a liability rule. Again, the impossibility of determining a priori what the necessary payment will be precludes protection of Alpha by a property rule. Alpha still has rights, but they are protected by a liability rule rather than a property rule.

The final manner in which Alpha's rights might be given protection is that of an inalienability rule. Here Beta may not interfere with Alpha under any circumstances; there is no price at which Alpha would agree to the interference. The example that comes to mind under the inalienability rule is the right to be free from dangerous toxic chemicals in domestic water supplies. When we find the outright banning of certain chemicals then we find Alpha protected by an inalienability rule.

Hence, within the rights-duties correlate there are three different ways in which Alpha may be protected, and thus there are three ways in which Beta might be bound by duties. When Alpha is protected by a property rule Beta has no choice but to approach Alpha to attempt to bargain. When Alpha is protected by a liability rule Beta may proceed to act—with the possibility that doing so will interfere with Alpha—but must be prepared to pay compensation set by a third party. Finally, when Alpha is protected by an inalienability rule there is no price that would permit Beta to interfere with Alpha; bargaining either ex ante or ex post is precluded.

Let us now turn to the second set of correlates, those pertaining to privileges and no rights. Recall that privilege is a situation in which Alpha may undertake actions that may be quite detrimental to Beta, but need hold no particular concern for the feelings of Beta about such interference. Here we have a situation in which Alpha may interfere with Beta and can only be stopped if Beta buys off Alpha. In this instance Alpha is the interfering party, while Beta is the receiving party; it is Beta upon whom costs are being imposed by Alpha's actions, yet it is Beta who must initiate ameliorative action to prevent the harm from being imposed. This action would consist of Beta somehow bribing (or buying out) Alpha. In this case we would say that Alpha's *privilege is protected by a property rule against Beta's no right*. To return to our earlier example concerning the color of my neighbor's house, the only way I can influence the way in which my neighbor chooses to paint the house is to agree to meet her price. If she decides to move and if I am terrorized by the prospects that she may sell to someone who likes purple houses then my only recourse—in view of my no-right position—is to meet her highest offer, and then resell the house to a more reliable buyer. But since I have no rights it costs me money to have my interests represented. When I do not have government (the law) on my side, my desires can only be given effect if I spend money.

The second property relation (entitlement) under the privilege-no right correlate is that where Beta may stop the interference by Alpha, but in doing so must be prepared to compensate Alpha (ex post) in an amount to be determined by a neutral third party. Alpha still has privilege over Beta—that is, Alpha may still impose costs on Beta. If Beta wants those costs terminated then it will be necessary to pay some compensation. As in the rights-duties correlate, this second form of protection for Alpha is one of a liability rule. Also, as above, the compensation is to be determined by a third party rather than as a process in which Alpha and Beta become engaged in bargaining. Property rules imply prior bargaining where both parties must agree to a price or there will be no change in the status quo. Liability rules imply efforts to redress grievances after the fact—with the settlement (the compensation) not being subject to the relative strength and wealth of the antagonists but rather set by the neutral eye of a third party (usually the state).

We can now return to the statement made earlier that property institutions sanctify the imposition of costs on others: property indicates which costs must be considered by the various decision making units in a society. In the early days of the Industrial Revolution workers had no property in their labor power, and so it was cheap for early capitalists to ignore the costs to those workers suffering injuring in the workplace; it was—of course—not unnoticed as an inconvenience to the families of the injured workers, but the workers had no rights, and the capitalists had privilege. A similar story could be told about early coal miners where mine safety could be ignored by the owners of the mines. Once it became more expensive for the owners to ignore mine safety—that is, once the workers had some property in their future income stream—then it became more costly for owners to be so cavalier about safety. It was then that a benefit-cost calculation by the owner would reveal that it suddenly would "pay" to invest in mine safety. The workers were able to convert their *no rights* situation to one of *rights* and the mine owners were moved from a position of *privilege* to one of *duty*.

We should not assume from this that the privilege-no right correlate is the only one in which costs are imposed on ungrateful victims. A binding labor contract—or slavery for that matter—are instances where the rights-duties correlate holds and yet those with duty may still be bearing some large unwanted costs.

The essence of protection by right and privilege—and the more specific protection by property rules, liability rules, or inalienability rules—is that one can disregard certain costs. Property arrangements define which of these costs might legally be ignored, and property legitimizes those costs that are so visited on others. It is the confrontation between those causing such costs and those on whom they fall that is at the heart of the conflict over social arrangements in general—and natural resources in particular. When people complain about "government interference" what they are really saying is that some costs which they were formerly able to ignore must now be internalized. One man's government interference is another's government protection [Samuels 1971].

This inability to continue to ignore certain costs is obviously uncomfortable to people who have often grown quite comfortable—literally as well as figuratively—with the status quo. Is it any wonder that they complain? When various states and the federal government began to outlaw child labor the factory owners screamed about government interference. But if government had not acted in the interests of the children would we label that inaction as "interference" in their lives? Unlikely. If government protects those who are currently able to ignore certain costs visited on others we do not consider it government "interference" with those now bearing such costs. On the other hand if government moves to protect those currently being visited with costs—those with duties or no rights—that action is referred to as government "interference." When the presumptive rights or privilege of certain economic agents is threatened then government becomes the enemy.

Factories had the presumptive "right" to treat children as their owners saw fit, and to discharge their effluent into the nearest river. Mine owners had the presumptive "right" to disregard the safety of those sent below. Farmers had the presumptive "right" to allow their cows' manure to wash into the stream. Meat packers had the presumptive "right" to sell any product on which they might make a profit—regardless of the health implications for those who might eat it. All of these presumptive "rights" have been challenged and changed. But not without an unrelenting gnashing of teeth from the captains of industry and others inconvenienced by the need now to absorb costs that were formerly imposed on others.

By way of summary, we have seen how two of four legal relations attributable to Hohfeld can be further categorized into property rules, liability rules, and inalienability rules. The obvious question becomes, which type of situation calls for which type of rule? One obvious place to start is with the nature of the transaction costs implied by each form of entitlement. Under a property rule it is necessary for the parties to negotiate prior to the action and to arrive at some bargain. Under a liability rule it is understood that actions with interfering aspects are going to occur, and compensation for the inconvenience follows the action.

For the property rule to be effective it must be possible for the parties to the interference to meet beforehand. When many individuals have an interest in the situation this is usually impossible. Thus, a liability rule would be more practical in that the interfering party could proceed, but with the knowledge that a subsequent payment would be necessary.

In a sense the 1972 amendments to the Federal Water Pollution Control Act (PL92-500) modified the structure of entitlements for pollution emissions into streams, lakes, and rivers by changing it from a privilege protected by a property rule for those who dump, to a right for recipients that is protected by either a property rule, a liability rule, or an inalienable entitlement for toxic substances. The National Pollution Discharge Elimination System calls for the issuance of permits for effluent discharges, with a graduated fee paid by the dumping party. This is neither an effluent tax so often advocated in the literature, nor is it compensation in the sense implied in the above discussion of the liability rules. Yet, it does represent a shift from the former situation, in which dischargers enjoyed a privilege.

It is also important to recognize that the tendencies for interference will differ between the two types of entitlements. Since the property rule requires a prior arrangement, we might assume that if my lake view is protected by a liability rule, my neighbor will have a greater incentive to build a fence in my line of sight than if I am protected by a property rule. Even when we assume that the required compensation from the neighbor under a liability rule exactly matches the bargained price under a property rule, under the latter entitlement the neighbor must approach me first and begin the (possibly) tedious bargaining process. The level of transaction costs for the neighbor is greater under a property rule than under a liability rule, hence we might expect interference to be greater under the latter. This difference in transaction costs arises since, under the liability rule, it is I (the "injured" party) who must initiate action that will result in compensation; I must actively initiate the compensation process, even though I did not initiate the action for which compensation is to be paid. Under an entitlement by which I am protected not by a liability rule but by a property rule, the active party must initiate the action to seek my approval.

The Policy Problem and Contemporary Analysis

The economist who wishes to say useful things about externalities is faced with several difficulties. Our models are most rigorous when concerned with incremental change within a constant institutional setup. Welfare theory—the explicitly normative branch of our science—offers direction for judging bargains struck by individual decision makers. The insights from much of this literature have been important in developing a coherent body of thought.

However, one senses that economists and those responsible for externality policy are, after all of this impressive progress, still failing to communicate. It would seem that as theorists we need to work harder to rationalize our own constructs, as well as to connect them more closely with the world of public policy.

The obvious place to start would seem to be with the explicit policy conclusions dervied from externality models—specifically the conclusion of Pareto-irrelevancy. Of course everyone—not just economists—should be interested in gaining efficiency. Let there be no mistaken view that I favor inefficiency. But it remains true that some economists have a tendency to celebrate efficiency to an extreme that ensures their isolation from the everyday policy struggle that is concerned with reconciling unwanted joint costs. The quest of economics as a social science has been unremittingly toward the idea of an objective—value free—discipline. The result of that search for truth has been to strip externality theory of any ethical content.

As theory, that is as it should be; as policy science, it leaves us with a sterile message. Pareto-irrelevancy as a theoretical justification to excuse us from the policy arena will continue to plague economists. Until we admit that externalities are about unwanted costs borne by members of a political system, and until we incorporate this reality into our theory, I fear that we will remain isolated.

A larger measure of the problem may be that economists have yet to come to grips with the relationship between the state and markets. The consistent liberal (in the traditional meaning of that term) economist starts with the notion that the state should setup the conditions for atomistic choice, and then step aside and let consensual bargainers get on with the business of maximizing aggregate satisfaction. The minimal state would—when new conditions require any modification of the prevailing institutional structure—follow Pareto–Wicksellian dictates by compensating those who were harmed by the change. This would protect the state from willy-nilly shifting economic advantage among the polity.

That this sanctifies the status quo should be obvious. In practice it means that all manner of offensive or dangerous activity, just because it is in existence, must be bought off by those who seek relief. Such economic theology is innocent of the constitutional distinction between eminent domain (which is compensable), and exercise of the police power (which is not). The tyranny of the status quo in externality policy, justified by the concept of Pareto-irrelevancy, is a serious matter.

Such a view of the world subjugates the political process to the market—a breathtaking convolution of reality. It also confuses the very essence of welfare economics, specifically that for any particular institutional structure there is a Pareto-efficient allocation of resources against which any number of externality situations might be judged Pareto-irrelevant. Since it is the institutional structure defining property rights that indicates which costs must be reckoned by atomistic agents we find ourselves using welfare theory inside of this very institutional structure to disregard certain unwanted costs as irrelevant.

It should be clear, therefore, that the concept of government "intervention" is thus stripped of any analytical—though not emotional—content. Just when did government intervene? When the prevailing market processes were first established? Or only when those currently protected by property rights see that they might be forced to internalize costs hitherto shifted to others? Alpha's intervention is Beta's relief.

One persistent puzzle in externality theory and policy concerns why we continue to see primary reliance upon pollution standards and quotas in the face of near unanimity among economists favoring effluent taxes? In this economists are opposed by both politicians and the industries currently imposing unwanted costs. Surely perceptions of the potential administrative costs of a system of effluent charges figure in shaping this particular policy outcome. But another measures of blame may go to us for failing to show that we understand the politics of unwanted costs. One might speculate that we see here the familiar ambivalence of business to real market processes. By that I mean the observation that those in business celebrate the metaphor of the market—but most vociferously when it is serving them well. When conditions turn less favorable it is not so easy to agree with market outcomes; indeed it is then that any number of erstwhile market apologists seek government relief. Consistency in such matters may be too much for us to require, or even expect.

The economist can regain currency in the political economy of externalities if we would focus the policy debate in a way that highlights the efficiency and distributional aspects of unwanted costs. That is, it should fall to us to frame the issues in a way that allows the policy process to reach of its own accord solutions that are equitable and yet avoid the most egregious inefficiencies. As Dahlman [1979] reminds us, workable policy prescriptions must be derived from comparison of the status quo with an attainable concept of the desideratum. To the extent that our usual view of the ideal world assumes away transaction costs and welfare (income) effects—conditions that preclude the existence of Pareto-relevant externalities in the first instance—then the policy goal can never be achieved.

But an alternative model that admits of the presence of transaction costs, income effects, and the very real fact of cost incidence on unwilling parties provides a feasible starting point from which to undertake an analysis of externalities and their resolution. The very fact that environmental control is still regarded as the *marginal* cost of a polluting commodity (coal, electricity produced with coal, paper, many products containing undesirable chemicals) indicates that we have not been successful in framing the issues. Until we convince those in charge of environmental policy that the full marginal social cost of offending products is not being paid by consumers then we have failed in our educational mission.

Yet another educational job is to be found in the matter of the cost incidence of the status quo while the search for decisive information continues. As indicated earlier, those benefiting from the current structure of institutional arrangements will continue to press for more research—all the while shifting costs to others. Those now bearing unwanted costs might be excused for growing impatient while the search goes on for the perfect data. The burden of transaction costs falls mainly on those currently not protected by rights. Economists would do well to study externalities from this perspective.

It seems a safe prediction that externalities will persist, and in fact become a more important element of economic life. Population density and certain technologies almost guarantee as much. There is yet another factor. One aspect of technology is the growth of knowledge that allows us to establish with greater precision causality of certain events hitherto blamed on "mother nature." As medical science advances we find out that certain outcomes were contributed to by all manner of human artifacts. These soon result in efforts to resolve the matter; such efforts being aimed at the legislative or judicial branches of government. While "acts of God" are not policy variables, actions taken by other individuals or groups clearly are. One ramification of science reducing the unexplained variation in the world around us is to bring ever more conflicts up for mediation. You feel differently about unwanted costs that are an "inexplicable part of life" than you do about unwanted costs visited on you by a neighbor—or, better yet, some distant corporation.

Economists will continue to have an important role to play in the domain of externality policy. That role will be enhanced to the extent that we understand the legal aspects of rights and duties, privileges and no rights, and inalienability. It will also be enhanced to the extent that we appreciate statutory and case law in matters of nuisance, tort, and property law. In short, it will require that we once again become political economists.

References

Bator, F. M. 1958. "The anatomy of market failure." *Quarterly Journal of Economics* 72:351–379.

Baumol, W. J. 1972. "On taxation and the control of externalities." *American Economic Review* 62:307–322.

Baumol, W. J., and W. E. Oates. 1975. "The theory of environmental policy." Englewood Cliffs, NJ: Prentice-Hall.

Bromley, D. W. 1978. "Property rules, liability rules, and environmental economics." *Journal of Economic Issues* 12:43–60.

Bromley, D. W. 1982. "Land and water problems: An institutional perspective." *American Journal of Agricultural Economics* 64:834–844.

Buchanan, J. M. 1962. "Politics, policy, and the Pigovian margins." *Economica* 29:17–28.

Buchanan, J. M. 1972. "Politics, property, and the law: An alternative explanation of Miller et al. v. Schoene." *Journal of Law and Economics* 15:439–452.

Buchanan, J. M., and W. C. Stubblebine. 1962. "Externality." *Economica* 29: 371–384.

Buchanan, J. M., and G. Tullock. 1975. "Polluters' profits and political response: Direct controls versus taxes." *American Economic Review* 65:139–147.

Burrows, P. 1980. "The Economic theory of pollution control." Cambridge: MIT Press.

Calabresi, G and A. D. Melamed. 1972. "Property rules, liability rules, and inalienability: One view of the cathedral," *Harvard Law Review* 85:1089–1128.

Coase, R. H. 1960. "The problem of social cost." *Journal of Law and Economics* 3:1–44.

Dahlman, C. J. 1979. "The problem of externality." *Journal of Law and Economics* 22:141–162.

Freeman, A. M., III. 1984. "Depletable externalities and Pigouvian taxation."

Journal of Environmental Economics and Management 11:173–179.
Hohfeld, W. M. 1917. "Fundamental legal conceptions as applied in judicial reasoning." *Yale Law Review* 26:710–770.
Kamien, M. I., N. L. Schwartz, and F. T. Dolbear. 1966. "Asymmetry between bribes and charges." *Water Resources Research* 1:147–157.
Marchand, J. R., and K. P. Russell. 1973. "Externalities, liability, separability, and resource allocation." *American Economic Review* 63:611–620.
Mishan, E. J. 1971. "The postwar literature on externalities: An interpretative essay." *Journal of Economic Literature* 9:1–28.
Polinsky, A. M. 1980. "On the choice between property rules and liability rules." *Economic Inquiry* 18:233–246.
Randall, A. 1971. "Market solutions to externality problems: Theory and practice." *American Journal of Agricultural Economics* 54:175–183.
Randall, A. 1974. "Coasian externality theory in a policy context." *Natural Resources Journal* 14:35–54.
Runge, C. F. 1981. "Common-property externalities: Isolation, assurance, and resource depletion in a traditional grazing context." *American Journal of Agricultural Economics* 63:595–607.
Samuels, W. J. 1971. "Interrelations between legal and economic processes." *Journal of Law and Economics* 14:435–450.
Samuels, W. J. 1972. "In defense of a positive approach to government as an economic variable." *Journal of Law and Economics* 15:453–459.
Tietenberg, T. H. 1980. "Transferable discharge permits and the control of stationary-source air pollution: A survey and synthesis." *Land Economics* 56: 391–416.

COMMENT 1

Wallace E. Oates

The Bromley chapter raises an issue of central concern to the proper functioning of a market economy: the existence of externalities and their implications for public policy. I shall argue in my comments here that there are compelling reasons for believing that a broad class of externalities will be the source of serious distortions in a purely market-determined allocation of resources. Moreover, as Bromley argues, "It seems a safe prediction that externalities will persist, and in fact become a more important element of economic life." In this context, William Baumol [1967] has shown that as the population in a given locality grows, the opportunity for interactions of all sorts (and particularly of external effects) rises with the *square* of the population, suggesting the potential for externally borne costs to grow at a disproportionate rate within an expanding community.

Bromley provides us with a careful and illuminating treatment of externalities. In particular, he calls our attention to the institutional setting and the important role that property rights and transaction costs play in determining the range and effects of externalities. His discussion, however, runs largely

I am grateful to the National Science Foundation for its support of my research on environmental policy.

in terms of a Coasian setting with two (or a few) participants trying to resolve successfully an externality through bargains (or other means) that realize the potential gains-from-trade. It is in this small-group setting that there exists the capacity for voluntary negotiations to correct the distortions that would otherwise result from the externality. These cases may, for this reason, be the least troublesome for the effective operation of the economy. However, even here (as Bromley notes) the presence of transaction costs can seriously impede the resolution of the externality. Moreover, the possibility of strategic behavior in the bilateral-monopoly case must reduce our confidence in a Coasian outcome. Nevertheless, one can at least argue that in the small-group setting the status quo will be likely to represent a reasonably successful handling of the problem.

There is, however, another class of externalities involving numerous participants for which the Coase analysis is simply inapplicable (and it is an important class). Where factories spew smoke over large metropolitan areas or where plants pollute bodies of water with large numbers of users, it is very hard to visualize a feasible process of negotiation among the large number of interested parties. For the large-group case, the Coase framework is simply irrelevant.

In the absence of Coasian negotiations, it is a straightforward exercise to show that activities involving external diseconomies (like pollution) will be extended to excessive levels [Baumol and Oates 1975, ch. 4]. For the large-group case, the presumption is not that the status quo (in the absence of public policy) will represent a Pareto-irrelevant externality; on the contrary, the market outcome will most certainly involve excessive degradation of the environment.

I shall try in my comments here to do two things: first, to explore the theory of externalities and its implications for the large-group case; and, second, to develop the policy relevance of this analysis with reference to some innovative new policy measures for the control of pollution.

Externalities Theory and the Large-Group Case

By the large-group case, I shall mean a setting in which there are a large number of *either* polluters or of victims. For purposes of discussion, I take as a prototype the standard illustration of the factory whose smoke emissions pollute the air over a substantial area with numerous residential and commercial units. The victims in this instance constitute the large group. Referring back to Bromley's figure 2-1, our prototype polluter will, in the absence of any policy measures or other inducements, extend his smoke emissions to

E_n. Moreover, the transaction costs inherent in attempts to organize the victims into a unit to negotiate effectively with the factory management are likely to be prohibitive; as Mancur Olson [1965] has shown, the incentives for free-riding by individuals in such a group can easily undermine efforts for collective action when dealing with a public good (or bad) such as pollution.

Thus, the presumption for the large-group case is pollution in excess of the socially optimal level. Economic analysis can provide some further insight into the nature of the problem and a potential remedy. Clean air is seen to be a scarce resource like the labor and raw materials employed in the manufacture of the firm's output, but unlike these other inputs, it is available without cost. The economic solution thus involves placing the appropriate price on this scarce resource. Referring again to figure 2-1, a unit tax (or effluent fee) on smoke emissions of vw will serve to *internalize* the externality and induce a cost-minimizing firm to reduce the level of pollution to the socially optimal level of E_2. This, of course, is the famous Pigouvian tax that has served as the basis for economic prescriptions for pollution control for many decades.[1]

As Bromley notes, the Pigouvian prescription has also been the subject of much criticism along Coasian lines. The Coasian position has validity but only for the case where voluntary bargains eliminate the potential distortions stemming from the externality. For this Coasian case, a Pigouvian tax can itself be the source of distortions [Coase 1960; Turvey 1963]. But again I emphasize that for the large-group case, the Coasian analysis is not applicable. In the large-number setting, it is a straightforward matter to demonstrate that a Pigouvian tax equal to marginal social damage at the optimal level of the externality can sustain a competitive equilibrium that satisfies the first-order conditions for an efficient outcome [Baumol and Oates 1975, ch. 4].[2]

The analysis provides some further insights. Bromley raises the tricky issue of compensation of victims by polluters. In the large-group case, the Pigouvian line of analysis provides an unambiguous answer to the compensation question: on economic efficiency grounds, victims must not, in general, receive compensation for damages. The rationale for this result is straightforward. Victims often have available to them ways to avoid or reduce the damages they suffer: they can, for example, insulate their homes against unwanted noise, or even relocate to avoid, say, pollution. Achieving the efficient levels of such alleviation activities is, in fact, an integral part of the externalities problem. But if victims are *fully* compensated for damages, they have no incentive to undertake alleviation activity. In fact, it can be shown [Oates 1983] that if victims receive no compensation whatsoever, they have precisely the right incentive to engage in the economically efficient levels of alleviation measures.

This proposition, incidentally, clarifies an issue raised in the original Coase paper. It was Coase's claim that under certain circumstances, victims need to be taxed to make them take into account the costs their decisions place on polluters. For example, a resident who moves closer to a smoky factory, thereby increasing the level of social damages with a resulting increase in the tax on the factory, should himself face some sort of levy equal to the cost that his move imposes on the factory. This, however, is simply wrong [Oates 1983]. What the Coasian analysis overlooks is that there is a fundamental assymetry in the pollution problem. As Bromley points out in his discussion of the definition of an externality, an argument in the victim's utility function is dependent upon an activity of the polluter (*but not vice versa*). And this asymmetry matters. It gives rise to the result that the polluter should be subject to a tax equal to marginal social damage, but the victim should neither receive compensation nor pay a tax. The level of the external damages itself provides the right signal for inducing the efficient pursuit of measures by the victim to alleviate the damages.

The Pigouvian analysis, as noted, runs in terms of a tax (i.e., an effluent fee in the case of waste emissions) per unit of the external diseconomy. However, we could adopt, instead of a tax on pollution, a subsidy for abatement. Such a subsidy, as Bromley indicates, is not a satisfactory alternative to the Pigouvian tax because of the long-run incentive it creates for the entry of new sources of pollution. But there is a further alternative. As the externalities literature makes clear [Weitzman 1974], it is possible to set "quantity" rather than "price." Instead of levying a Pigouvian tax equal to marginal social damage, the environmental authority could issue emission permits that, in the aggregate, result in the efficient level of pollution. Such permits could either be auctioned off by the authority or simply assigned initially to sources (or others). But they would be marketable so that sources would be free to buy and sell them. Such a marketable permit system has the capacity to realize the same efficient outcome as the Pigouvian tax.[3] In short, the environmental agency can either levy the Pigouvian tax or introduce tradeable permits and let the forces of supply and demand determine the market-clearing price.

Externalities Theory and Policy Realities

In spite of having a systematic and compelling perspective on the problem of pollution (and other externalities issues like congestion), economists really have not, as Bromley notes, had much influence on actual policy determination. This has been something of a puzzle to the profession. Part of the answer is perhaps attributable to a failure of communication—a failure on the part of economists to make clear to policy makers the basic rationale for Pigouvian tax measures. Steven Kelman [1981], in an extensive series of interviews with policy makers and lobbyists, was unable to find a single person who could explain the economist's efficiency argument for the use of effluent fees!

There is, I think, more to the story. As Buchanan and Tullock [1975] have argued, polluters may have a real stake in the existing command-and-control system. In spite of the burdensome nature of the prescribed regulations (often involving mandated treatment procedures), existing sources may easily find such measures preferable to Pigouvian taxes. A tax after all represents an additional cost to the polluter; sources are understandably not overly enthusiastic with a proposal that would introduce a further form of taxation on them. In addition, Buchanan and Tullock point out that these regulations can frequently represent effective barriers-to-entry into the industry so that existing sources can make use of such measures to fend off potential competition. The lack of interest in, or active opposition to, a system of effluent fees may not be an irrational response by industry sources.

However, in the last few years, there has emerged an intriguing and innovative alternative for the introduction of economic incentives for pollution control. As I noted in the preceding section, the theory of externalities suggests that we can seek to regulate externalities either through the levying of Pigouvian taxes or the adoption of marketable permits. With full information and zero transaction costs, both instruments have the desired efficiency properties.

But from the perspective of an actual regulator trying to formulate and enforce effective control measures, the two approaches are far from equivalent. After several years of advocacy of effluent charges, I am now coming to realize that the permit approach has some very compelling advantages over a system of fees. In the remainder of this section, I want to discuss these advantages and to suggest that they can explain why some recently emerging policies for the control of pollution are taking the form of systems of marketable emission permits rather than fees.

It is important to recognize at the outset that the setting for the determination of environmental policy is typically rather different from the rarified atmosphere of pure externalities theory. In particular, environmental policy typically proceeds through two stages: the first involves the setting of standards for environmental quality and the second entails the design of a regulatory system to attain these standards. My concern here will be with the second stage: the design of a system to achieve predetermined standards in the least costly and most effective way.

From the perspective of a regulator, permits promise more direct control over the level of emissions. The setting of fees, in contrast, puts the regulating agency in the less comfortable position of influencing quantity only indirectly through price. If the fee is set too low, the resulting emissions will be excessive with the consequent failure to achieve the mandated level of environmental quality. In a policy setting in which the regulator must ensure that specified levels of pollutant concentrations are not exceeded (as under the Clean Air Act in the U.S.), a preference for control over quantity to control over price is easily understandable.

Of course, an effluent fee can always be raised should the associated level of emissions prove to be excessive. But such adjustments are neither popular nor costless. Moreover, in a dynamic setting of economic growth and inflation, an appropriate fee today will be inadequate tomorrow. This puts on the regulator the unhappy burden of altering the fee as economic conditions change. No such burden exists under a permit system: quantity is fixed and the price of permits adjusts to clear the market.

Even if frequent adjustments to fees were not required, the regulator faces a further formidable problem in the design of a fee system: spatial differentiation. For most of our major air and water pollutants, the effects of emissions on environmental quality depend not only on their level but also on their location. This implies that an efficient system of control must tailor the penalty on emissions to the location of the source; the environmental authority, in short, must levy a fee appropriate to each polluter. The feasibility of such a differentiated structure of fees within an air shed or water basin is, needless to say, open to serious question. I would add that an alternative, a compromise involving a uniform fee over the entire area, can be highly unsatisfactory. Existing simulation studies of specific pollutants indicate that systems of uniform fees can be enormously costly—in some cases even more costly than the command-and-control systems they seek to replace. Marketable-permit systems, in contrast, can incorporate the spatial aspect of the pollution problem in a less objectionable way by requiring trades of permits to reflect relative contributions to levels of pollution. (See, for example, Krupnick et al. [1983].)

The design and administration of a system of marketable permits thus has some compelling advantages for the environmental agency relative to a fee system. Permits can also be more appealing to sources. As noted, one unhappy prospect for sources under a fee regime is a new form of costs: the fee bill. Not only must polluters bear their costs of abatement, but they must also pay a fee on their remaining emissions. While such payments represent a transfer from the perspective of society, they are nevertheless a cost to sources. On this point, existing simulation studies suggest some rather staggering estimates for potential fee bills. In a RAND study [Palmer et al. 1980] of chlorofluorocarbon emissions into the atmosphere, the control costs under a hypothetical CAC program were estimated to be $230 million per annum. A prospective fee program promised large savings in abatement costs—about 50 percent—with control costs estimated at $110 million. But the associated fee payments were estimated by the RAND group at $1400 million. These results suggest that a fee program would impose costs on sources over six times as large as the CAC regime. Another study of nitrous oxide emissions in the Chicago AQCR by Eugene Seskin and his colleagues [1983] reaches similarly dramatic results: they estimate that fee payments under a system of uniform effluent fees would total $414 million as compared to total control costs under a representative CAC program of $132 million.

Such figures are disturbing. For feasible policy reform, we typically search for proposals that represent a Pareto improvement. Based on existing studies, it is hard to believe that a fee system will typically make sources better off. However, a permit system need not impose additional costs on existing polluters. Instead of auctioning off the permits, the system can be set in motion with an initial distribution of permits to sources. Trading can then proceed from this initial allocation. Some have objected on equity grounds to a distribution to polluters of "property rights" to the environment. However, the equity issue is a complex one. We should recall, for instance, that most sources have already been required to institute extensive control measures to reduce their waste discharges. Starting from the existing CAC equilibrium, the proposal is to allocate entitlements only for the remaining, or residual, discharges.

Finally, the permit approach offers to both regulators and sources the attraction of a certain familiarity. The introduction of a fee system involves a wholly new form of environmental management with uncertain consequences from the perspectives of the administering agencies and polluters. Permits, in contrast, already exist. It would seem a much less radical move to make permits transferable than to supplant permits altogether by a new system of effluent fees.

For all these reasons, it is not surprising to find the evolution of environmental policy moving in the direction of marketable permits instead of fees. The excessive cost and cumbersome character of our historic CAC programs for pollution control have become increasingly evident and have intensified the search for more efficient alternatives. In the United States, an intriguing (and potentially quite revolutionary) response has been the adoption of two schemes that allow the transfer of emissions entitlements:

Emissions Trading for the control of air pollution and a system of Transferable Discharge Permits (TDP's) for the management of water quality in the State of Wisconsin.[4] While it is too early to herald these measures as introducing a widespread movement toward pricing incentives for pollution control, they do represent innovative and exciting new experiments with a market approach.

At the same time, ongoing research by environmental economists and others has clarified the properties of alternative structures of marketable permit systems. Some alternative forms of such permit systems possess the desired formal property that their competitive equilibria satisfy the first-order conditions for cost-minimization. Once, however, the element of transactions costs enters the analysis, certain forms seem preferable to others. In sum, we are developing a good grasp of (at least) the static properties of these kinds of permit markets. (See, for example, Krupnick et al. [1983].)

But I should not overstate the case. There are potential difficulties that need to be resolved. In their important work in California, Robert Hahn and Roger Noll [1983] have explored the extent of distortions that can arise from market imperfections. In particular, the presence of one large polluter with substantial power in the permit market can result in an inefficient pattern of abatement activity across sources. On another issue, Scott Atkinson and Tom Tietenberg [1982] have raised the concern that proposed market systems, although meeting the formal standards for ambient air quality, will result in degradation of local air quality in places where, under existing CAC systems, it is currently cleaner than the standards require. However, by introducing a further constraint on trading, it has been shown that such increments to air pollution can, in principle, be avoided. In fact, it is not hard to design a marketable permit system that, starting from an initial CAC equilibrium, can bring *both* improved environmental quality and reduced abatement costs to sources. (See McGartland and Oates [1985].) Such a system represents a Pareto improvement from the perspectives of both environmentalists and polluters.

The response of sources to the opportunities for trading in these markets remains to be seen. This, of course, will be the real test of the ability of systems of marketable emission permits to achieve our environmental objectives at relatively low cost. We have had some experience with emissions trading that suggests certain start-up problems, including a reluctance in some instances to engage in trades. However, as all this becomes more familiar, these markets should become more active.

Finally, I don't want to be too hard on effluent fees. There are undoubtedly cases where fees represent an attractive alternative. Where, for example, marginal social damages (MSD) are readily measured and are fairly constant over the relevant range, a fee equal to MSD can generate both the efficient level and the pattern of abatement activity. My sense, however, is that the range of application for this policy instrument may be rather limited. Particularly where the location of polluters is important (which is true for most of the major air and water pollutants), I suspect that it would be difficult to design and introduce the system of differentiated fees that is required for an efficient resolution of the pollution problem. For such cases, marketable permits appear much the more promising approach.

Notes

1. The optimality properties of the Pigouvian tax depend upon a perfectly competitive setting. If our polluter is not a perfect competitor in his output market, then things become more complicated (see Baumol and Oates [1975, ch. 6] and Barnett [1980]). Likewise, the Pigouvian prescription assumes a constant marginal social damage (MSD) over the range of emissions of any single polluter. Where MSD varies for the emissions of a particular source, some further modifications (namely, a tax schedule) are needed (see Collinge and Oates [1982]).

2. For some qualifications to this proposition regarding second-order conditions, see Baumol and Oates [1975, chs. 7 and 8].

3. In a setting of imperfect information where there is some uncertainty on the part of the environmental authority regarding polluters' abatement cost functions, the choice between a fee system and marketable permits can matter. As Weitzman [1974] shows, the expected welfare gain from the two policy instruments will, in general, differ, depending upon the shapes of the damage and abatement cost functions.

4. For a description of the emissions trading and Wisconsin TDP systems, see Oates [1984].

References

Atkinson, S., and T. Tietenberg. 1982. "The empirical properties of two classes of designs for transferable discharge permit markets." *Journal of Environmental Economics and Management* 9 (June):101–121.

Barnett, A. 1980. "The Pigouvian tax rule under monopoly." *American Economic Review* 70 (December):1037–1041.

Baumol, W. 1967. "Macroeconomics of unbalanced growth: The anatomy of urban crisis." *American Economic Review* 57 (June):415–426.

Baumol, W., and W. Oates. 1975. *The Theory of Environmental Policy*. Englewood Cliffs, NJ: Prentice-Hall.

Buchanan, J., and G. Tullock. 1975. "Polluters' Profits and Political Response: Direct Controls Versus Taxes." *American Economic Review* 65 (March):139–147.

Coase, R. 1960. "The problem of social cost." *Journal of Law and Economics* 3 (October):1–44.

Collinge, R., and W. Oates. 1982. "Efficiency in pollution control in the short and long runs: A system of rental emission permits." *Canadian Journal of Economics* 15 (May):346–354.

Hahn, R., and R. Noll. 1983. "Barriers to implementing tradable air pollution permits: Problems of regulatory interactions." *Yale Journal on Regulation* 1 (1):63–91.

Kelman, S. 1981. *What Price Incentives? Economists and the Environment.* Boston: Auburn House. For a condensed treatment, see S. Kelman, "Economic incentives and environmental policy: Politics, ideology, and philosophy." In *Incentives for Environmental Protection.* Ed. T. Schelling. Cambridge, MA.: MIT Press, 1983. Pp. 291–331.

Krupnick, A., W. Oates, and E. Van De Verg. 1983. "On marketable air-pollution permits: The case for a system of pollution offsets." *Journal of Environmental Economics and Management* 10 (September):233–247.

McGartland, A., and W. Oates. 1985. "Marketable permits for the prevention of environmental deterioration." *Journal of Environmental Economics and Management* 12:207–228.

Oates, W. 1984. "Markets for pollution control." *Challenge* (May/June):11–17.

Oates, W. 1983. "The regulation of externalities: Efficient behavior by sources and victims." *Public Finance* 38 (3):362–375.

Olson, M. 1965. *The Logic of Collective Action* (Cambridge, MA: Harvard University Press.).

Palmer, A., et al. 1980. *Economic Implications of Regulating Chlorofluorocarbon Emissions from Nonaerosol Applications.* Santa Monica, CA: Rand.

Seskin, E., R. Anderson, and R. Reid. 1983. "An Empirical analysis of economic strategies for controlling air pollution." *Journal of Environmental Economics and Management* 10 (June):112–124.

Turvey, R. 1963. "On divergences between social cost and private cost." *Economica* 30 (August):309–313.

Weitzman, M. 1974. "Prices vs. quantities." *Review of Economic Studies* 41 (October):477–491.

COMMENT 2

Thomas H. Tietenberg

Playing the curmudgeon's role, Professor Bromley has leveled a barrage at the state of externality theory. This theory is characterized in his essay at various points as politically naive, misguided and, in perhaps the most devastating criticism of all, unhelpful in the design of public policy.

It is ironic that this attack on the theory comes at a time when economics is having its greatest impact on environmental policy. I take this new-found policy interest in economic approaches as evidence that the situation is not as bleak as Professor Bromley would have us believe. Indeed in my view the central contribution of this essay is not the condemnation of externality theory, but the refinement and extension of it. In particular the fusion of ideas from legal scholarship with those of externality theory is a most promising avenue for future research. Though some of the historical branches of the theory identified in this essay have certainly led to intellectual dead ends, the main body of externality theory has in the past, and will continue to have, important implications for public policy.

In the first part of my comments I shall briefly review the Bromley message to isolate what I see as the strengths and weaknesses in the argument. In the second part I shall show how the various aspects of externality theory as elaborated and refined by Bromley can be used to forge a new, more pragmatic approach to environmental policy. These arguments will be cast in the context of a particular case study—EPA's growing reliance on marketable emission permits.

The Bromley Thesis

Professor Bromley's most severe criticism is leveled at the concept of Pareto-irrelevancy, particularly when it is coupled with the presumption that any policy changes in the status quo should be Pareto-superior moves. According to the proponents of this branch of externality theory, any external cost that cannot be eliminated without hurting one or more of the involved parties should be ignored. As Bromley correctly points out and illustrates with a large number of examples, this restriction on the set of permissible outcomes gives an unfortunate amount of weight to the status quo and ignores the important question of whether the status quo is a morally defensible point of departure for evaluating the desirability of externality correction policies.

A familiar story conveys the essential point rather well. If I throw someone in a pit full of vipers and then offer a ladder in return for his wealth, the victim and I could probably consummate a voluntary trade which would make us both better off, given the starting point of the trade. But the fact that the starting point is morally repugnant cannot be ignored! This negotiated trade may support a Pareto-superior change, but that does not mean it is desirable in some larger ethical sense and, therefore, supportable. In the legal system this contract would be said to have been negotiated under duress and therefore would be unenforceable.

Bromley points out that this heavy reliance on the status quo creates in practice a series of presumptive rights. Coupled with the difficulty in overcoming them once established, the existence of these rights provides a basis for inaction. He laments the fact that this situation is not seen for what it really is—the unfair imposition of unwanted costs on unwilling victims.

With this as a motivating belief, Bromley quite properly attacks Ronald Coase's classic article "The Problem of Social Cost." One of Coase's fundamental contributions was to show that in a world of no transaction costs and zero income effects, there would exist a basic symmetry in how these conflicts could be resolved. Regardless of how the rights, duties, and privileges were initially assigned, as a result of negotiation the final allocation would be the same.

Bromley's attack on this point of view comes at several levels. First, since in a world of no transaction costs there would be no externalities (because they would have been bid away), he argues that Coase's point has no merit. In my view this is going too far because the Coase analysis can be seen as showing that the pressures for bidding the externalities away can come from either party, depending on the assignment of the initial entitlements. That is pedagogically a useful point.

Bromley's other criticisms relate more to the practical and philosophical implications of the Coase theorem. On the practical level Bromley points out that because transaction costs are never really zero, Coasian symmetry does not exist; the assignment of presumptive rights by historical accident could well determine the outcome. In particular the outcome could be affected by any asymmetry in the transaction costs between the parties to the conflict.

Philosophically Bromley argues that even if a symmetry of outcomes among various initial allocations of rights and duties were to exist, morally there may be a basis for preferring one allocation to another. Those who inflict unwanted costs on others, he argues, have a preeminent duty to protect the rights of innocent victims. The fact that victims could conceivably bribe injurers to prevent the damage is of little practical interest.

The Unwanted Cost Principle

This analysis leads Bromley to his key normative prescription—that innocent victims should have presumptive rights while injurers should have a general duty to protect victims from unwanted costs. As appealing and uncontroversial as this prescription may appear at first glance, closer examination reveals some potential problems, particularly when this principle is extended to cover the entire range of potential external cost situations.

Professor Bromley's case seems most convincing when he evokes the image of a factory dumping pollution on nearby residents who had located there before the factory started polluting. But not all images yield as clear a result. Suppose for example that I am especially sensitive to light. Anyone in a public meeting I am attending who turns on the light inflicts an unwanted cost on me. According to the Bromley criterion they should compensate me in return for my agreement for the light to be on. Yet it is not clear that this is the most morally defensible solution. Since I am in the best position to identify both the problem and the appropriate remedy (sunglasses) and implement it, time and resources are saved if I know in advance that I will bear the cost and simply show up with my sunglasses.

This example suggests an alternative general principle. Rather than imposing a general duty to protect all parties from unwanted costs, the duty should be imposed on the least-cost avoider. For the industry emitting pollutants, it, not the victims, would be in the best position to assess the alternative means of control and to act on that assessment; therefore it makes sense to impose the duty on them while assigning the right to be protected to the nearby residents. For this type of externality the unwanted-cost principle and the least-cost-avoider principle lead to the same outcome.

The two principles would suggest rather different outcomes, however, for the light-sensitivity example. Since the light-sensitive victim would also be the least-cost avoider, he or she would bear the cost according to the least-cost-avoider principle, but not according to the unwanted-cost principle.

To a large extent the least-cost-avoider principle has been followed in air pollution and toxic substance control policy. The polluter-pay principle is rather firmly established in current air pollution control legislation; emitters are recognized as the least-cost avoiders. Similarly, toxic substance legislation allocates the burden of proof to those parties who can most easily bear it.

But the least-cost-avoider principle does not always lead to outcomes that are universally recognized as moral. A case in point is provided by a recent legal case. Because of the vulnerability of a fetus to environmental hazards, pregnant women face special workplace risks. In 1978, responding to this fact, American Cyanamid decided to ban all fertile women from jobs in the section manufacturing lead chromate pigment at its Willow Island, West Virginia Plant. Since the displaced women were not able to secure comparable jobs, this least-cost-avoider solution did not command universal support. The women's union sued on the grounds that the women had been unfairly discriminated against.

In other areas the principle has stood the test of application rather well. One such area, a major focus of my own research, is in the application of the economic concept known as marketable emission permits to air pollution control. Probing this area in more detail allows us to examine the applicability of many of the points raised by Professor Bromley in a specific policy context. In particular it illustrates the importance of the status quo in creating presumptive rights, the difficulties in overcoming those rights, the role of transaction costs, and the degree to which these transaction costs may dictate the final outcome.

Applying the Least-Cost-Avoider Principle

Hailed by Senator Pete Domenici (R–New Mexico) as "The one bright idea that has emerged in the 1980s," the emissions trading program initiated by the Environmental Protection Agency (EPA) is a particularly interesting example of the application of the principles discussed by Professor Bromley. In order to gain acceptance this program had to overcome a good deal of resistance by lowering transaction costs and by recognizing and incorporating presumptive rights. While it is appropriate to lament the excessive importance of the status quo, as a practical matter it is difficult to implement any policy that ignores it. Pontificating about how unfortunate the existing system of serendipitious rights and duties is does little to correct the situation. The political feasibility of any change in policy depends in an important way on how the various parties to the change are treated by the status quo as well as by the change.

Prior to the inception of this program, all attempts to use policy instruments based upon economic incentives as a means of controlling pollution in the United States had been decisively rejected. The emissions trading program not only was able to overcome this traditionally powerful resistance within Congress (and even within some offices in EPA) to become a centerpiece in air pollution policy, but it has now made limited inroads in water pollution control policy as well. The story behind this achievement illustrates the dilemmas faced by those who seek to implement the least-cost-avoider principle.

The Emissions Trading Program

Stripped to its bare essentials the Clean Air Act's approach toward controlling pollution from stationary sources prior to the emissions trading program involved the specification of a separate emission standard (legal emission ceiling) for each pollutant discharge point (such as a stack, a vent, or a production process). The stringency of these standards depended on whether the facility was in a region where the air quality was worse than required by law (called a nonattainment area), or was in a region with air quality better than required by law (called a prevention-of-significant-deterioration or PSD area). The enormity of the regulator's task becomes clear when it is realized that the typical industrial facility may contain as many as one hundred discharge points. Identifying the mix of least-cost avoiders is far from a trivial task.

The emissions trading program has attempted to provide a feasible means of imposing the control costs on the least-cost avoider by encouraging sources to seek alternative, cheaper means of reducing emissions as long as the substitute means produce equivalent or better effects on air quality. Sources are allowed to use excess emission reductions at some set of cheaper-to-control, discharge points to offset equivalent increases at other more difficult-to-control discharge points.

Specifically, any source reducing its emissions at any discharge point more than required by regulation can apply to have this excess reduction certified as an emission reduction credit. Once certified this becomes available for sale or use as a means of meeting the assigned control responsibilities for that source (at other discharge points) or for other sources.

In one sense this was a radical reform. Whereas traditionally the pollution control authorities retained the exclusive authority to stipulate the amount of emissions allowed at each discharge point, under the emissions trading program the responsibility for picking the mix of discharge point reductions used to achieve the stipulated overall emission reduction was transferred to the managers of the pollution sources. Environmentalists feared, and no doubt some industrialists hoped, the program would open a large number of loopholes, leaving a legacy of reduced compliance.

This reform package did not comand an immediate constituency and building one was not easy. The status quo is not easily overcome. Even industrial sources, the most natural constitutents in light of the flexibility offered by the program, were far from unanimous in their enthusiasm. To some extent they feared that any gain in flexibility introduced greater risk. For example, when an EPA-recommended technology failed to live up to standards, the source could claim it had lived up to its responsibilities by following the EPA recommendation, but when the control mix was up to the source, it would lose this defense.

Though this was a voluntary program, requiring the full cooperation of state control agencies, state cooperation was not inevitable. State authorities feared that the new programs would be more difficult to administer and saw it as a threatening departure from their comfortable, customary way of doing business.

Overcoming the Status Quo

Because any change in policy has its own set of costs, it is difficult to overcome the inertia of the status quo. New grounds for legal challenge are exposed. Bureaucratic staffs trained in one set of procedures must learn new ones. The comfort of familiarity is lost to both regulators and sources.

The political feasibility of implementing this particular reform depended not only on its potential to lower compliance costs, but also on its potential to prevent participants from being injured by the transition. The major participants in this case included the emitters and those charged with the responsibility for implementing and enforcing the reforms.

A several-pronged implementation procedure was designed to fulfill this potential. First, although marketable emission permits can be allocated by auction, EPA chose a grandfathering approach. After the inception of the emissions trading program, existing sources were permitted to continue to emit as much as they could under the emission standards established prior to the reform without incurring any additional financial obligation. By allowing existing sources to escape the negative cash flow implications of having to pay for the auctioned permits, existing emitters (and the jobs they represented) were given a presumptive right.

Coupled with the rather large cost savings that were possible with this reform, grandfathering stimulated a good deal of interest in the program on the part of existing emitters. The good news is that this particular approach allowed a significant amount of headway to be made on allocating the burden to the least-cost avoider; the status quo inertia had begun to be overcome. The bad news is that this approach disadvantages new sources. New sources have to bid emission reduction credits away from existing sources before they can contribute any new emissions to a nonattainment area. By being forced to purchase permits that were given free-of-charge to existing sources, new sources incur a financial burden existing sources can avoid. This has served both to diminish competition from potential entrants and to retard the introduction of those innovative pollution control processes most easily embodied in new plants.

The relatively slow pace of trading following these initial initiatives convinced EPA that these substantive reforms would have to be accompanied by procedural reforms if the program was to live up to its potential. Originally the bubble policy could be only be used if the approving state included the intended trade in a formal revision to its state implementation plan (SIP). Because the SIP approval process is the primary means by which EPA exercises its responsibility for assuring state compliance with the Clean Air Act, SIP revisions are bureaucratically cumbersome. When the Reagan administration took office, for example, a backlog of some 643 proposed changes in SIP's were awaiting approval by EPA.[1] Because any SIP revision has to fulfill a large number of procedural requirements, state control authorities are reluctant to file revisions except when absolutely necessary. Requiring emission trades to be approved through SIP revisions was a surefire way to limit state control authority interest in the program. The transactions cost were too high. EPA reacted to this situation, not by concluding that these costs rendered the potential trades Pareto irrelevant, but rather by reducing the transaction costs.

In 1981 EPA significantly lowered this procedural burden by approving generic rules as an alternative to approving each individual trade. By approving the generic rules states intended to use to govern possible emissions trades, EPA eliminated the need for states to obtain SIP revision approval for each trade. As long as subsequent trades conformed to these rules, no SIP revision was necessary. The resulting dramatic reduction in transaction costs allowed state control authorities to see this policy as something other than a procedural nightmare.

An Appraisal

There is little doubt that this program has improved upon the command-and-control policy that preceded it. EPA has estimated that in excess of 2500 emission-trading transactions have taken place since the inception of the program. Each of these trades represents an affirmation of the basic premise of emissions trading—allowing sources to trade emission-reduction credits reduces the cost of complying with the law.

One of the substantial subsidiary benefits of this lower compliance cost has been an increase in the ease with which sources can be brought into compliance. In a large number of cases emissions trading was the means by which sources achieved compliance for the first time. In two cases the actions taken under the bubble policy contributed to the ability of state authorities to demonstrate that the ambient standards in the affected nonattainment areas would be achieved.[2]

One of the hopes held out for emissions trading was that by making excess emission reductions valuable, it would stimulate the introduction of new, innovative means of controlling pollution. Although the majority of emission-reduction credits have been created on the basis of such noninnovative techniques as fuel substitution and changes in the degree of control of already controlled discharge points, four innovative bubbles have been approved. All involved the conversion of a solvent-based process (high in VOC's) to a solventless process.[3] Emissions trading created the environment that made these substitutions possible.

Although on balance it substantially improved upon the policy that preceded it, the emissions-trading program has fallen short of fulfilling the expectations for it articulated in the theoretical and empirical economics literature. A price was paid for survival. Paradoxically the very attributes that allowed it to overcome the status quo and therefore to gain a permanent place in U.S. environmental policy are responsible for its failure to fully locate the mix of least-cost avoiders.

The enduring role that EPA's emissions trading program is currently playing is directly attributable to the fact that it was preceded by a very cost-ineffective regulatory policy. Not only did the predecessor policy—because of its deficiencies—create a demand for approaches that offered to reduce cost, but the policy also provided a ready-made baseline for the trades, making the transition to emissions trading rather smooth. Had the previous command-and-control policy been more cost effective, it is doubtful that the emissions-trading policy could have gained the foothold it has.

Although the ability to overlay this program on an existing, but cost-ineffective policy was a key to its political success, it has also diminished the effectiveness of the program in several specific ways:

1. In response to command-and-control regulation, a great deal of capital equipment had already been installed prior to the inception of the emissions-trading program. Since much of this installed durable capital not only was cost ineffective, but was also unable to benefit from the emissions-trading program, this has reduced the degree of cost savings achievable by the program below what would have been possible if the program had started with a clean slate.
2. A particularly unfortunate side effect of overlaying emissions trading on a preexisting command-and-control allocation arises when some sources comply rather rapidly with the command-and-control allocation and others prove more recalcitrant. Because the emissions-trading option appeared late in the game, sources which had chosen to immediately comply with the command-and-control regulations were precluded from using the emissions-trading policy to their greatest advantage, while those who were able to fend off early, expensive standards could, with the advent of emissions trading, reach compliance at a substantially lower cost. In this way the introduction of an emissions-trading program rewarded slow compliance, which strikes many potential supporters as patently unfair.
3. By choosing a grandfathered version of emissions trading, the bias against new sources which characterized the command-and-control policy has persisted (albeit to a lesser degree) in the emissions trading program. Under this policy new sources not only face more stringent control responsibilities and are given less flexibility in meeting these responsibilities than existing sources, they have to purchase sufficient emission reduction credits in nonattainment areas to offset any remaining emissions after the control is applied. This bias in the regulations has the effect of delaying the replacement of older heavier-polluting facilities with newer, less-polluting facilities.
4. The notion that firms might have a property right in surplus emission reductions was not a part of the command-and-control system and

has been hard for some control authorities to swallow. In some jurisdictions confiscation of certified credits is a distinct possibility, destroying much of the incentive to create additional emission reductions.

This brief survey of our experience with the emissions-trading program suggests several points of relevance to the Bromley essay. The status quo does exercise a very large influence on environmental policy. Yet the presumptive rights that are created need not be the basis for a policy of inaction. Action is possible, though rarely to the extent suggested by our least realistic externality models. The existence of potential gains from trade in any external-cost situation creates the preconditions for applying the least-cost-avoider principle. Furthermore, combining an initial command-and-control assignment of the control responsibility with an "emissions-trading after-market" permits the least-cost-avoider principle to be implemented in a way that is generally consistent with conventional ethical norms. Though this principle may be applied in practice with less grace and finesse than we might have been led to expect from theory, its application does represent progress. The realm of the desirable and the realm of the possible rarely, if ever, completely overlap, but it is comforting to close by noting that the overlap is not inconsequential.

Notes

[1] See Robert W. Crandall and Paul R. Portney, "The Environmental Protection Agency in the Reagan Administration," in Paul R. Portney, ed. *Natural Resources and the Environment: The Reagan Approach* (Washington, DC: Urban Institute Press, 1984), p. 48.

[2] See the approved bubbles for Armco, 46 FR 19468 (31 March 1981) and Shenango, 46 FR 62849 (29 December 1981).

[3] The innovative bubbles include McDonnell Douglas, 46 FR 20172 (3 April 1981); 3M, 46 FR 41778 (August 1981); Fasson-Avery International, 46 FR 61653 (18 December 1981); and U. S. Steel, 48 FR 54347 (2 December 1983).

3 THE VALUATION PROBLEM

Glen D. Anderson
and
Richard C. Bishop

Economists are often asked to determine the values of commodities as part of cost-benefit analyses. Many goods and services are traded in organized markets, and it is reasonably straightforward to derive values for these commodities. Consumer surplus is given by the area under the inverse Marshallian demand curve and above the good's market-clearing price. This so-called "welfare triangle" is an estimate of what consumers would be willing to pay for incremental units of the good (X_i) up to the actual level (X_i^*) minus the amount they actually pay, which in turn equals X_i^* multiplied by the market price, P_{xi}^*.

Marshallian consumer surplus is not an ideal welfare measure because a

This work was funded in part by the College of Agricultural and Life Sciences of the University of Wisconsin-Madison. Support was also provided by the University of Rhode Island Sea Grant Program and the University of Wisconsin Sea Grant Institute under grants from the National Sea Grant Program, National Oceanic and Atmospheric Administration, U.S. Department of Commerce, and from the States of Rhode Island and Wisconsin. Rhode Island Sea Grant Project R/ME-3. Federal Grant (to Wisconsin Sea Grant) NA84AA-D00065, Wisconsin Project R/PS-32. Kevin Boyle, Daniel McCollum, Richard Ready, and Michael Welsh made many helpful suggestions on earlier drafts. Their contributions are gratefully acknowledged.

change in the commodity's price involves a change in the real purchasing power of consumers. If the price of X_i falls to $\hat{P}_{xi}$ from P^*_{xi}, the consumer can continue to purchase X^*_i units and subsequently increase utility by purchasing additional units of X_i or other goods with the residual income $[(P^*_{xi} - \hat{P}_{xi})\ X^*_i]$. If more accurate measures of willingness to pay are needed, utility or income compensated welfare measures can be obtained from the Hicksian compensated demand functions [Deaton and Muellbauer 1980] or by making use of Willig's result to adjust Marshallian consumer surplus measures (see [Willig 1976; Just, Hueth, and Schmitz 1982]).

Environmental assets are more difficult to value. Information on Marshallian or Hicksian demand curves is seldom available because organized markets for these goods do not exist. To understand the reasons that markets are lacking, it is useful to compare the characteristics of environmental assets with those of private goods.

In the usual utility maximization framework, the consumer is assumed to make allocative decisions over the vector of commodities, $\bar{X}$. In private goods cases, X_i is a choice variable and is rival in consumption; that is, once X_i has been acquired by a consumer, other consumers are excluded from enjoying the purchased units unless a second transaction occurs. Finally, the price of X_i is assumed to be exogenous to the consumer and, in a perfectly competitive economy, reflects the marginal cost of providing additional units of X_i.

By contrast, quantities of environmental goods are seldom choice variables for the individual. The level (if quantifiable) of the environmental asset, rather than its price, is exogenous. Ownership and control of access to the resource is often vested in a national, state, or local unit of government. Hence, units of the environmental asset are often not for sale or are provided at nominal charges. Dissatisfaction with the level of resource supply must be expressed through appropriate public choice mechanisms. However, it is also important to recognize that, while individuals do not freely choose the level of the environmental good, they may make market purchases in order to use it. For example, costs may be incurred to visit a recreation site. Likewise, environmental attributes such as air and water quality may be accessible only to those who own property in an area. Such related market purchases may provide clues to environmental values, as will soon be shown.

Furthermore, unlike private goods, environmental assets are often nonrival in consumption. If congestion effects are negligible, efficient pricing suggests a zero price for nonrival goods, since the marginal opportunity cost of providing the resource to an additional consumer is zero. Hence, even if an environmental good can be privatized (i.e., potential consumers can be excluded), the market information generated is unlikely to be germane to the determination of its social value. Under the nonrivalry assumption, the social value of the resource is equal to the sum of individuals' willingness to pay for a given level of the good. Hence, only a pricing scheme such as a set of Lindahl prices provides sufficient market information to value the resource.[1]

In attempting to overcome the valuation problem, economists have developed techniques for valuing environmental goods. Two approaches—the travel-cost method (TC) and hedonic-price techniques (HP)—are termed "related-market approaches" because they are based on the linkages between environmental assets and markets for related private goods and services. TC utilizes recreational trip expenditures as a proxy for market prices in demand estimation. HP attempts to ferret out environmental values that may be reflected in differential real estate values and wages. A third approach—the contingent-valuation method (CV)—employs personal interviews, telephone interviews, or mail surveys to ask people about the values they would place on environmental commodities if ideal markets did exist or other means of payment such as taxes were in effect. That is, consumers are asked about the values they would place on the commodity *contingent* on the existence of a market or other means of payment. Although there are other nonmarket approaches (see [Freeman 1979]), the majority of environmental valuation studies employ one or more of these three techniques.

In this chapter, we will present an overview of TC, HP, and CV. Each of the next three sections begins with the elementary mechanics of the valuation technique under consideration. That is, we attempt first to explain on a somewhat simplified level how valuation is accomplished. Next, some of the more important refinements in each technique are explained. Each section closes with an evaluation of the technique. The final section explores the question of which technique—TC, HP, or CV—is best. There has been a tendency to prefer the related-market approaches because they are based on actual economic behavior, while CV involves only hypothetical behavior. We intend to challenge this bit of conventional wisdom and foster a more balanced view.

A brief warning is in order about what this chapter does not do. First, space constraints made it difficult to provide a complete set of references on each topic. We tried to cite key works, particularly those that are most accessible, so that the reader is provided a basis for beginning a full bibliography. Second, TC and CV frequently involve primary data gathering through surveys. Without throwing stones at any one study, we would assert that, in general, economists have not taken sufficient advantage of the expertise and experience of trained survey researchers. Better data could have been assembled in many studies for equal or less money. It would have been desirable to include a section on survey methodology in this chapter. However, it will have to suffice to explicitly encourage newcomers to valuation research to give as much attention as possible to sampling, choice of survey technique, survey design, assuring an adequate response, and full reporting of survey procedures and results in papers and reports. Advice from competent survey researchers on all these topics is highly desirable.

The Travel-cost (TC) Method

The idea of inferring consumers' willingness to pay for recreational services from travel expenditures was originally suggested by Hotelling in a 1947 letter to the National Park Service. The idea was then developed and applied by Trice and Wood [1958] and by Clawson and Knetsch [Clawson, 1959; Knetsch, 1963; Clawson and Knetsch, 1963, 1966]. All applications of TC that we know of have involved outdoor recreation. We will begin by examining the basic logic of TC, following the approach of Clawson and Knetsch closely.

The basic logic

Consider a single recreation site surrounded by a number of travel zones. The zones may be defined by concentric rings around the site or other geographic areas such as counties. The important characteristic of zones is that travel costs from all points within each zone to the site are sufficiently close in magnitude to justify neglecting the differences. Let TC_i equal the average round-trip travel cost from zone i to the site. Intuitively, TC_i must be an *average marginal cost*. That is, residents of zone i have marginal costs of making such trips and TC_i equals the average across zonal residents of these marginal costs. By assumption, TC_i is a constant with respect to the number of trips taken per unit of time. While TC_i is termed the *travel cost*, clearly it could include such items as food, lodging, and access fees.

TC can be visualized as a two-step process. The first step entails estimation of the *trip demand curve*, a regression equation relating trips per capita from each zone to the travel cost from the zone. Let V_i equal the total number of trips by residents of zone i per unit of time and N_i equal the population of the ith zone. Assume that there are a total of Z zones of origin for those using the site. Mathematically, the general form of the trip demand

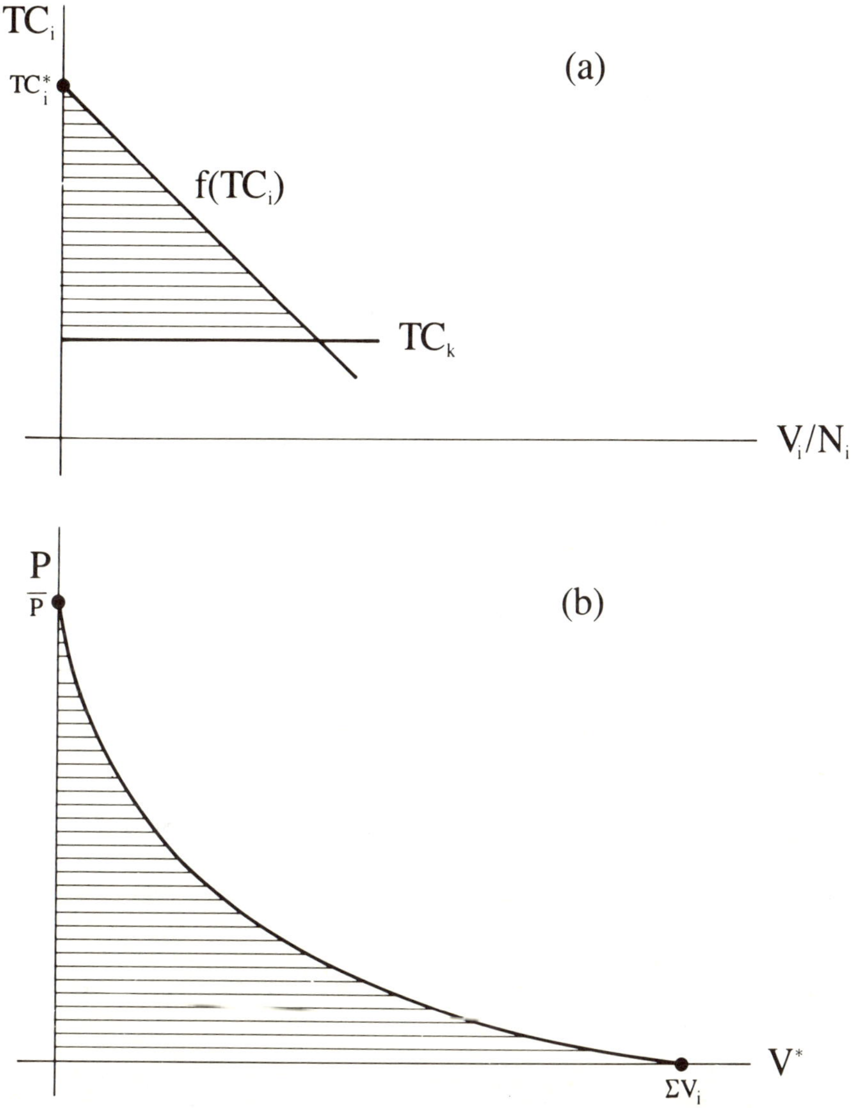

Figure 3-1. Trip demand curve is shown in part (a), while part (b) illustrates the aggregate curve. Shaded areas show alternative ways to measure consumer surplus.

curve can be stated as

$$V_i/N_i = f(TC_i)$$

A linear version of $f(\cdot)$ is portrayed in figure 3-1a.

The second step involves derivation of the *aggregate demand curve*, a function that shows the estimated trips by all recreationists at various prices. For simplicity, assume that, at present, the admission fee to the site is zero. One point on the aggregate demand curve corresponds to the currently observed number of trips, $\Sigma_{i=1}^{z} V_i$. Additional points can be found by adding assumed entry fees to TC_i. Resulting visits per capita for each zone as estimated from the trip demand curve are multiplied by zonal population and summed across all zones. When the functional form of $f(\cdot)$ may lead to negative predictions, as in the case of the linear form in figure 3-1a, it is necessary to constrain visits per capita to nonnegative values. Let P symbolize the assumed entry fee and $V_i^*(P)/N_i^*$ equal predicted visits per capita from zone i. Then

$$N_i^* V_i^*(P) = \begin{cases} f(TC_i + P) & \text{if this value is} \geqslant 0 \\ 0 & \text{otherwise} \end{cases}$$

Next, to get the point on the aggregate demand curve associated with P, let $V^*(P)$ equal aggregate visits, defined by

$$V^*(P) = \sum_{i=1}^{z} [V_i^*(P)/N_i^*]N_i$$

P is increased incrementally to obtain additional points until the fee, $\bar{P}$ is found such that $V^*(\bar{P}) = 0$ or until the trips function, $V^*(P)$, asymptotically approaches zero. Such an aggregate demand function is depicted in figure 3-1b. Note that the aggregate demand curve shown there is not linear even though $f(\cdot)$ as pictured in figure 3-1a is linear. This is because, at progressively higher values of P, $f(\cdot)$ will be negative for more and more zones and these negative values have been excluded. Even if $f(\cdot)$ is linear, $V^*(P)$ will in general not be linear. Once the aggregate demand curve is obtained, an estimate of the Marshallian surplus associated with recreation at the site would be given by

$$\text{total consumer surplus} = \int_0^{\bar{P}} V^*(P)\, dp$$

This value is depicted as the shaded area in figure 3-1(b).

While aggregate demand functions are sometimes developed in actual studies and are useful for teaching purposes, there is an alternative method of deriving consumer surplus that is simpler because it utilizes the trips demand function directly. This makes it unnecessary to deal with negative values and the aggregate demand curve need not be derived. Let TC^* equal the intercept of the trip demand curve. The integral of the trip demand curve between a zone's travel cost and TC^* is an estimate of consumer surplus per capita for that zone. The shaded area in figure 3-1a is such an estimate for the kth zone. Multiplying each such value by zonal population and summing across all zones gives a total consumer surplus estimate. Mathematically,

$$\text{Total consumer surplus} = \sum_{i=1}^{z} N_i \int_{TC_i}^{TC^*} f(TC)dTC$$

Even in this simple model, the logic of TC is clear. Using the aggregate demand curve, the problem is to predict how rapidly trips would decline if admission fees really were increased. In TC, this is accomplished for people in zones with lower travel costs by examining the actual behavior of people in more distant, higher-cost zones. To see this, consider two zones, say arbitrarily zone 5 and zone 9 where $TC_5 < TC_9$. Suppose further that we are looking for the point on the aggregate demand curve where $P = P'$ and that, by coincidence, $TC_5 + P' = TC_9$. Visits per capita from zone 5 would then be predicted as $f(TC_5 + P')$. But, by assumption,

$$f(TC_5 + P') = f(TC_9)$$

Thus, for the case $P = P'$, trips per capita from zone 5 are being predicted based on the actual behavior of people in zone 9. Stated more generally, at the heart of TC is the assumption that people in the different zones would visit at the same rates if they had the same travel costs.

This assumption may be violated for a number of reasons. Clearly, if there are differences in preferences or incomes across zones, the simple version of the trip demand curve could lead to biased predictions of trips per capita and hence consumer surplus. Thus, at a minimum, the basic model should be modified to

$$V_i/N_i = f(TC_i, Y_i, \overline{S}_i)$$

where Y_i is average income in zone i and $\overline{S}_i$ is a vector of socioeconomic characteristics of people living there. Additional modifications of the basic model have been required to deal with variation in travel time, differences in the availability of substitutes and complements across zones, and changes in environmental quality at recreation sites. These refinements will require a bit more discussion.

Allowing for travel time

The problem here is that those living farther from the site not only have higher money costs per trip, they must expend more time getting there. It would seem intuitive to assume that the travel time to and from the site has some opportunity cost either in terms of wages or an alternative leisure activity foregone. If so, the trip demand curve, as we have specified it, will underestimate participation rates as P is increased. To see why, refer again to the example involving zones 5 and 9 when $P = P'$. Assume that round-trip travel time is one hour from zone 5 and two hours from zone 9. When P is set at P' to get a point on the aggregate demand function, the basic model, it will be recalled, predicted a trips-per-capita rate from zone 5 equal to current actual visits per capita from zone 9. This would be an underestimate since people from zone 5 have lower travel times and would come more often, other things being equal. Thus, the basic model needs to be modified to read

$$V_i/N_i = f(TC_i, T_i, Y_i, \bar{S}_i)$$

where T_i is travel time from zone i to the recreation site being studied.

In more formal terms, this can be viewed as a problem of an omitted relevant variable. Participation rates are determined not only by dollar travel costs but also by travel time; and travel costs and time are often positively correlated. This correlation implies that the least-squares regression coefficient on TC_i in the basic model may be biased.

While it is easy to insert T_i into the general form of the trip demand function, handling it in a regression context is more difficult. The econometric problem is that TC_i and T_i may be highly correlated. It is usually impossible to efficiently estimate separate coefficients for both, particularly when the data are aggregated by zone as in the basic model. Two solutions for dealing with multicollinearity have been suggested: disaggregation of the model and monetization of time costs.

Brown and Nawas [1973] disaggregated their data to the individual level, so that trips by individuals in the sample became the dependent variable. This reduced the multicollinearity sufficiently to allow them to estimate significant coefficients on both travel cost and travel time. With a few exceptions (see, for example, Gum and Martin [1975]), other investigators have not been so successful. Even with individualized data, serious multicollinearity persists. Furthermore, disaggregation may have some pitfalls of its own, as we shall later see.

The more usual solution is to translate travel time into monetary units and add it into TC_i. Cesario [1976] surveyed urban transportation studies and concluded that the value of nonwork time spent in transportation usually fell between one-fourth and one-half the wage rate. The typical travel cost study today includes travel time at a value in this range in the TC_i variable.

Substitutes and complements

Recreation sites usually have substitutes. The angler who could not go to Lake A would go to Lake B and likewise for campers, birdwatchers, and other recreationists. Though the discussion here will be framed in terms of substitutes, it should be recognized that complementary relationships are also conceivable, as when two nearby lakes jointly enhances utility from fishing. Problems can be created for TC analysis if zones farther from the site in question are also closer to or farther from substitute sites. Suppose, for example, that zones with higher travel costs to a study site also have lower travel costs to a substitute site. This would mean that participation at the study site would decline as TC_i increases not only because travel (and time) costs are rising, but also because zones with higher TC_i's will have lower travel costs to the substitute. As a result, as P is increased for the study site, the trip demand equation will underestimate how many trips per capita will be taken to that site. Similar scenarios can be described for cases where TC_i and travel costs to the substitute are positively related and for cases where sites are complements.

As in the case of travel time, this can be thought of as an omitted relevant-variable problem [Caulkins, Bishop, and Bouwes 1985]. The trip demand function for the kth site thus needs to be respecified as

$$V_{ik}/N_i = f(\overline{TC}_i, \overline{T}_i, Y_i, \overline{S}_i)$$

where V_{ik} = the trips from zone i to site k, $k = 1, \ldots, K$,
$\overline{TC}_i$ = a vector of travel costs from zone i to the K sites,
$\overline{T}_i$ = a vector of travel times from zone i to the K different sites,
and all other variables are as previously defined.

At the risk of stating the obvious, the fact that sites are substitutes creates no problem unless the sites are *imperfect* substitutes. If sites were perfect substitutes, recreationists would choose to visit only one site, the one with the lowest TC_{ik}. That sites are imperfect substitutes is another way of saying that they have different qualitative characteristics, a relevant point in the next subsection.

Two TC techniques have been devised to deal with substitutes: single-equation gravity models and multiple-equation models. Gravity models try to account for substitutability among sites by including measures of the qualitative characteristics of sites (i.e., site attributes) in the trip demand equation. That is, a single equation of the form

$$V_{ik}/N_i = f(\overline{TC}_i, \overline{T}_i, Y_i, S_i, \overline{A})$$

would be estimated using data from all sites, where $\overline{A}$ is a vector of attributes of the K sites. Many variations on this form of TC appear in the literature, as reviewed by Dwyer, Kelly, and Bowes [1977] and Mendelsohn [1985]. Usually some form of *attractiveness index* is used to represent substitutes. Stated generally, for any site, say site k, the equation used would be

$$V_{ik}/N_i = g[TC_{ik}, T_{ik}, h(\overline{TC}_{im}, \overline{T}_{im}, \overline{A}_k, \overline{A}_m), Y_i, \overline{S}_i]$$

where $\overline{TC}_{im}$ = a vector of travel costs to all sites other than k;
$\overline{T}_{im}$ = a vector of travel times to sites other than k;
$\overline{A}_k$ = a scalar or vector of attributes of site k;
$\overline{A}_m$ = a vector of characteristics of sites other than k;
$h(\cdot)$ = the attractiveness index where relative atrractiveness depends on the attributes of site k, all other sites, and travel costs and times to other sites.

Assuming positive relationships between site attributes and utility from consuming a visit to that site, the following signs would be expected:

$$\frac{\partial[V_{ik}/N_i]}{\partial TC_{ik}} < 0; \quad \frac{\partial[V_{ik}/N_i]}{\partial T_{ik}} < 0; \quad \frac{\partial[V_{ik}/N_i]}{\partial h(\cdot)} > 0; \quad \frac{\partial[V_{ik}/N_i]}{\partial A_{kn}} > 0;$$

$$\frac{\partial[V_{ik}/N_i]}{\partial A_{mn}} < 0, \quad \text{all } m \neq k; \qquad \frac{\partial[V_{ik}/N_i]}{\partial TC_{im}} > 0, \quad \text{all } m \neq k;$$

$$\frac{\partial[TC_{ik}/N_i}{\partial T_{im}} > 0, \text{ all } m \neq k$$

where A_{kn} and A_{mn} are the nth attributes of the kth and mth ($\neq k$) sites, respectively. In an application of this approach one would array the travel cost, travel time, attribute, and other data for each site and estimate coefficients for a *single* equation. An application of this sort of model can be found in Cesario and Knetsch [1976].

The multiple-equation approach explicitly treats alternative sites that are either imperfect substitutes or complements as different products. Theoretically, demands for different products are normally reflected in different demand functions, with substitutability and complementarity reflected in cross-price terms. Applying this principle for K recreation sites, there would be K demand equations:

$$V_{i1}/N_i = f_1(\overline{TC}_i, \overline{T}_i, Y_i, \overline{S}_i)$$
$$\vdots \qquad \qquad \vdots$$
$$V_{iK}/N_i = f_K(\overline{TC}_i, \overline{T}_i, Y_i, \overline{S}_i)$$

Examples of this approach may be found in Burt and Brewer [1971], Cicchetti, Fisher, and Smith [1976], and Samples and Bishop [1985]. Furthermore, it may not be necessary to actually estimate the full set of equations [Hof and King 1982, 1983; Ward, 1983].

Once the trip demand equation or set of equations has been estimated, the estimation of aggregate demand functions for the sites is conceptually parallel to the procedure already outlined for a single site. Trips to any given site are estimated by increasing P_k, the hypothetical admission price to the kth site, holding travel costs and times to all other sites constant and the hypothetical admission fees for all other sites at zero. Consumer surplus for any one site is estimated in the usual way. If two or more sites are to be valued together, a *line integral* must be calculated. This explicitly accounts for substitutability or complementarity between sites. For a discussion of welfare theory and valuation of more than one product, see Just, Hueth, and Schmitz [1982].

Theoretically speaking, the multiple-equation models are probably superior to gravity models. The latter, with their single trip demand equation are much less like the set of simultaneous demand functions for imperfect substitutes that theory suggests would describe consumer behavior. Note, for example, that the cross price elasticities of the gravity model are equal across sites. This is hard to rationalize theoretically. Furthermore, the theoretical rationale for the attractiveness index is not clear. Practically speaking, several sites are needed to get enough variation in attributes and travel costs to estimate the model coefficients, yet as more and more sites are considered the amount of information that must be crammed into a single equation also grows. This leads one to question whether the set of aggregate demand functions derived from the gravity model's single-trip demand function will capture the demand relationships across sites to a reasonable approximation.

Before becoming too confident about the multiple-equation approach, however, it is worth pointing out that it is not necessarily completely consistent with theory either. In the model, as presented here, the aggregate demand functions are not derived from estimates of the individual demand functions. Instead, they are specified in terms of per capita trips from the zones. Though a relationship between trips per capita and individual demand functions must exist, the nature of the relationship is not explicit. One potential solution would be to disaggregate the zonal data to the individual level. Unfortunately this may not solve the problem [Bockstael, Hanemann, and Strand 1984], a point to which we will return in a moment. First, however, it is important to recognize that, at least at present, gravity models do have the advantage in dealing with changes in environmental quality.

Valuing quality changes

Thus far in this chapter, the value calculations have dealt with total site value. The welfare triangle under the aggregate demand function estimates the total value of the recreational experiences to all consumers from having the site rather than doing without it completely. Such all-or-nothing values do have relevance to actual policy issues. For example, if a dam will flood the course of a trout stream and thus change the site from stream trout fishing to reservoir bass fishing, the welfare triangle under the trout fishing aggregate demand function would be an estimate of the loss to trout fishermen, while the welfare triangle for bass fishing would be an estimate of the gain to that segment of the fishing population. However, such values are of less relevance when the proposed policy or project will not add or destroy a site, but change the quality of recreation at an existing site.

Conceptually, quality may be viewed as a demand shifter. Suppose that through a fish stocking program angler success rates for species normally caught at a given site are improved and that success is the only determinant of angling quality affected by the program. Suppose, referring to figure 3-2, that the aggregate demand for trips is D_1 for "low success" and D_2 for "improved success." Assume further than the actual admission fee is zero. Then, improved fishing will increase consumer surplus by area *ABCE*. This is a measure of anglers' maximum willingness to pay for the improvement in success provided that a certain condition, "weak complementarity," holds. Quoting Freeman [1979, 197], "a public good and a private good are weakly complementary if, when the private good consumption is zero, the marginal value or marginal willingness to pay for the public good is also zero" (see, also, Mäler [1974]). In the present case, catchable fish are the public good and the various inputs required to generate trips are the private goods. Weak complementarity holds if anglers get utility from improved fish stocks only at sites they actually visit. If anglers would get positive utility from knowing that more fish are present in a lake even if they could not fish there, then weak complementarity conditions are not fulfilled and *ABCE* would underestimate the value of the quality change to them. Such "existence

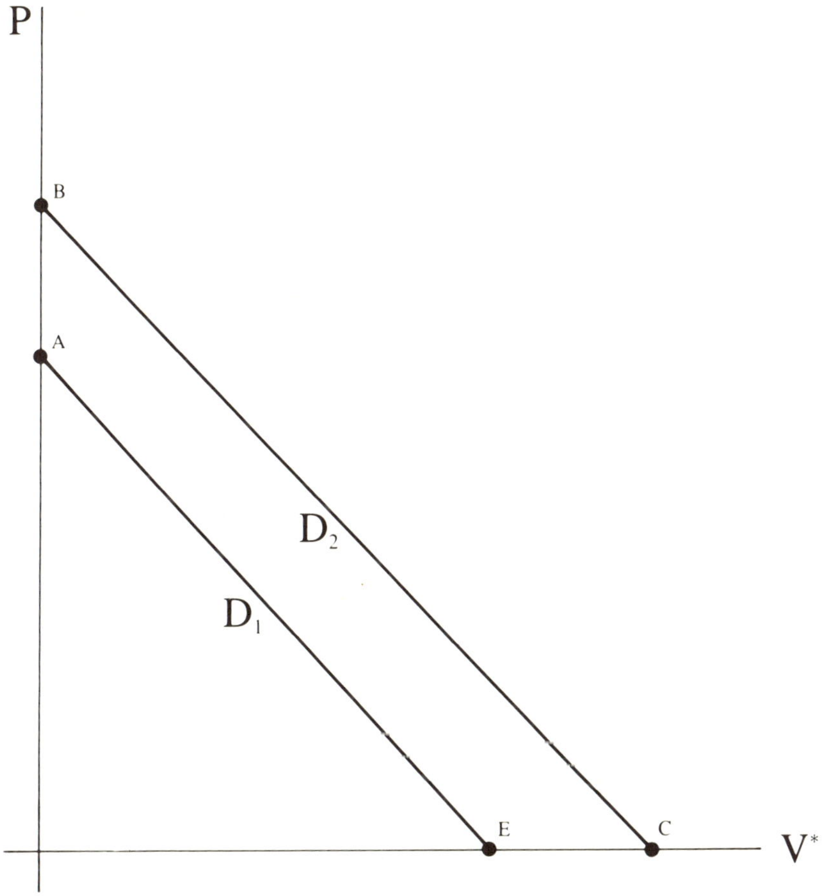

Figure 3-2. Improvement in environmental quality shifts aggregate demand curve from D_1 to D_2, yielding increased consumer surplus of *ABCE*.

values" are discussed in more detail later.

The problem, assuming that weak complementarity holds, is to determine how a qualitative change will shift the aggregate demand curve. This could be accomplished with gravity models. Such a model would first be estimated under present conditions and the aggregate demand function for trips to the site in question estimated. Then, the new quality level would be "plugged in" in place of the old one, a new, shifted aggregate demand function estimated, and the change in consumer surplus calculated. Though it is much more elaborate than the procedures just outlined, an interesting example of the overall approach is found in Sutherland [1982].

The varying-parameter model is another version of this overall approach, but it treats site quality in a two-step procedure. In its simplest form and assuming linearity, the first step would involve estimation of a trip demand equation:

$$V_{ik}/N_i = \alpha_{0k} + \alpha_{1k}\, TC_i$$

Parameters of this equation would be estimated for K different sites of differing quality, with each site having its own parameters (α_{jk}, $j = 0,1$). Each site also would have its own set of origin zones, so that origins are in general different for each recreation site. The second step would then be to regress the α_{jk} on site attributes

$$\alpha_{jk} = \bar{\beta}_j \bar{A}_k, \qquad j = 0,1; k = 1, \ldots, K$$

where $\bar{\beta}_j$ is a vector of parameters and $\bar{A}_k$ is a vector of site attributes. To evaluate a change in quality at a given site, the new attribute bundle would be used via the second equation to estimate parameters for the new, shifted trip demand curve. Recent applications of this approach involving water quality are studies by Vaughan and Russell [1982] and Desvousges, Smith, and McGivney [1983].

It should in principle be possible to infer something about quality shifters from multiple-equation models, since the existence of more than one demand equation implies that sites are qualitatively different. However, exact procedures for valuing quality shifts are not so clear as in the gravity model, since site characteristics are not represented as explicit arguments in the equations but rather are implicit influences on coefficients. For this reason, multiple-equation models have more often been used to evaluate new sites. One exception is the paper by Samples and Bishop [1985]. They regressed average consumer surplus per day at each site on qualitative characteristics and developed elasticities of consumer surplus with respect to qualitative change. Talhelm [1973, 1981] has developed a more elaborate approach where "products" are defined through a combination of a priori definitions and empirical tests. Each product then has its own demand equation in a multiple-equation system. Qualitative changes at any set of sites are handled by changing the product supplied at those sites. In this way, quality changes are dealt with in a rather complicated simulation model.

In sum, gravity and/or multiple-equation models are needed for at least three reasons: to avoid omitted relevant variable bias, to evaluate new sites, and to estimate demand shifts related to environmental quality changes.

Having examined the basics of TC and summarized some of its major refinements, let us turn to broader issues. Given the current state of the art, to what extent has TC solved the valuation problem? What is the future outlook?

Evaluation of TC

TC has been applied in many studies. These applications have been successful in the sense that plausible estimates of policy-relevant values have been provided. TC is attractive because it is based on actual behavior of recreationists as they adjust to real economic parameters. However, it is apparent that sources of potentially significant error are present.

For one thing, arbitrarily setting the value of time at some percentage of the wage rate is a compromise that leaves most researchers feeling uneasy. That the link is weak between gravity and multiple-equation models, on the one hand, and economic theory, on the other, has already been mentioned. A number of other unresolved issues could have been discussed as well: the role of time at the site; how to deal with multiple-purpose and multiple-site trips; the choice of functional form; heteroskedasticity in the zonal model; the potential problems created by using individual observations rather than zonal ones; definition of the travel cost and trip variables; and alternative methods of calculating consumer surplus. This is not to say that TC values are *necessarily* bad, but, when all these potential problems are added together, it is difficult to say how good such values are.

Fortunately, major research efforts are underway to strengthen the theoretical roots of TC and develop improved ways of applying it. Full treatment of trends here would take us far beyond the scope of this chapter, but a few remarks on a general level, along with selected references, are appropriate.

One general feature of current research is its emphasis on firming up the link between TC and consumer theory. Working in a household production framework [Desvousges, Smith, and McGivney 1983; Bockstael and McConnell 1981, 1983] is helping to clarify some key assumptions that have previously remained implicit. This is yielding criteria for judging when TC is inappropriate, as, for example, when recreation site quality is endogenous to the consumer's decision calculus. It is also helping to clarify the nature of the costs to be included. TC researchers have recognized for many years that the marginal cost of trips might need to include more than transportation costs, and a theoretical framework now exists to provide guidance for empirical definition of this important variable. In addition, time can be included explicitly in household production models. This, combined with the labor supply literature [Bockstael Hanemann, and Strand 1984], should improve the treatment of both travel time and time at the site.

Forging a stronger link with theory is also providing insights into econometric specification of TC models. It is becoming quite clear that models based on individual rather than zonal data are called for. Recall the basic logic of TC: the consumer surplus of those with lower travel costs is estimated based on the behavior of those with higher travel costs. This link between low-travel-cost and high-travel-cost consumers is based on the assumption that, except for shifters such as income and socioeconomic characteristics, the researcher is dealing with a typical consumer who takes a certain number of trips, plus or minus some randomly distributed error, as a function of the vector of travel costs. Give a person from location A the same travel cost vector as a person from location B and, by assumption, the person from A will behave just like the person from B except for random error and the shifter variables. To the extent that the trip demand function at the individual level is consistent with consumer theory, the researcher can be more confident that the typical-consumer assumption holds and that, therefore, consumer surplus estimates are valid welfare measures. These requirements include additivity, homogeneity of degree zero of demand, and integrability. The appropriateness of separability and other assumptions can also be tested. Aggregation of individual behavior to the zonal level obscures these relationships. Individual demand functions derived from explicitly stated utility functions assure consistency with theory and provide exact (i.e., Hicksian) welfare measures, provided, of course, that they fit the data.

Individual demand models also seem more promising for resolving a second issue, nonparticipation. Normally, the data gathered for TC applications are from a sample of site visitors, yet increasing travel costs are likely to cause some consumers to decide against any participation at all. While this is one of the major concerns about use of individual, as opposed to zonal, models [Brown, et al. 1983], Bockstael, Hanemann, and Strand [1984] show that zonal models do not provide a satisfactory solution since visits per capita are determined by the same individual decisions regarding participation. Nor is this simply a sampling problem. Even if the sample is drawn from the population as a whole—rather than users only—the participation decision must still be modeled. Furthermore, in most multiple-site cases, not all consumers visit all sites, so that the possibility of corner solutions must be incorporated in the analysis. Both the participation decision and the choice of sites seem more easily and naturally modeled at the individual level, rather than the zonal level. For all these reasons, and to reduce multicollinearity and heteroskedasticity as well, the TC models of the future are likely to involve data disaggregated to the individual level that explicitly incorporate the participation decision and corner solutions.

There is also currently a tendency toward models that estimate the *share* of trips to each site rather than directly estimating the number of trips to each site. *Share models* are not theoretically different from *trip models* in the sense that the simultaneous solution of a set of demand functions for trips implies a corresponding set of shares of trips to each site. Share models do open some promising econometric possibilities from recent developments in probabilistic models.[2]

Finally, as we turn our attention to the hedonic price method (HP), a couple of attempts to link HP and TC should be noted. Smith, Desvousges, and McGivney [1983] have adapted a hedonic wage model to the problem of valuing travel time. Brown and Mendelsohn [1984] have attacked the problem of site quality valuation by developing what they term an "hedonic travel cost model." Thus, the principles of HP are not only important for their own sake but may hold clues for resolving problems in TC.

Hedonic-price (HP) method

As we saw in the last section, TC is based on the premise that travel expenditures and travel time *ration* access to some environmental goods such as recreation sites. Yet, many environmental commodities can be readily accessed from one's home without incurring travel costs. Examples include air quality, views, and water frontage. Households often pay substantial premiums to acquire homes that afford access to these amenities. If the demand for such amenities could be inferred from housing prices, the value of the unmarketed environmental good would be obtained. This is what the hedonic-price (HP) method as applied to real estates values attempts to accomplish.

In HP, individual characteristics of goods are valued based on the satisfaction they provide. HP was first used by Griliches [1961] to estimate the value of quality changes in automobiles. The first study to attempt to infer environmental values from residential property values was Ridker [1967] (see also Ridker and Henning [1967]). A number of later environmental studies are discussed by Freeman [1979]. While our exposition will be developed in terms of property values, it should also be recognized that HP has been applied to wage rate differentials as related to environmental risks in a number of studies. Relevant literature on wage models is cited by Smith and Gilbert [1985]. We will begin this section by examining the basic hedonic theory presented by Rosen [1974].

The basic hedonic theory

Rather than deal with the many complexities of real-world real estate markets, let us consider the basic concepts of HP in a more simple, abstract world. Consider a class of goods each member of which is completely defined by an n-dimensional vector of characteristics, $Z = (Z_1, Z_2, \ldots, Z_n)$. For example, if the class of goods is automobiles, Z_1 might be horsepower, Z_2 might be cargo capacity, and so on. To avoid unneeded complexity, it will be assumed that characteristics are perfectly divisible. Also, all characteristics are assumed to be positive in the sense that consumers view larger values of Z_i as preferable to smaller values for all i.

Our goal is to develop the theoretical arguments for how the prices of various members of such a class of highly differentiated products would be determined under conditions of perfect competition. Since the vector Z completely describes each good's characteristics, a function, $P(Z)$, can be written expressing the perfectly competitive price of each good as a function of its characteristics. $P(Z)$ is termed the hedonic or *implicit price function*. The "prices" of the characteristics may be thought of as being implicit in the price of the good.

To describe how the implicit price function would be generated, we must deal with the decision processes of individual firms and consumers. Under competition, individual firms and consumers will treat $P(Z)$ as a set of parameters. The implicit price function confronting any one firm or consumer may be visualized as a surface in an $n + 1$-dimensional space with price on one axis and the quantities of the various characteristics on the other n axes. A slice of this surface for one characteristic, say Z_1, can be seen in two-dimensional space by setting $Z_2^*, \ldots, Z_n^*$ at fixed amounts and then letting $P(Z_1, Z_2^*, \ldots, Z_n^*)$ vary as Z_1 varies. This slice of the implicit price function is illustrated in figure 3-3. For the time being θ_1, θ_2, and θ_3 can be ignored. The shape of $P(Z)$ will be discussed later. At this point assume strict concavity.

Now consider a utility-maximizing consumer confronting the problem of choosing Z. In this sort of model, consuming multiple units from the class of goods in question adds additional complexity which will not be needed here. Assume instead that each consumer buys exactly one unit. Thus, the utility function can be described as $U(X, Z)$ where X is the consumption of all other goods measured in dollars and Z is the bundle of characteristics of the one unit purchased from the class of goods in question. Given money income of M, utility is maximized subject to the budget constraint $M = X + P(Z)$.

To begin to think about the consumer's willingness to pay for alternative bundles Z, define a bid function of the form

$$\theta = \theta(Z; u, M)$$

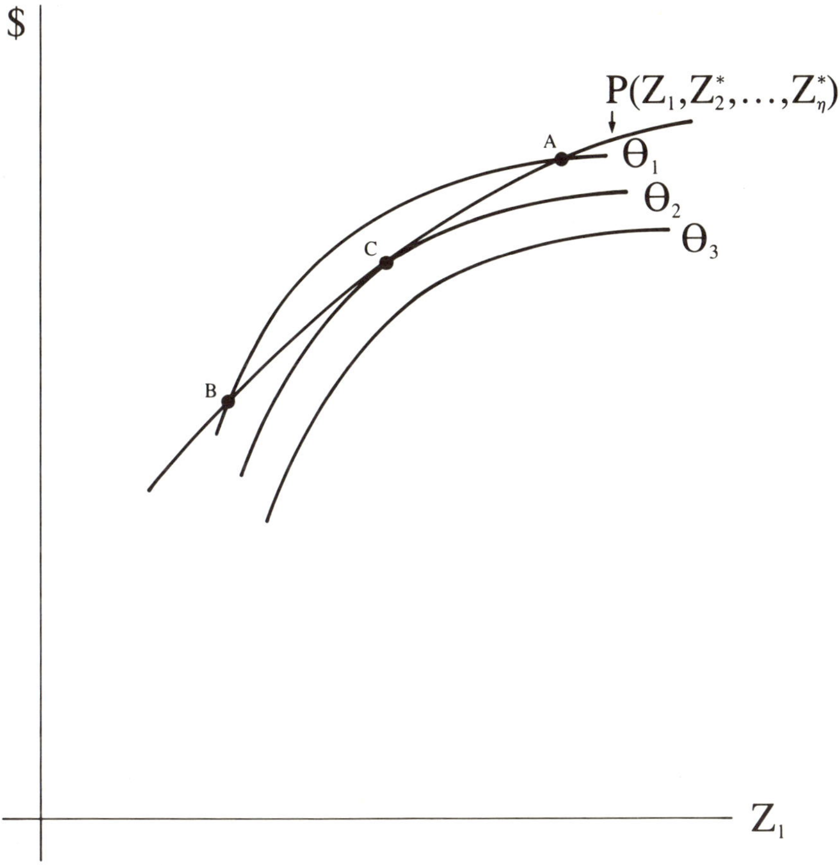

Figure 3-3. The implicit price function and a consumer's indifference curves.

where θ is defined implicitly such that

$$U(M - \theta, Z) = u$$

where u is a predetermined level of utility. Given M and some bundle, Z, the consumer could pay up to θ and still achieve utility level u. Notice that $M - \theta$ is the amount left to be spent on X. The properties of θ(·) are explored by Rosen [1974, 38].

Return again to the $n + 1$-dimensional space in dollars and characteristics. θ(·) can be expressed as a family of bid surfaces, one for each utility level. This can be seen in two-dimensional space by looking again at a slice where all characteristics except Z_1 are held constant at $Z_2^*,\ldots,Z_n^*$. The result is a set of indifference curves like θ_1, θ_2, and θ_3 in figure 3-3. These can be viewed as indifference curves between X and Z_1 except that they are upside down. The amount of X consumed would be measured *down* the vertical axis from a point representing money income. Thus, the indifference curves θ_1, θ_2, and θ_3 reflect increasing levels of utility. Measuring up along the vertical axis from the origin yields the amount spent on Z (and thus unavailable to be spent on X). Stated differently, the θ curves portray the marginal rate of substitution between Z_1 and money to be spent on other goods.

Continuing to examine the graph, reconsider the implicit price function, $P(Z_1,Z_2^*,\ldots,Z_n^*)$. Points lying above and to the left of this function are feasible in that they involve combinations of X and Z_1 that are within the budget constraint of the consumer. Thus, all points between A and B on θ_1 are feasible while none of the points on θ_3 is feasible. Given Z_i^* for $i = 2,\ldots,n$, the optimal level of Z_1 to add to the bundle occurs at point C, where θ_2 is tangent to $P(Z)$.

With all the Z_i's and X as variables, the consumer can be thought of as exploring the various $\theta(\cdot)$ surfaces until one is found that is tangent to $P(Z)$. Different consumers may choose different bundles, Z, for two reasons: differences in tastes and differences in money incomes. Thus, in figure 3-4a, three different bid curves θ^1, θ^2, and θ^3 are shown as tangent to $P(Z)$ where superscripts denote different consumers who choose different amounts of Z_1.

The analysis of firms is in many ways symmetrical to the consumer case. Let $Q(Z)$ = the number of units produced by a firm with characteristic bundle Z. Assume, for simplicity, that each firm specializes in only one product. That is, all output from any one firm has the same characteristics. Total costs are given by $C(Q,Z)$. Given competition, the price is treated as a parameter and the profit of an individual firm is simply $\pi = P(Z)Q - C(Q,Z)$.

Now define a set of offer or iso-profit functions comparable to the consumer's bid curves. Let ϕ equal the price at which a firm can bring a marginal unit of output with characteristics Z onto the market given total output Q and a given profit level, $\hat{\pi}$. That is,

$$\phi = \phi\,(Z;\,Q,\hat{\pi}).$$

Given a value of Q, we can visualize a family of such offer functions in $n+1$-dimensional space, each one depending on a different level of $\hat{\pi}$. Setting all members of the vector Z, except the first, at $Z_2^*,\ldots,Z_n^*$, a two-dimensional slice such as ϕ^1 in figure 3-4a can be drawn.

ϕ^1 has a positive slope because additional units of Z_1 can be provided only at higher offer prices if profits are to remain constant. Convexity of ϕ^1 follows from the conventional assumption of diminishing returns at higher

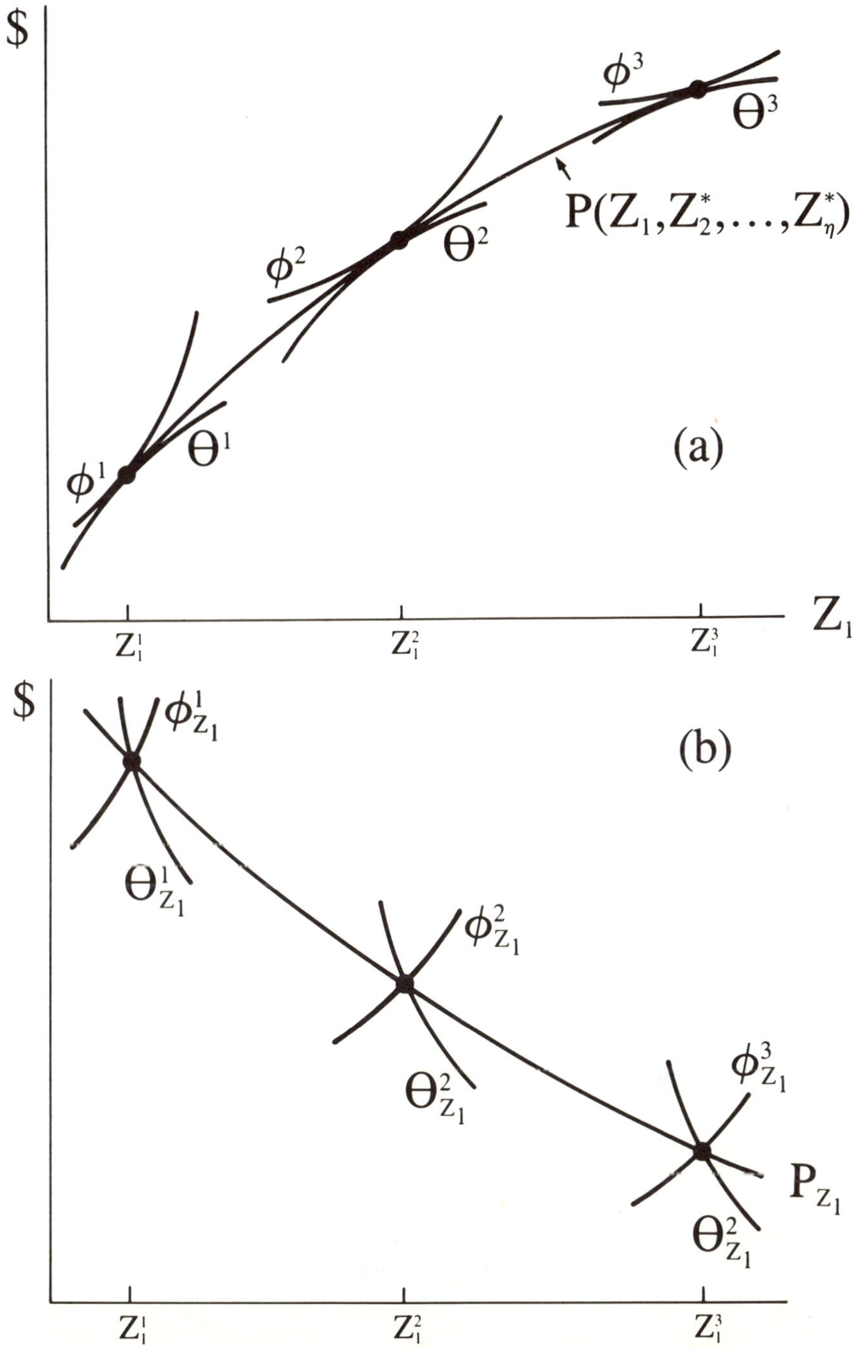

Figure 3-4. Market forces generate implicit price function (a) and associated marginal implicit price function (b).

levels of Z_1 production holding other characteristics constant. ϕ^1 is a single-offer curve but additional ones could have been shown with higher curves reflecting higher profit levels. Thus, profits are maximized by choosing that level of Z_1 that places the firm on the highest possible offer curve. This occurs at the offer curve that is just tangent to $P(Z)$. For firm 1 this is Z_1^1 in the figure. Other firms, because of different technical capabilities or differences in access to factor markets, seek out tangencies on offer functions like ϕ^2 and ϕ^3.

It is now possible to expand the field of vision to many consumers and many firms interacting in a competitive market. $P(Z)$ is no longer a set of parameters, but is determined by the market process. Consumers seek to get on the lowest possible bid function in order to maximize utility. Firms seek to get on the highest possible offer function to maximize profits. Where a tangency between a bid function and an offer function is reached, a market transaction involving a specific Z vector occurs and a point on $P(Z)$ is established. The combination of all such transactions determines the full implicit price function, $P(Z)$, across all relevant bundles of characteristics. It is assumed that there are enough firms and consumers operating at each point to maintain competition.

By assuming that there is a subset of consumers and firms that has already settled on $Z_2^*, \ldots, Z_n^*$, we can portray the process in two-dimensional space. Firm 1 and consumer 1 in figure 3-4a bargain and decide to produce and consume Z_1^1. Similar agreements occur at Z_1^2, Z_1^3, and other points of tangency. All these points combine to form $P(Z_1, Z_2^*, \ldots, Z_n^*)$, the implicit price function in the figure.

The same process can also be depicted in terms of marginal bid and offer curves. Differentiating and noting that points of tangency imply equal slopes, shows that, in market equilibrium, at each output level for Z_1

$$\frac{\partial \Theta_{Z_1}^1}{\partial Z_1} = \frac{\partial \phi}{\partial Z_1}$$

Equilibrium outputs occur where marginal bid equals marginal offer. Such points are shown in figure 3-4b. The marginal bid curves such as $\theta_{Z_1}^1$ have special significance. Because they hold utility constant and express marginal willingness to pay for characteristics, the marginal bid functions can be interpreted as Hicksian compensated demand functions for characteristics. Also, tracing out the points of intersection between marginal bid and marginal offer curves yields the *marginal implicit price function*, P_{Z_1}, and it follows that

$$P_{Z_1} = \frac{\partial P(Z)}{\partial Z_1}$$

evaluated, in this case, at $Z_2^*, \ldots, Z_n^*$.

Armed with these concepts, HP, as utilized in environmental economics, can be presented and interpreted. Applied to real estate, housing prices or equivalent annual rental rates are regressed on housing and site characteristics, such as number of rooms, square footage, distance from central business district, and the like. Also included are measures of environmental quality. Letting Z_1 equal a measure of air quality and $Z_2, \ldots, Z_n$ equal other characteristics, $P(Z)$ is the implicit price function for housing and $\partial P(Z)/\partial Z_1$ is the marginal implicit price of air quality.

Some a priori requirements for $P(Z)$ in the real estate case seem necessary. As before, if Z_1 measures air quality (as opposed to air pollution), $P(Z)$ should have a positive or at least a nonnegative slope in air quality. Furthermore, in general, one would not expect $P(Z)$ to be linear for housing [Freeman 1979, 122]. In terms of environmental characteristics, linearity would imply that marginal willingness to pay is the same regardless of the existing level of environmental quality. It seems more likely that, at least above some threshold, willingness to pay for improvements in environmental quality declines as quality increases. That is, a person whose residential location has poor air quality will probably be willing to pay more for a marginal improvement that he/she would pay if the air were nearly perfect. Thus, $P(Z)$ is drawn as concave in figure 3-4 and P_{Z_1} slopes downward.

Once $P(Z)$ is estimated it could be used to predict housing prices [Butler 1982]. Here, we are more interested in the valuation of changes in environmental quality. Could P_{Z_1} be used for this purpose? Caution is warranted at this point. As Rosen [1974, 54] concluded, "Estimated hedonic price-characteristics functions typically identify neither demand nor supply." This can be seen clearly in the lower portion of figure 3-4. Assuming that $P(Z)$ could be accurately estimated and P_{Z_1} derived, it would not necessarily follow that the individual Hicksian compensated demand functions, $\theta^1_{Z_1}$, $\theta^2_{Z_1}$, $\theta^3_{Z_1}, \ldots$, could be identified. Since the marginal implicit price function passes through the equilibrium point on each of the demand functions, it could be used to predict the value of a marginal change in air quality at one particular location, but for nonmarginal changes and simultaneous changes at several locations, the underlying demand functions would have to be determined if theoretically defensible values are to be estimated.

In econometric terms, $P(Z)$ is a reduced form for simultaneous sets of bid and offer functions. To use HP for valuation of most environmental quality changes, the underlying structural equations would have to be identified.

Thus, whether HP can be used for environmental valuation depends to a large extent on whether the identification problem can be solved. We will also look at some issues relating to specification and functional form before assessing HP's potential as a valuation technique.

The identification problem

For valuation purposes, we are interested in the simultaneous equation system:

$$P_Z^D = P_Z^D\,(Z,M,t)$$
$$P_{Z_i}^{iS} = P_{Z_i}^{iS}(Z,\hat{\pi},s)$$

where the superscripts D and S refer to demand and supply, respectively, and t and s are shifters. To estimate his system, Rosen [1974] proposed a two-step procedure. First, the implicit price equation is estimated using the best specification and functional form available. From this equation, marginal implicit prices would be calculated and used in the second stage as endogenous variables in the supply and demand equations. By treating these estimated marginal implicit prices as direct observations, Rosen (p. 50) contended that the second step is just a "garden variety identification problem." However, later work, including Brown and Rosen [1982] and Parsons [1984], has shown that the problem may not be so easily dispensed with. It is instructive to outline the two approaches that have been most often used to achieve identification, indicate their shortcomings, and examine appropriate identification alternatives.

One identification approach is to exclude a variable from the demand equation such as a supply shifter. This will be referred to as the *exclusion restriction model*. Following Parsons [1984], let's focus on a single attribute (Z_i) of housing and demand (t) and supply (s) shifters. For simplicity assume that t and s are scalars. The structural equations for the model are:

$$\text{marginal bid:} \qquad P_{Z_{ij}} = \beta_0 + \beta_1 Z_{ij} + \beta_2 t_j + u_{ij} \tag{3.1}$$
$$\text{marginal offer:} \qquad P_{Z_{ij}} = \gamma_0 + \gamma_1 Z_{ij} + \gamma_2 s_j + v_{ij} \tag{3.2}$$

where j = observations $1,\ldots,N$; u_{ij} and v_{ij} are random disturbance terms; and β and γ are structural coefficients. Also, assume the implicit price function is nonlinear and the marginal implicit price function is linear:

$$P_{Z_{ij}} = \delta_0 + \delta_1 Z_{ij} + w_i \tag{3.3}$$

where w_i is a random disturbance term. Is the demand-supply system (equations 3.1 and 3.2) identified? Parsons shows that t and s are observationally equivalent and the marginal bid function is underidentified.[3] Intuitively, the problem is that each point on $P(Z)$ where bid and offer curves are tangent represents unique values for both t and s. We cannot, so to speak, hold the influence of t constant while varying s or vice versa. Thus, it is still impossible to discern the separate influences of supply and demand. The individual demand functions cannot be identified.

The second approach is to assume exogenous attribute supply. The structural model consists of equations 3.1 and 3.3. In this case, the marginal bid function is underidentified because the number of excluded exogenous variables is less than the number of included endogenous variables minus one.

Parsons [1984] has pointed out that the demand–supply system includes not two but three equations: the marginal bid and offer functions plus the equilibrium equation or marginal implicit price function. Once the three-equation system is specified, identification might be achieved in at least three ways. First, if identical preferences and incomes are assumed for all households (i.e., t can be ignored), the marginal bid equation is identified for either the exogenous supply or the exclusion restriction model. Second, identification can be achieved if a segmenting factor is included in the marginal implicit price equation and excluded from either the marginal bid or the offer function. A number of segmenting factors have been suggested including geographical location, race of purchaser, and time of purchase. Finally, identification can be achieved in some cases through restrictions on the functional form of the implicit price equation [Brown and Rosen 1982]. In many instances market segmentation offers the best prospects for identification. The assumption of identical preferences and income is often not appropriate and there appears to be no theoretical justification for imposing Brown and Rosen's restrictions on the marginal implicit price function.

Once the identification problem is solved and the attribute demand function has been estimated, it is straightforward to determine the aggregate value of the attribute. The welfare triangles under the attribute demand curves are summed. We will now examine two additional topics concerning HP and then assess the technique.

Specification

As we have seen, the implicit price function is the cornerstone of the hedonic valuation method. Thus, the specification of this equation is critical to HP applications. Butler [1982] suggests that, in principle, all characteristics that provide utility to consumers and are costly to produce should be included in the hedonic price equation. Typically, explanatory variables must be selected—from a long list of site and structural characteristics, which appear in sales abstracts or in tax descriptions of the property—as well as access and amenity variables, which can be generated once the location of a property is known. A variety of access and amenity attributes have been specified in empirical studies including locational and neighborhood variables [Li and Brown 1980; Linneman 1980], quality of public schools [Johnson and Lea 1982], property tax rates [Oates 1969], air quality [Brookshire et al. 1982], and water frontage and waterviews [Brown and Pollakowski 1977; Edwards and Anderson 1984a; Shabman and Bertelson 1979].

With such a variety of candidate attributes available to the researcher, there are necessarily trade-offs between a "true" specification and the restricted specifications that are feasible given data availability. Butler [1982] argued that a restricted specification may still provide a reasonable fit and reduces collinearity between variables. He suggested several tests for estimating the size and importance of biases when a restricted model is used and found specification bias (for one data set) to be within prescribed tolerance limits. Use of a restricted specification may also reduce the costs of collecting data and estimating coefficients in the hedonic price equation.

Functional form

Once the model has been specified, the researcher must select a functional form for the hedonic price equation. Economic theory provides little guidance for selecting the appropriate functional form. As noted earlier, a linear functional form is usually rejected because it generates constant attribute prices.

As a result, the hedonic price equation is often estimated using nonlinear functional forms such as logarithmic, semilog, or quadratic. Some writers, including Rosen [1974], have argued that functional form be selected on the basis of statistical criteria. Halvorsen and Pollakowski [1981] proposed a Box-Cox maximum-likelihood procedure to test statistically for the functional form that involves a quadratic flexible form with second-order terms. Others [Edwards and Anderson 1984a; Milon et al. 1984] have rejected the quadratic form because of high computational costs and used a simplified Box-Cox procedure suggested by Goodman [1977] and Linneman [1980]. All of the nonlinear functional forms listed above are just special cases of the Box-Cox equation. A maximum-likelihood estimation procedure is used on various power transformations of P and Z. The "best" functional form is that power transformation that maximizes the value of the likelihood function. In both empirical studies mentioned above [Edwards and Anderson 1984a; Milon et al. 1984], all commonly used nonlinear (as well as the linear) forms fall outside of the confidence interval for the "best" functional form. Hence, use of the more flexible forms may become the standard procedure.

Evaluation of HP

Like TC, HP can be used to value certain types of environmental commodities. In judging HP's applicability to a specific problem, two relationships must be considered. First, is the link between the environmental good (e.g., clean air) and the corresponding environmental attribute (e.g., particulate concentrations) firmly established in the minds of property owners? Second, is the environmental good likely to be valued by buyers and sellers of housing? Let us consider three examples.

For an environmental good such as air quality, researchers have used pollutant concentration levels in hedonic studies. Where households have good information about air quality differentials, air quality variables have provided good results when used in HP (see Brookshire et al. [1982]). Also, qualitative differences in air quality are readily visible to most people and may affect a person's eyes and breathing, as well.

For water quality of a lake or river, the link to an attribute can be established, but some kinds of water quality differentials may not be obvious to households [Willis and Foster 1982]. Part of the problem with water quality is seasonal fluctuation. Also, poor water quality may be evident only to recreational users. A more subtle problem with water quality concerns buyers' access to information. When convenient, most sellers will list houses when they are most attractive. For a house near a nutrient-rich lake, the house will be less likely to be listed when weeds and algae are present.

A third environmental good for which HP might be employed is accessibility to an ocean beach [Edwards and Anderson 1984a]. The beach might be linked to HP through an access variable such as distance from the property to the beach. Households do seem to recognize the value of access in the market but there are still problems when HP is used. First, HP is likely to underestimate the value of the beach. Better access has value but users must nevertheless incur travel costs to visit the beach. Second, the locational variable may represent other attributes besides access to the beach. For example, distance to a beach may be a proxy for microclimatic differences between locations or be collinear with other important destinations such as employment centers and schools. In summary, the researcher must exercise caution in using HP to value environmental goods.

A second issue concerning the use of HP is the cost of resolving the identification problem. In most instances, the researcher cannot assume identical preferences and income. For example, air quality in some metropolitan areas is probably collinear with household incomes (or could even be used as a segmenting factor). When identification is achieved through market segmentation, the data collection costs may increase substantially. In some cases, the use of several markets may force restricted specifications of the attribute list. Thus, the identification problem can be a major impediment to the use of HP for valuation.

One alternative to the standard HP method of valuation is the utility approach proposed by Quigley [1982]. Assuming appropriate data can be assembled on consumers, this approach uses marginal implicit prices in the consumer's budget constraint. If parameters of the utility function can be identified, compensating or equivalent variation measures can be calculated. For an application of Quigley's method, see Edwards [1984].

A final consideration in using HP is whether a marginal or nonmarginal change is being valued. For small changes in an environmental attribute, we would expect HP to provide acceptable estimates of welfare changes if competently applied. One concern with examining marginal changes is whether consumers could be expected to perceive such changes in the variable (e.g., air and water quality). When the researcher must evaluate nonmarginal changes in the attribute, HP may provide erroneous estimates. The marginal implicit price function is based on an existing aggregate distribution of attributes. Suppose, to take an extreme case, that we want to value a proposed substantial improvement in air quality over the entire study area. The extant distribution of sites of given air quality levels determines $P(Z)$. If air quality improves dramatically, the distribution changes and we would expect $P(Z)$ to shift. For this hypothesized improvement, we would expect the HP for a single market to overestimate the benefits of improvements, since the value of each site is related to how poor air quality is at other sites.[4] Thus, HP can be expected to work well for small localized changes in environmental quality, but these may not be perceived by households. It may work less well for changes that are large enough for households to perceive and value, particularly if broad areas are affected.

Contingent Valuation (CV)

Both TC and HP involve elaborate sets of assumptions and complicated econometrics to arrive at values. Instead of all this fuss and bother, why not just ask people what values they place on environmental assets? This is exactly what CV does. The simpler CV techniques attempt to get values directly from "the horse's mouth," so to speak, rather than by inference. Following the same format as in previous sections, we will first examine the basics of CV, then introduce several refinements, and finally attempt to evaluate its strengths and weaknesses.

The basic approach

To our knowledge, the first economist to suggest valuation of nonmarket environmental resources by asking people directly about their values was Ciriacy-Wantrup [1952, 241–242]:

> Individuals of a sample or of a social group as a whole may be asked how much money they are willing-to-pay for successive quantities of a collective good....

The first person to actually implement this suggestion was Davis [1963, 1964]. Davis devised a question format that has since been employed in many studies—the *bidding game*. Maine big game hunters in a specific area were asked whether they would continue to hunt if their expenses rose by a specified amount. If the response was affirmative, Davis increased the amount to successively higher levels until a maximum willingness-to-pay amount was reached. Likewise, if the original level of expenses (the so-called "starting bid") received a negative response, Davis lowered the amount iteratively until the respondent indicated the maximum level of expenses that was tolerable before participation would cease. The resulting estimate of maximum willingness-to-pay of hunters was then used for comparison with timber values. A second pioneering CV study was that by Randall, Ives, and Eastman [1974]. Their study involved environmental damages from coal development in the Four Corners area. They also used bidding games.

A great deal of research has been devoted to CV since the Davis and Randall studies. We propose to discuss the major refinements in CV by focusing on six issues that must be dealt with in any good CV study: (1) What will be the population of people whose values will be estimated? (2) How will the "product" to be valued be defined? (3) What payment vehicle will be used? (4) How will CV questions be posed (i.e., in a bidding-game format or using some other technique)? (5) How will the data be analyzed? (6) And, what supplemental data will be obtained?

For the sake of simplicity and brevity, the discussion will concentrate on CV measures of willingness to pay. Willingness to accept compensation is, of course, an equally valid measure of economic welfare from a theoretical point of view. This point notwithstanding, most studies that employ CV have not attempted to measure willingness to accept. One reason is that those studies that have included willingness-to-accept questions invariably obtain values much larger than corresponding willingness-to-pay estimates (see Cummings, et al. [1984], for a summary). This phenomenon is generally interpreted to mean that CV does not work well when applied to willingness to accept. Not all of the empirical evidence supports this view (see, for example, Bishop et al. [1984]). Nevertheless, except for the caveat that more research is desirable, this chapter will take the easier route of focusing only on willingness to pay.

Population definition

In CV research, the first question is always, whose values are to be measured? In TC and HP, this decision is made more or less automatically. TC studies focus on those who take trips to the site. When applied to real estate values, HP studies focus on property owners. Likewise, most early CV studies dealt with obvious resource users. For example, hunters, anglers, people living in a city affected by air pollution, or park visitors would be the relevant populations. More recently, there has been growing interest in "nonuser" or "intrinsic" values [Fisher and Raucher 1984]. People who are not currently using the resource may still value the option to use it in the future or the knowledge that the resource exists. Thus, there is a trend toward broadening the population of subjects in CV studies to include those with option and existence values [Boyle and Bishop 1985].

Product definition

If people are to express valid values, the object being valued must be clear in their minds. A good CV study must include a carefully worded description of the resources or change in environmental quality that is to be valued. In addition, visual aids such as photographs, charts, and maps are often used. An example is the water quality ladder shown in figure 3-5. It has been used by Mitchell and Carson [1981] and Desvousges, Smith, and McGivney [1983] to describe various levels of water quality during CV interviews. Vague or overly technical descriptions are to be avoided since they make surveying difficult and results hard to interpret. The goal here and elsewhere in CV studies is to give respondents enough information to motivate informed judgements about value without biasing their answers.

Payment vehicle definition

CV researchers have generally argued that, in order for respondents to come up with realistic values, some specific mechanism for payment must be specified. Various payment vehicles have been used. For recreational

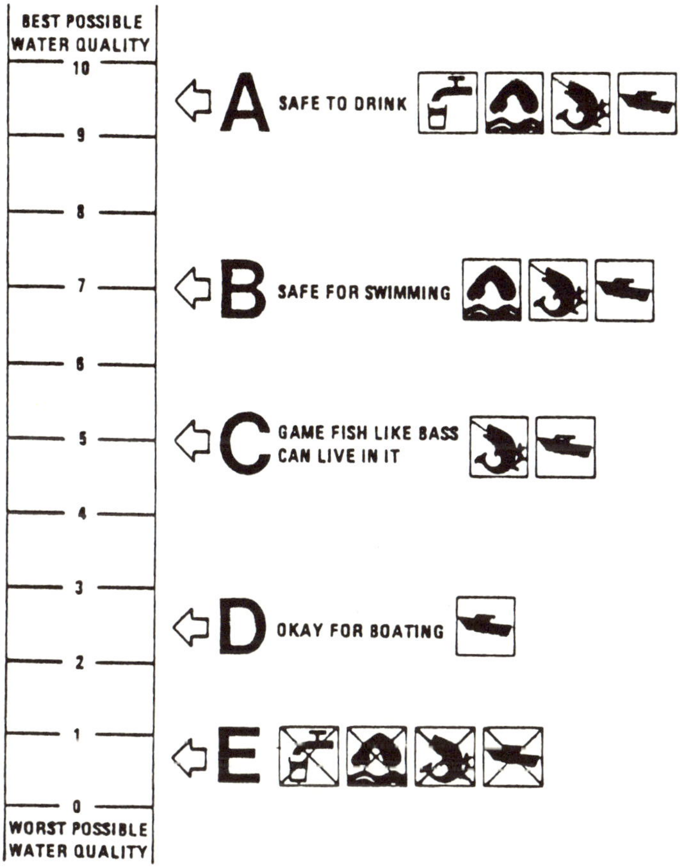

Figure 3-5. The water quality ladder is one way to describe the product in CV surveys. (From Desvousges, Smith, and McGivney 1983).

outings, the vehicle has often been increased expenses per trip. For environmental improvements, a realistic vehicle is higher taxes and prices of manufactured goods. Other examples include property taxes, sewerage fees, hunting and fishing licenses fees, and prices in newly created markets for the good in question.

Two criteria are involved in the choice of a vehicle [Mitchell and Carson 1981]. The first is realism. A priori, it seems reasonable to assume that the more realistic the situation, including the mechanism for payment, the easier it will be for people to accurately respond to CV questions. This viewpoint argues in favor of using the actual means of payment if possible.

Using higher taxes and prices in water pollution control studies, for example, is a reflection of this rationale.

The second criterion for choosing vehicles is neutrality. The hope is that people will respond to CV questions in ways that will reflect their underlying values for the resource, and not their emotional reaction to the payment vehicle itself. Use of taxes as the payment vehicle may be a case in point. The concern is that people will use the CV question to express general dissatisfaction with tax rates rather than to express a value for the resource.

As the tax example indicates, the realism criterion and the neutrality criterion may conflict. The most realistic vehicle may not be neutral. In such cases, compromises are necessary, but such compromising often leaves the researcher uncomfortable about the resulting values.

Alternative valuation techniques

Once a vehicle has been chosen, the researcher must determine the mechanics of using it in actually eliciting values. Past work has placed considerable emphasis on this problem and five different approaches can be identified: bidding games, open-ended questions, payment-card formats, dichotomous-choice questions, and contingent ranking. Each of these merits a brief explanation.

Bidding games, as described above, have been applied in the majority of CV studies. Still, there has been considerable dissatisfaction with the technique. For one thing, personal and telephone interviews are necessary in order to carry out the bidding process. This has led to research on techniques that can be utilized in less-expensive mail surveys. Also, fears of starting-point bias have been repeatedly expressed. The starting bid is a tool for initiating the bidding process. Starting-point bias exists when the initial bid, as stated by the interviewer, influences the final value stated by the respondent. Starting-point bias may occur if the starting bid is sufficiently different from respondents' true values that they become bored and terminate the bidding process before their maximum willingness-to-pay is reached. Another plausible explanation is that the initial bid suggests an appropriate range of final bids to respondents [Brookshire et al. 1981].

Empirical evidence on starting-point bias has not been convincing to all investigators. Cummings et al. [1984] argue that the evidence is still inconclusive, while Mitchell and Carson [1984a] and Boyle, Bishop, and Welsh [1985] are convinced that starting-point bias is a serious flaw in bidding games and have set out to develop alternative techniques.

One such technique is the *open-ended question*. Once the product and vehicle have been described, the respondent is left to state a value without the aid of additional information, iterative bidding, or other processes. This technique is amenable to mail surveys and avoids influencing responses by stating a starting bid. Perhaps the best known study employing open-ended questions was Hammack and Brown's [1974] study of waterfowl values.

Despite its simplicity and avoidance of starting-point bias, many researchers have been reluctant to use open-ended questions. This is presumably due to a fear that open-ended questions do not provide sufficient stimuli and enough information to encourage people to thoroughly consider the value they would place on the resource if a market were created. After all, in most cases, people have not valued the resource before and many never have considered what its economic value to them might be. To expect them to come up with an accurate value "out of the blue" may be expecting too much. Cummings et al. [1984] reported results from a number of CV studies that used both bidding games and open-ended questions. The latter consistently produced lower values, a result, they argued, of inadequate stimuli for full exploration of preferences when open-ended questions were used. They further argued that bidding games help provide the necessary stimuli.

To avoid starting-point bias, yet provide some information to help respondents think the valuation issue through, Mitchell and Carson [1981] proposed the *payment-card* method. Their study involved nationwide improvements in water quality. After defining the product with the help of the water quality ladder and explaining the vehicle (increases in taxes and prices), their interviewers handed respondents a payment card like that shown in figure 3-6. (Actually, this particular card is from Boyle and Bishop [1984].) Notice that the card is anchored, in that it shows amounts spent for things like highways and public education. Note also that it is tailored to the respondent's income category. After considering the card, each respondent was asked the maximum she or he would pay each year for various changes in water quality.

One obvious concern here is whether there might be an anchor-point bias in payment-card results analogous to possible starting-point bias in bidding games. That is, might respondents be influenced by the choice of anchors in ways that cause them to distort their expressed values compared to true willingness to pay? One test [Mitchell and Carson 1981] failed to find evidence of such a bias, but further research would be desirable before the payment-card technique receives wide, uncritical adoption by CV researchers.

A fourth alternative for asking CV questions is the *dichotomous-choice*

$20,000 - $29,000

		Average Annual Taxpayer Expenditures for Selected Public Services			
$ 0		$300		$ 870	
	- National Parks				
30		360		960	
60	- Space Program	420		1050	
90	- Highways	480		1140	
	- Public Education				
120		540		1230	
150		600	- Health Care	1320	
180		66C		1410	
210		720		1500	
					-Defense
240		780		1590	

Figure 3-6. Sample payment card (From Boyle and Bishop 1984).

format. The three previously mentioned techniques all require respondents to express exact amounts. As an alternative, Bishop and Heberlein [1979] asked Wisconsin goose hunters whether they would willingly pay a specific amount. Different hunters were assigned different amounts at random. The rationale here is that respondents to CV surveys may find it difficult to come up with exact amounts, but may be able to respond "yes" or "no" to fixed amounts. This approach is very easily incorporated into mail surveys and can be used in interviews as well. Analysis of the data is more difficult than for the previously mentioned techniques, as we shall see below.

Another relatively new approach is *contingent ranking*. Here, respondents are not asked to value environmental commodities directly, but rather to rank various combinations of environmental quality and fees. The method was developed by Rae [1981a, 1981b] and applied also by Desvousges, Smith, and McGivney [1983]. Rae's work dealt with visibility in two National Parks. Respondents the personal interviews were typically given eight cards depicting various fees, various levels of visibility, and various other recreational characteristics. No clearly dominant combinations (e.g., low fee, high visibility and low congestion) were included. Respondents ranked the alternatives from most-preferred to least-preferred. Values were then inferred through statistical analysis of the rankings.

No consensus currently exists about which technique for asking CV questions is best. Each researcher has his or her preference, and variations on the five basic techniques discussed here are constantly appearing. In fact, it is not even clear whether question format has a significant effect on results. Bishop et al. [1984] used open-ended questions and bidding games and found no significant difference. Boyle and Bishop [1984] have compared bidding-game, payment-card, and dichotomous-choice results. The bidding-game and payment-card results were not significantly different. Dichotomous-choice values were significantly lower, but the difference may be due to an interviewer bias problem and a starting-point bias in the bidding game. On the other hand, Cummings et al. [1984] cite results that seem to indicate that open-ended questions produce lower values and that iterative bidding tends to raise values regardless of whether a starting bid is specified or subjects set their own starting bids. To our knowledge, only Desvousges, Smith, and McGivney [1983] have compared contingent-ranking results with those from bidding games and open-ended questions. In that case, contingent ranking yielded magnitudes that were roughly comparable to those of the other techniques. At this stage in the development of CV, choice of questioning technique is still largely a matter of the individual researcher's judgement.

Data analysis

For data from bidding games, open-ended questions, and payment-card questions, analysis of the data to develop value estimates is normally rather straightforward. The most difficult problem is to decide what to do about extreme values, including both zeroes and expressions of willingness to pay that seem unusually high. Current practice calls for presenting zero bidders with follow-up questions to ascertain whether they really place no value on the resource, are expressing a protest bid against valuation, found it too difficult to arrive at a value, or what. Zeroes that are judged to be legitimate expressions of value are included in the analysis, while others are excluded. Traditionally, expressed values that were judged, by rather arbitrary standards, to be excessive were excluded from the data set as protest bids. More systematic approaches to identifying true outliers have been suggested by Desvousges, Smith, and McGivney [1983] and Edwards and Anderson [1984b]. Once protest bids and other outliers are taken care of, sample means and standard errors are generally adequate to estimate values for the population.

Econometric analysis becomes more difficult for responses to dichotomous-choice questions. Here, the data provide yes/no responses to specific, randomly assigned values. How are such yes/no responses to be used to infer maximum willingness to pay? Current approaches involve econometric models, such as the logit model, that predict the probability of accepting a given price as a function of the stated level of the price and other socioeconomic variables. then values are calculated as either the mathematical expectation of maximum willingness to pay or the median value. Unfortunately, detailed exploration of procedures and issues here would immediately embroil us in a technical discussion that is beyond both the scope and space limitations of this chapter. It must suffice to say that major issues regarding functional form and truncation remain and to refer the reader to Bishop, Heberlein, and Kealy [1983], Boyle and Bishop [1984], and Hanemann [1984].

The contingent-ranking method also requires special attention to econometrics. Again, the approach is probabilistic. In this case, probabilities reflect the likelihood that a typical respondent will rank one scenario over another. Values are inferred from these probabilities. Details on the analysis of contingent-ranking results are given by Desvousges, Smith, and McGivney [1983, ch. 6].

What supplementary data will be gathered?

It is conceivable that a CV survey might include only valuation questions, but most studies gather additional data. Several objectives may be satisfied here. One might hypothesize that if CV values are valid, they should be systematically related to other variables. Income is an obvious example. For recreational assets, annual days of use might be correlated. Bishop, Heberlein, and Kealy [1983] have included measures of commitment to the recreational activity in their analysis. Age of the respondent and location of residence (urban/rural) are often included among CV survey questions. Such variables can be included in bid equations with CV values as the dependent variable. To the extent that hypotheses are supported by significant coefficients with the expected sign, the CV results take on additional credibility. Data can also be gathered on CV surveys to do complementary TC or HP analyses. To the extent that samples are necessarily nonrandom, additional data may be gathered to facilitate estimate of population values from sample statistics. Resource managers frequently find it desirable to gather information in addition to dollar values.

Evaluation of contingent valuation

The striking positive characteristic of CV is its flexibility. Assuming that people's answers are accurate measures of willingness to pay, a very wide variety of resource and environmental issues are amenable to CV techniques. The only apparent limitations are in the ability of researchers to describe the product and vehicle in terms that noneconomists can understand. In the extreme, it is hard to imagine how some kinds of values could be estimated by any other means. An example is existence value, a concept that has been explored by Krutilla [1967], Randall and Stoll [1983], McConnell [1983], Fisher and Raucher [1984], Boyle and Bishop [1985], and others. While definitions are still somewhat in a state of flux, existence values are, in general terms, values people place on resources quite apart from any desire they personally have to consume them or enjoyed them in any other conventional sense. An often cited example is the blue whale. Worldwide concern for the species indicates that people who never hope to consume whale products or even see blue whales are still willing to pay something to know that the whales will continue to exist. If this willingness does exist, there would be no market values, travel costs, or property values on which to base an estimate of such values. Thus, CV appears to be adaptable to a much broader set of environmental and resource issues than the other techniques.

Nevertheless, many within the economics profession have been reluctant to accept CV. Perhaps the concerns of most economists were summed up by Scott's [1965, 37] statement: "Ask a hypothetical question and you get a hypothetical answer." CV estimates reflect hypothetical transactions and many economists question whether people are both *willing* and *able* to respond in ways that reflect how they would really behave in a well-functioning market. Regarding the willingness to respond accurately, fears have focused on possible "strategic bias" in CV results. Regarding the ability of people to respond, concerns might be lumped, for lack of a better term, under the heading of "hypothetical bias."[5]

Strategic bias would be present if respondents intentionally misled researchers in order to further their own ends. The arguments are drawn from the literature on public goods. If respondents believe that their expressed CV values will affect policy, and hence their own welfare, and that expressed amounts will never be collected, they may report values larger or smaller than their true values. Suppose, for example, that you are answering a willingness-to-pay question about air quality in your neighbourhood. Suppose also that you know that if further clean-up measures are adopted, taxpayers in general will pick up the full cost so that the effect on your taxes will be negligible. You might well be tempted to report a value higher than your true willingness to pay in the hope that this will support adoption of the clean-up measure. Likewise, if people perceive, rightly or wrongly, that the fees or taxes they actually do pay will be affected by their CV values, they may under-report.

On the other hand, even if people do want to express their values accurately, they may still find it difficult or impossible to do so. Quoting Bishop, Heberlein, and Kealy:

> Prior to being confronted by an interviewer or mail survey, subjects may never before have attempted to express how they feel about environmental assets in monetary terms. While constrained utility maximization is a useful construct, conversion of utility into monetary terms in the real world may involve repeated market transactions over time, consultation within peer groups, assessment of markets for complements and substitutes, consultations within the household, and references to consumer information. It is questionable whether the interviewer or questionnaire designer can fully compensate for the lack of such experience and information in the limited time and space available. Hence, subjects are forced to deal with a situation which seems quite artificial from their point of view in comparison to situations where they normally arrive at market values. While the researcher hopes they will follow the same mental processes they would in real markets, the social context within which contingent valuation occurs may be so artificial that people will be unwilling or unable to do so [Bishop, Heberlein, and Kealy 1983, 627]

To the extent that resulting values differ from values that would be obtained from well-functioning markets, hypothetical bias is present.

Despite widespread a priori fears that strategic and hypothetical biases are large, empirical research has been at least moderately encouraging about the accuracy of CV estimates. Several laboratory studies from the public goods literature have involved attempts to set up situations where theory predicts that people will behave strategically. (See, for example, Scherr and Babb [1975]; Smith [1977]; Marwell and Ames [1979, 1980, 1981]). Strategic behavior appears to be the exception rather than the rule. Some CV studies have attempted to discern whether strategic behavior was having an effect and could find none [Schulze, d'Arge, and Brookshire 1981].

Furthermore, CV results have been roughly comparable in magnitude to results from studies employing other valuation techniques including TC models [Knetsch and Davis, 1966; Desvousges, Smith, and McGivney, 1983; Sellar, Stoll, and Chavas, 1985], surveys of the costs and prices of substitutes [Thayer, 1981], and HP [Brookshire, et al. 1982].

A number of laboratory and field experiments have now been completed where CV results could be compared with value estimates from actual cash transactions [Bohm, 1972; Bishop, Heberlein, and Kealy 1983; Bishop et al. 1984; Coursey et al. 1984]. Statistically significant differences sometimes emerge between CV values and actual cash values. However, the contingent values and actual cash values are usually in the same ballpark, at least for willingness to pay.

Without doubt, the weight of all this evidence has increased confidence in CV. Still doubts remain. For example, Freeman [1984] and Kahneman [1984] have voiced concerns about whether results relating to the validity of use values can be generalized to existence values. Further research, especially involving laboratory and field experiments, will help resolve these questions. In the meantime, it can be concluded that CV is becoming more and more firmly established as a major tool for valuation of nonmarket commodities.

Comparing the Valuation Approaches

Having discussed the basic mechanics of TC, HP, and CV and summarized some of the strengths and weaknesses of each, this chapter will close by examining the issue of selecting the best approach for specific applications. Most economists would agree that the valuation problem for nonmarket goods would be solved if values were estimated comparable to those that would be obtained if a well-functioning market could be established. Which approach will come closest to realizing this goal?

Most often the choice is between CV and one of the related-market approaches, either TC or HP. There are few, if any, instances where the researcher must choose between HP and TC.

In choosing between CV and a related-market approach, the views of many economists can be summarized in the proverb, "Actions speak louder than words." People bring real preferences for environmental commodities and real money to bear when they choose a home site, decide to make a recreational trip, or engage in other market activities in order to consume environmental amenities. By comparison, CV involves only words. The implication is that related-market measures are superior where the necessary data exist. Such a view may be reflected in a recent statement by Freeman:

> . . . it appears that [CV] is likely to work best for those kinds of problems where we need it the least, that is, where respondents' experience with changes in the level of the environmental good have left a record of trade-offs, substitutions, and so

> forth, which can be the basis of econometric estimates of value. But for those problems for which we need something like [CV] most, that is, where individuals have little or no experience with different levels of the environmental good, [CV] appears to be least reliable. [Freeman 1984]

Thus, Freeman implies that CV may be a usable tool for valuing some types of environmental goods, but these are precisely the cases where data are available to apply related-market methods. Freeman seems to imply that, in such cases, related-market methods are likely to yield results that are at least as reliable as CV. It would follow that where the researcher has a choice, related-market approaches are to be preferred over CV. Is such a conclusion warranted?

That some environmental preferences are visible in market decisions is undeniable. On a superficial level, the inference of environmental values from related-market data appears to be straightforward. The deeper one goes, however, the more visible are a whole host of theoretical and empirical issues. We have already attempted to summarize many of these issues and to do so again would be redundant. The point here is that, despite great progress, applied researchers still face a formidable array of potential pitfalls in trying to infer accurate environmental values from related-market data.

A second source of concern about related-market methods has to do with data quality. It is sometimes argued that related-market methods are superior because they can utilize secondary data whereas CV requires primary data gathering through surveys. In our judgement, this alleged advantage is quite often an illusion. Available secondary data on recreation, property values, wages, and other variables of potential value in TC and HP analyses are typically collected for purposes unrelated or peripheral to valuation. Researchers are subsequently forced to perform econometric acrobatics, apologize for omitted variables, and specify models that make tenuous assumptions about consumer behavior. In one instance, the 1980 National Survey of Fishing, Hunting and Wildlife and Associated Recreation, data for TC applications was purposely generated (see Miller and Hay [1984] for a discussion). While such efforts are to be encouraged, the 1980 data were necessarily so highly aggregated that their usefulness has been limited. For the time being at least, high quality related-market applications, no less than CV, will require primary data collection except under unusual circumstances.

A third drawback of related-market methods should also be noted: they tend to be quite limited in their applicability. TC appears to be applicable only to recreational pursuits where travel is a major household input. Furthermore, TC seems most easily adapted to values of recreation sites. Valuation of changes in site quality has been attempted, as noted above, but major unresolved questions remain. Though potentially applicable to wages and possibly other prices, in environmental economics HP has thus far been most often applied to property values. Environmental values of those not owning property do not get counted even through they may be substantial. Furthermore, given what has been said regarding the identification problem, one has to question whether HP, at least as it is currently practiced, is applicable to nonmarginal changes in environmental quality, especially nonmarginal changes across numerous sites within the housing market or markets covered by the study.

It is *not* our intent to argue that CV is necessarily superior to the related-market approaches. On the contrary, CV has potential pitfalls of its own. The assumption that people are both willing and able to reveal the values that they would bring to bear in a well-functioning market for environmental amenities may be violated to some degree, particularly when, as the Freeman quotation indicates, respondents have limited experience with the amenity levels in question.

Thus, we would conclude that all three of the techniques discussed in this paper are imperfect. Lacking a fully operational market to generate a standard for value comparisons, it seems best to make no general conclusions about which techniques are more or less accurate. For applied research, the upshot is that where related-market transactions exist, *both* related-market and CV approaches can be profitably applied. Both have imperfections, yet each provides some insights into the value of environmental amenities.

What about cases where related-market transactions are not apparent and where respondents have few, if any, market activities to help them in arriving at values? Existence values of natural areas and wildlife populations are cases in point. Here the choice is whether to use CV or simply admit that monetary valuation is scientifically impossible, at least for the time being. The latter course of action would be the safest and would be warranted if CV had been judged invalid when applied to more conventional valuation problems (e.g., recreational opportunities at well-known sites and environmental amenities at levels and locations familiar to respondents). However, as we have pointed out, research of CV validity has been rather encouraging. To the extent that strategic behavior is having any influence at all, the magnitude does not appear to be large. Inaccuracies may be present due to the hypothetical circumstances within which CV is applied, but for more conventional environmental values the magnitude of the errors in competently done studies appears to be within tolerable limits. Though a healthy amount of scientific skepticism is desirable, attempts to extend CV to the less-conventional values are warranted.

That more research is desirable on a broad array of topics relating to valuation is obvious. The shortcomings of TC, HP, and CV should not blind us to the solid progress that has been made toward solving the valuation problem or to the additional progress that is in the offing. In a world where market values have tremendous clout in the political arena and where non-economists all too often treat unpriced environmental commodities as if they had either zero or infinite values, the policy relevance of nonmarket valuation is assured. In this research agenda CV deserves a high priority because of its potential adaptability to a very wide range of environmental issues.

Thus, our conclusion regarding the preferredness of related-market approaches vis-à-vis CV might be summarized in a new title for the chapter as a whole. Paraphrasing Willig [1976], we might well have entitled this chapter, "Contingent Valuation Without Apology."

Notes

[1]For a discussion of Lindahl prices, see Lindahl [1958], Roberts [1974], or Boadway and Wildasin [1984].

[2]For work involving specific utility functions and share models, see Bockstael, Hanemann and Strand [1984], ch. 9 and 10; Hanemann [1978]; Morey [1981, 1984]; and Caulkins, Bishop, and Bouwes [1984].

[3]To see this result, solve 3.3 in terms of Z_i, and substitute for Z_i in 3.1 and 3.2. Rearrange 3.1 and 3.2 in terms of Z_i then solve for s in terms of t.

[4]To see this point, marginal implicit price functions for air quality from different regions with different distributions of air quality levels might be estimated and compared. Alternatively, air quality differences might be used as a segmenting factor.

[5]"Hypothetical bias" as used here is a rather vague, catch-all category of problems used for the sake of convenience. The quest for a more rigorous, useful taxonomy of biases continues. For some recent thoughts on the topic, see Mitchell and Carson [1984b].

References

Bishop, R. C., and T. A. Heberlein. 1979. "Measuring values of extramarket goods: Are indirect measures biased?" *American Journal of Agricultural Economics* 61: 926–930.

Bishop, R. C., T. A. Heberlein, and M. J. Kealy. 1983. "Contingent valuation of environmental assets: Comparisons with a simulated market." *Natural Resources Journal* 23:619–633.

Bishop, R. C., T. A. Heberlein, M. P. Welsh, and R. M. Baumgartner, 1984. "Does Contingent Valuation Work? Results of the Sandhill Experiment." Invited paper, joint meetings of the Association of Environmental and Resource Economists, the American Agricultural Economics Association, and the Northeast Agricultural Economics Council. New York: Cornell University, August 5–8.

Boadway, R. W., and D. E. Wildasin. 1984. *Public Sector Economics*. Boston: Little, Brown.

Bockstael, N. E., and K. E. McConnell. 1981. "Theory and estimation of the household production function for wildlife recreation." *Journal of Environmental Economics and Management* 8:199–214.

Bockstael, N. E., and K. E. McConnell. 1983. "Welfare measurement in the household function framework." *American Economic Review* 73:806–814.

Bockstael, N. E., W. M. Hanemann, and I. E. Strand, Jr. 1984. "Measuring the benefits of water quality improvements using recreation demand models. Volume II: Benefit Analysis Using Indirect or Imputed Market Methods." Draft report to the Office of Policy Analysis, Office of Policy and Resource Management, U.S. Environmental Protection Agency, Washington, D. C.

Bohm, P. 1972. "Estimating demand for public goods: An experiment." *European Economic Review* 3:111–130.

Boyle, K. J., and R. C. Bishop. 1984. "A Comparison of Contingent Valuation Techniques." Department of Agricultural Economics Staff Paper no. 222, University of Wisconsin-Madison.

Boyle, K. J., and R. C. Bishop. 1985. "The Total Value of Wildlife Resources: Conceptual and Empirical Issues." Invited paper, Association of Environmental and Resource Economists Workshop on Recreational Demand Modelling, Boulder, Colorado, May 17–18.

Boyle, K. J., R. C. Bishop, and M. P. Welsh. 1985. "Starting point bias in contingent valuation bidding games." *Land Economics*, 61:188–194.

Brookshire, D. S., R. C. d'Arge, W. D. Schulze, and M. A. Thayer. 1981. "Experiments in valuing public goods." *Advances in Applied Micro-Economics*, vol. 1, ed. V. K. Smith. Greenwich, CT: JAI Press, pp. 123–172.

Brookshire, D. S., M. A. Thayer, W. D. Schulze, and R. C. d'Arge. 1982. "Valuing public goods: A comparison of survey and hedonic approaches." *American Economic Review* 72:165–177.

Brown, G. M., Jr., and R. Mendelsohn. 1984. "The hedonic travel cost method." *Review of Economics and Statistics* 66:427–433.

Brown, G. M., Jr., and H. O. Pollakowski. 1977. "Economic valuation of shoreline." *Review of Economics and Statistics* 59:272–278.

Brown, J. N., and H. S. Rosen. 1982. "On the estimation of structural hedonic models." *Econometrica* 50:765–768.

Brown, W. G., and F. Nawas. 1973. "Impact of aggregation on the estimation of outdoor recreation demand functions." *American Journal of Agricultural Economics* 55:246–249.

Brown, W. G., C. Sorhus, B. Chou-Yang, and J. A. Richards. 1983. "Using individual observations to estimate recreation demand functions: A caution." *American Journal of Agricultural Economics* 65:154–157.

Burt, O. R., and D. Brewer. 1971. "Estimation of net social benefits from outdoor recreation." *Econometrica* 39:813–827.

Butler, R. V. 1982. "The specification of hedonic indices for urban housing." *Land Economics* 58:96–108.

Caulkins, P. P., R. C. Bishop, and N. Bouwes, Sr. 1984. "A Comparison of Two Travel Cost Models for Valuing Lake Recreation." Department of Agricultural Economics Staff Paper no. 227, University of Wisconsin-Madison.

Caulkins, P. P., R. C. Bishop, and N. W. Bouwes. 1985. "Omitted cross-price variable biases in the linear travel cost model: Correcting common misperceptions." *Land Economics* 61:182–187.

Cesario, F. J. 1976. "Value of time in recreation benefit studies." *Land Economics* 52:32–41.

Cesario, F. J., and J. L. Knetsch. 1976. "A Recreation Site Demand and Benefit Estimation Model." *Regional Studies* 10:97–104.

Cicchetti, C. J., A. C. Fisher, and V. K. Smith. 1976. "An economic evaluation of a generalized consumer surplus measure: The Mineral King controversy." *Econometrica* 44:1259–1276.

Ciriacy-Wantrup, S. V. 1952. *Resource Conservation: Economics and Policy*. Berkeley and Los Angeles: University of California Press.

Clawson, M. 1959. "Methods of Measuring the Demand for and Value of Outdoor Recreation." Reprint no. 10. Washington, D. C.: Resources for the Future, Inc.

Clawson, M., and J. L. Knetsch. 1963. "Outdoor recreation research: Some concepts and suggested areas of study." *Natural Resources Journal* 3:250–275.

Clawson, M., and J. L. Knetsch. 1966. *Economics of Outdoor Recreation*. Baltimore: John Hopkins University Press.

Coursey. D. L., et al. 1984. *Experimental Methods for Assessing Environmental Benefits*. Report to U.S. Environmental Protection Agency, contract Cr-8110077-01-0, Washington, DC.

Cummings, R. G., D. S. Brookshire, D. L. Coursey, and W. D. Schulze. 1984. *Valuing Environmental Goods: A State of the Arts Assessment of the Contingent Valuation Method*. Washington, DC: Office of Policy Analysis, Office of Policy, Planning and Evaluation, U.S. Environmental Protection Agency.

Davis, R. K. 1963. "Recreation planning as an economic problem." *Natural Resources Journal* 3:239–249.

Davis. R. K. 1964. "The value of bid game hunting in a private forest." *Transactions of the Twenty-Ninth North American Wildlife and Natural Resources Conference.* 29:393–403.

Deaton, A., and J. Muellbauer. 1980. *Economics and Consumer Behavior*. Cambridge, England: Cambridge University Press.

Desvousges, W. H., V. K. Smith, and M. P. McGivney. 1983. *A Comparison of Alternative approaches for Estimating Recreation and Related Benefits of Water Quality Improvement*. Washington, DC: Economic Analysis Division, U.S. Environmental Protection Agency.

Dwyer, J. F., J. R. Kelly, and M. D. Bowes. 1977. "Improved Procedures for Valuation of the Contribution of Recreation to National Economic Development." University of Illinois at Urbana-Champaign, Water Resources Center, UILU-WRC-77-0128.

Edwards, S. F. 1984. "An Analysis of the Non-Market Benefits of Protecting Salt Pond Water Quality in Southern Rhode Island: An Application of the Hedonic Price and Contingent Valuation Techniques." Unpublished Ph.D. dissertation, Department of Agricultural Economics, University of Rhode Island.

Edwards, S. F., and G. D. Anderson. 1984a. "Land-use conflicts in the coastal zone: An approach for the analysis of the opportunity costs of protecting coastal resources." *Journal of the Northeast Agricultural Economic Council* 13:73–81.

Edwards, S. F., and G. D. Anderson. 1984b. "Valuing Non-Marginal Changes in the Water Quality of the Rhode Island Salt Ponds." University of Rhode Island, Department of Resource Economics Staff Paper.

Fisher, A., and R. Raucher. 1984. "Intrinsic benefits of improved water quality: Conceptual and empirical perspectives." *Advances in Applied Micro-Economics*, vol. 3. ed. V. K. Smith and A. D. Witte, Greenwich, CT: JAI Press, pp. 37–66.

Freeman, A. M., III. 1979. *The Benefits of Environmental Improvement: Theory and Practice*. Baltimore: John Hopkins University Press.

Freeman, A. M., III. 1984. "On assessing the state of the arts of the contingent valuation method of valuing environmental changes." In *Valuing Environmental Goods: A State of the Arts Assessment of the Contingent Valuation Method*, R. G. Cummings, D. S. Brookshire, D. L. Coursey, W. D. Schulze. Washington, DC: U.S. Environmental Protection Agency, pp. 180–195.

Goodman, S. A. 1977. "Measuring the value of housing quality." *Journal of Regional Science* 17:107–115.

Griliches, Z. 1961. "Hedonic price indices for automobiles: An econometric analysis of quality change." *Price Statistics of the Federal Government*. Washington, DC: U.S. Government Printing Office.

Gum, R. L., and W. E. Martin. 1975. "Problems and solutions in estimating the demand for and value of rural outdoor recreation." *American Journal of Agricultural Economics* 57:558–566.

Halvorsen, R., and H. O. Pollakowski. 1981. "Choice of functional form for hedonic price equations." *Journal of Urban Economics* 8:37–49.

Hammack, J., and G. M. Brown. 1974. *Waterfowl and Wetlands: Toward Bioeconomic Analysis*. Baltimore: Johns Hopkins University Press.

Hanemann, W. M. 1978. "A Methodological and Empirical Study of the Recreation benefits from Water Quality Improvement." Unpublished Ph.D. dissertation, Department of Economics, Harvard University.

Hanemann, W. M. 1984. "Welfare evaluation in contingent valuation experiments with discrete responses." *American Journal of Agricultural Economics* 66:332–341.

Hof, J. G., and D. A. King. 1982. "On the necessity of simultaneous recreation demand equation estimation." *Land Economics* 58:547–552.

Hof, J. G., and D. A. King. 1983. "On the necessity of simultaneous recreation demand equation estimation: Reply." *Land Economics* 59:459–460.

Hotelling, H. 1947. Letter to the National Park Service, June 18. Reprinted in: *Economic Studies of Outdoor Recreation*, Outdoor Recreation Resources Review Commission, Study Report no. 24, Washington, DC, 1962, p. 56.

Johnson, M. S., and M. J. Lea. 1982. "Differential capitalization and public service characteristics." *Land Economics* 58:189–203.

Just, R. E., D. L. Hueth, and A. Schmitz. 1982. *Applied Welfare Economics and Public Policy*. Englewood Cliffs, NJ: Prentice-Hall.

Kahneman, D. 1984. "Comments on the Review Panel's assessment." *Valuing Environmental Goods: A State of the Arts Assessment of the Contingent Valuation Method*, R. G. Cummings, D. S. Brookshire, D. L. Coursey, W. D. Schulze. Washington, DC: U.S. Environmental Protection Agency. pp. 226–235.

Knetsch, J. L. 1963. "Outdoor recreation demands and benefits." *Land Economics* 39:387–396.

Knetsch, J. L., and R. K. Davis. 1966. "Comparison of methods for recreation valuation." In *Water Research*. Ed. A. V. Kneese and S. C. Smith. Baltimore: Johns Hopkins University Press.

Krutilla, J. V. 1967. "Conservation reconsidered." *American Economic Review* 57:777–786.

Li, M. M., and H. J. Brown. 1980. "Micro-neighborhood externalities and hedonic housing prices." *Land Economics* 56:125–141.

Lindahl, E. 1958. "Just taxation: A positive solution." In *Classics in the Theory of Public Finance*. Ed. R. A. Musgrave and A. T. Peacock, London: Macmillan pp. 168–177.

Linneman, P. 1980. "Some empirical results on the nature of the hedonic price function for the urban housing market." *Journal of Urban Economics* 8:47–68.

Mäler, K. G. 1974. *Environmental Economics: A Theoretical Inquiry*. Baltimore: Johns Hopkins University Press, 1974.

Marwell, G., and R. E. Ames. 1979. "Experiments on the provision of public goods. I. Resources, interest group size, and the free-rider problem." *American Journal of Sociology* 84:1335–1360.

Marwell, G., and R. E. Ames. 1980. "Experiments on the provision of public goods. II. Provision points, stakes, experience, and the free-rider problem." *American Journal of Sociology* 85:926–937.

Marwell, G., and R. E. Ames. 1981. "Economists free ride, does anyone else? Experiments on the provision of public goods. IV." *Journal of Public Economics* 15:295–310.

McConnell, K. E. 1983. "Existence and bequest value." In *Managing Air Quality and Scenic Resources at National Parks and Wilderness Areas*. Ed. R. D. Rowe and L. G. Chestnut. Boulder, CO: Westview Press, pp. 254–264.

Mendelsohn, R. 1985. "Modelling the demand for outdoor recreation." Invited paper, Association of Environmental and Resource Economists Workshop on Recreational Demand Modelling, Boulder, Colorado, May 17–18.

Miller, J. R., and M. J. Hay. (1984) "Estimating substate values of fishing and hunting." *Proceedings of the 49th North American Wildlife and Natural Resources Conference*.

Milon, J. W., J. Gressel, and D. Mulkey. 1984 "Hedonic amenity valuation and functional form specification." *Land Economics* 60:378–387.

Mitchell, R. C., and R. T. Carson. 1981. *An Experiment in Determining Willingness to Pay for National Water Quality Improvements.* Report prepared for U.S. Environmental Protection Agency, Washington, DC.

Mitchell, R. C., and R. T. Carson. 1984a. "Some comments on the state of the arts assessment of the contingent valuation method draft report." In *Valuing Environmental Goods: A State of the Arts Assessment of the Contingent Valuation Method*, R. G. Cummings, D. S. Brookshire, D. L. Coursey, W. D. Schulze, Washington, DC: U.S. Environmental Protection Agency, pp. 284–296.

Mitchell, R. C., and R. T. Carson. 1948b. "Willingness to Pay for National Freshwater Quality Improvements." Draft report to U.S. Environmental Protection Agency, Contract CR-810224-01-4. Washington, DC: Resources for the Future.

Morey, E. R. 1981. "The demand for site-specific recreational activities: A characteristics approach." *Journal of Environmental Economics and Management* 8:345–371.

Morey, E. R. 1984. "The choice of ski areas: Estimation of a generalized CES preference ordering with characteristics." *Review of Economics and Statistics* 66:584–590.

Oates, W. E. 1969. "The effects of property taxes and local public spending on property values: An empirical study of tax capitalization and the Tiebout hypothesis." *Journal of Political Economy* 77:957–971.

Parsons, G. R. 1984. "Estimating Demand Functions for Attributes of a Differentiated Product." Unpublished Ph.D. Dissertation, University of Wisconsin-Madison.

Quigley, J. M. 1982. "Nonlinear budget constraints and consumer demand: An application to public programs for residential housing." *Journal of Urban Economics* 12:177–201.

Rae, D. A. 1981a. *Visibility Impairment at Mesa Verde National Park: An Analysis of Benefits and Costs of Controlling Emissions in the Four Corners Area.* Report prepared for the Electric Power Research Institute. Boston, MA: Charles River Associates.

Rae, D. A. 1981b. *Benefits of Improving Visibility at Great Smoky National Park.* Report prepared for the Electric Power Research Institute. Boston, MA: Charles River Associates.

Randall, A., and J. R. Stoll. 1983. "Existence value in a total valuation framework." In *Managing Air Quality and Science Resource at National Parks and Wilderness Areas*. Ed. R. D. Rowe and L. G. Chestnut, Boulder, CO: Westview Press, pp. 265–274.

Randall, A., B. Ives, and C. Eastman. 1974. "Bidding games for valuation of aesthetic environmental improvements." *Journal of Environmental Economics and Management* 1:132–149.

Ridker, R. G. 1967. *Economic Costs of Air Pollution: Studies in Measurement.* New York: Praeger.

Ridker, R. G., and J. A. Henning. 1967. "The determinants of residential property values with special reference to air pollution." *Review of Economics and Statistics* 49:246–257.

Roberts, D. J. 1974. "The Lindahl solution for economies with public goods."

Journal of Public Economics 3:23–42.

Rosen, S. 1974. "Hedonic prices and implicit markets: Product differentiation in pure competition." *Journal of Political Economy* 82:34–55.

Samples, K. C., and R. C. Bishop. (1985) "Estimating the value of variations in anglers' success rates: An application of the multiple-site travel cost method." *Journal of Marine Resource Economics*. 2:55–74.

Scherr, B. A., and E. M. Babb. 1975. "Pricing public goods: An experiment with two proposed pricing systems." *Public Choice* 23:35–48.

Schulze, W. D., R. C. d'Arge, and D. S. Brookshire. 1981. "Valuing environmental commodities: Some recent experiments." *Land Economics* 57:151–173.

Scott, A. 1965. "The valuation of game resources: Some theoretical aspects." *Canadian Fisheries Reports* no. 4, Ottawa.

Sellar, C., J. R. Stoll, and J. P. Chavas. 1985. "Validation of empirical measures of welfare change: A comparison of nonmarket techniques." *Land Economics* 61:156–175.

Shabman, L. A., and M. A. Bertelson. 1979. "The use of development value estimates for coastal wetland permit decisions." *Land Economics* 55:213–222.

Smith, V. K., and C. C. S. Gilbert. (1985) "The valuation of environmental risks using hedonic wage models." In *Horizontal Equity, Uncertainty and Economic Well Being*. Ed. M. David and T. Smeeding, National Bureau of Economic Research. Chicago: University of Chicago Press.

Smith, V. K., W. H. Desvousges, and M. P. McGivney. 1983. "The opportunity cost of travel time in recreation demand models." *Land Economics* 58:259–278.

Smith, V. L. 1977. "The principle of unanimity and voluntary consent in social choice." *Journal of Political Economy* 85:1125–1139.

Sutherland, R. J. 1982. "A Regional Approach to Estimating Recreation Benefits of Improved Water Quality." *Journal of Environmental Economics and Management* 9:229–247.

Talhelm, D. R. 1973. "Defining and evaluating recreational quality." *Transactions of the 38th North American Wildlife and Natural Resources Conference* 38:183–191.

Talhelm, D. R. 1981. "Defining angling supply, the key to recreational fishing evaluation." *Allocation of Fishery Resources*. Ed. J. Grover. New York: UNFAO, pp. 443–451.

Thayer, M. A. 1981. "Contingent valuation techniques for assessing environmental impacts: Further evidence." *Journal of Environmental Economics and Management* 8:27–44.

Trice, A. H., and S. E. Wood. 1958. "Measurement of recreation benefits." *Land Economics* 34:195–207.

Vaughan, W. J., and C. S. Russell. 1982. "Valuing a fishing day: An application of a systematic varying parameter model." *Land Economics* 58:450–463.

Ward, F. A. 1983. "On the necessity of simultaneous recreation demand equation estimation: Comment." *Land Economics* 59:455–458.

Willig, R. D. 1976. "Consumer's surplus without apology." *American Economic Review* 66:587–597.

Willis, C. E., and J. H. Foster. 1982. "The hedonic approach: No panacea for valuing water quality changes." Journal of the Northeastern Agricultural Economics Council 12:53–57.

COMMENT 1

A. MYRICK FREEMAN III

In his letter inviting my contribution to this volume, the editor asked for commentaries that would "highlight the differences that exist among economists" on the topic under discussion. This may prove to be a rather difficult assignment. Anderson and Bishop (hereafter referred to as A & B) and I accept the basic premises of neoclassical welfare economics as the basis for deriving valuation measures. The neoclassical framework is well developed and it provides a basis for deriving conceptually valid models for estimation and measurement. A & B have provided a very competent discussion of three models and measurement techniques, all based on the neoclassical framework. Rather than attempt to find points of difference or disagreement with what they have written, a major portion of my commentary will be an effort to identify some important aspects of the value problem that A & B did not discuss.

My commentary will consist of three sections. In the next section I identify some additional issues and problems that might have been addressed in a discussion of the natural resource evaluation problem. The third section consists of some specific comments concerning the three techniques that A & B discussed. In the final section I comment on their comparative assessment and their conclusions concerning the contingent valuation method.

Additional Topics and Issues

Other valuation models

A & B have chosen to discuss in some detail the travel cost, hedonic price, and contingent valuation models. They say that "the majority of environmental valuation studies employ one or more of these three techniques." I think that the proportion of studies based on these models may be as high as two-thirds or three-fourths. However there are other categories of benefits and other useful and conceptually valid models and techniques for estimating values.

One important category of natural resource values is what I choose to call production or market values. Production or market values arise in those cases where some attribute of the environment is an argument in the production and cost functions for a marketed good. A beneficial environmental change is reflected in an increase in economic productivity and a reduction in the cost of producing the marketed good. This in turn results in changes in marketed quantities, product prices, factor prices, rents, and/or profits. Some interesting economic models have been used to derive measures of benefits from these market changes.

The duality or cost function model is one example. The technique requires the estimation of cost or supply functions for affected firms with the level of the environmental resource as one argument. The demand function for the market output must also be estimated if price effects are significant. With these functions known, it is a straighforward matter to calculate changes in producers' and consumers' surpluses for postulated changes in the environmental resource. Examples of this approach include Mathtech [1982].

There are several advantages to the cost function approach. First it is not necessary to determine damage functions for specific materials. Second, it is not necessary to estimate the stock of each material exposed to pollution. And finally, it is not necessary to determine specific producers' responses to air pollution—such as material substitution and preventive actions. All of these relationships are embodied implicitly in the estimated cost functions. On the other hand this approach is subject to all of the econometric problems associated with the specification and estimation of cost and supply functions. And relatively weak but not insignificant pollution effects may be difficult to sort out from the statistical noise in equations that involve a substantial degree of aggregation.

An alternative approach to estimating market benefits to both consumers and producers involves explicitly modeling the optimization problem of producers. In principle this approach is capable of taking account of producers' opportunities for changing the mix of outputs and changing input combinations in response to changes in pollution levels. These producer adjustments are captured implicitly in the cost function model, but they can be made explicit and perhaps can be represented more accurately in micro or firm level optimization models. For examples of this approach see Adams, Thanavibulchai, and Crocker [1979] and Adams, Hamilton, and McCarl [1984].

Another category of models and techniques for estimating the values of environmental change to individuals involves variations on the household production framework first applied to the problem of valuing public goods by Hori [1975]. The household production framework is based on the assumption that there is a set of technical relationships among goods used by households in the implicit production of utility yielding final services. Changes in various measures of environmental quality can affect individuals through a variety of channels. This is equivalent to saying that there are a variety of alternative specifications of individual utility functions and household production functions that can be used to estimate the values of particular types of environmental change.

The simplest form of technical relationship involves the assumption that an individual can defend himself or herself against the adverse effects of pollution by increasing purchases of some other good (e.g., paint, air conditioning equipment), or by increasing spending on some other activity. The increased spending is a direct cost or a defensive expenditure. Direct costs or defensive expenditures have been the basis of several estimates of the benefits to households in the form of reduced materials damages and soiling due to air pollution. [Benedict et al. 1973; Booz, Allen, and Hamilton 1970; Gillette 1975; Liu and Yu 1976; Michelson and Tourin 1966]. However, more formal analysis of the individual utility maximization problem has shown that whether changes in defensive spending are good approximations of individual values or seriously over-or underestimate values, depends on the specific properties of the utility function, and the production relationships between the environmental resource and goods purchased through markets. (See for example Courant and Porter [1981] and Harrington and Portney [1983]).

There has been at least one attempt to implement a variation of Hori's model based on household production theory. In a recent study for the U.S. Environmental Protection Agency, Mathtech [1982] used household expenditure data to estimate a system of demand functions for market goods and the underlying demands for final services flows. This study provides evidence of both the strengths and the limitations of the household production approach. On the plus side this approach provides an opportunity within the context of the model to capture the rich variety of possible substitutions between marketed goods and attributes of the environment, and among various types of final service flows. In this regard, the model is conceptually superior to the defensive expenditure or direct cost techniques. However this model makes severe demands for data, and it requires sophisticated econometric techniques.

Uncertainty

The presence of uncertainty can affect the values individuals place on environmental resources in a variety of ways. For example, individual users of a contaminated ground water aquifer may face a higher probability of cancer. Individuals may be uncertain as to whether a particular unique and irreplacable environmental resource will be available for their use on some future date. And individuals may also be uncertain as to whether they will actually want to use that resource in the future. In such cases the analytical problem is to incorporate uncertainty explicitly into the measurement of values.

Much of the literature on the effect of uncertainty on the valuation of environmental resources has focused on the concept of option value. The nature of option value might best be illustrated with the following example. Consider a national park containing unique scenic and ecological resources. Suppose that at the beginning of each year all individuals are uncertain ex ante as to whether they will wish to visit the park during that year. But during the course of the year, some people will in fact visit the park. An indirect technique, such as TC can be used to estimate the maximum willingness-to-pay of those who actually visit the park. These consumer surpluses represent an ex post measure of the value of the park to users. This value can also be interpreted as the expected value of the consumer surpluses of the population as a whole. Alternatively, we could ask each individual at the beginning of the year for his maximum willingness-to-pay to preserve the right to visit the park during the year. This ex ante payment is option price. The early literature on option value was concerned with the question of whether the aggregate option price would be greater than the aggregate expected consumer surplus. If option price was greater, the excess was termed option value.

More recent theoretical analysis has identified three sets of issues which collectively make the role of option value in environmental valuation much more complicated than the preceding example suggests. First, it has been shown that in the context of the preceding example, option price can be either greater or less than the expected consumer surplus depending on the nature and source of uncertainty concerning demand [Schmalensee 1972; Bishop 1982; Smith 1983]. Furthermore the difference between option price and expected surplus (whether positive or negative) might be trivially small or quite large, also depending on the circumstances [Freeman 1985]. This raises the question of whether something that can be either positive or negative should be termed a "value."

The second question involves the nature of uncertainty of supply or availability of the environmental resource to potential users. The early option-value models assumed that if the individual paid the option price, the resource would be available with certainty; and if the individual did not pay his option price, he would be excluded from the resource. But other conditions of supply uncertainty are possible. For example there may be a nonzero probability of availability in the absence of payment of option price by the individual. And policies may only reduce the uncertainty of supply, not eliminate it. It has been shown that even in the case of certainty of demand on the part of the individual, the relationship between option price and the expected surplus of the project is ambiguous, that is, such "supply side option values" can be either positive or negative [Freeman 1985].

The third issue has only recently begun to receive much attention in the literature on natural resource and environmental valuation. It has implication for the analysis of all forms of uncertainty, not just the demand uncertainty of the option value literature. The issue concerns whether it is more appropriate to use ex ante or ex post welfare measures for policy making. This issue was first identified by Smith and Desvousges [1983] and further analyzed by Smith, Desvousges, and Freeman [1985]. The context for these analyses was the valuation of reducing the risk of death through the prevention of contamination of an environmental resource such as a ground water aquifer.

The expected value of consumer surplus is an ex post welfare measure in that it focuses on the realized outcomes of policy choices. Expected utility is the basis for ex ante welfare measurement. Option price is an ex ante measure since it is defined as that state independent payment that makes the expected utility with the project just equal to the expected utility without the project. But as Graham [1981, 1984] (see also Mendelsohn and Strang [1984]) has shown, there is an infinite number of state dependent payment schemes that can provide the basis of ex ante welfare measurement. The choice of which one to use depends upon the nature of the uncertainty and the mechanisms open to individuals for diversifying risk, for example, contingent claims markets.

Space limitations will not permit an extensive discussion of these issues here. My purpose is simply to call attention to this set of problems and to suggest that in some cases—for example, policies to regulate the handling and disposal of hazardous and radioactive materials in the environment—uncertainty is perhaps the central issue that must be addressed in developing measures of value.

Problems with the neoclassical framework

A & B accept without discussion the premise that economic value is to be measured by compensating income changes to individuals. They recognize the possibility of existence values, that is, willingness to pay unrelated to present uses. But there are some issues and problems in applying the neoclassical framework to the valuation of living environmental resources not directly used by people. Some of these problems involve lack of information on ecological relationships and future patterns of needs and resource uses. But some involve more fundamental challenges to the neoclassical premise itself.

Existence values for living species means a willingness to pay to prevent the extinction of or to preserve a regional population of some species of symbolic or aesthetic significance. The most frequently mentioned examples of such species are the blue whale, the bald eagle, and the grizzly bear. But what about other species which lack the symbolic or aesthetic significance and may even be nuisances in some cases. If there is a policy relevant value to the preservation of such species, we have to look elsewhere rather than in individuals' expressed willingness to pay. There are several possible avenues for such a search.

One possibility is to look for an ecological link between the threatened species and a species that is valued by individuals. For example the extinction of the black fly might lead to a substantial decline in the population of landlocked salmon and trout in some streams, thereby diminishing recreational values. The value of the threatened species can be estimated through a kind of marginal productivity analysis of its contribution to some use value. For an example of an effort to value wet lands on the basis of their marginal contribution to a commercial fishery (see Lynn et al. [1981]).

Another avenue is to realize that the extinction of any species means the irreversible loss of specific genetic information. The value of that information could in principle be estimated by examining possible future uses of that information [Brown and Goldstein 1984; Fisher and Hanemann 1986].

This approach requires information on future technologies and patterns of demand and resource use. This approach will probably find only limited application to specific cases where information on technologies and demands is available.

The neoclassical framework does not recognize a concern for the existence of a species out of ethical considerations. Ethical philosophers are not in agreement as to the validity and proper form of such concern [Norton 1982; Rescher 1980; Sagoff 1980]. But if people do hold such ethical beliefs or values, they are policy relevant. And the challenge to neoclassical value theory is to find a way to incorporate these beliefs into measures of economic value.

The search for an acceptable basis for valuing ecological resources is taking on a practical significance not only as a basis for policy making (benefit-cost analysis), but also because of the changing legal environment. Now those responsible for causing oil spills and discharges of hazardous materials to the environment are liable under the law for the damages caused to natural resources. Although economists and ecologists may not be ready to provide the methods and data necessary to determine the magnitude of those damages in particular cases, the courts will be assigning liability and settling claims involving hundreds of millions of dollars in the next few years.

Commentary on A & B

In this section I offer some brief comments on A & B's discussion of the travel-cost, hedonic-price, and contingent-valuation models.

The travel-cost method

A & B mention the problem of using multiple-site individual models when some individuals choose not to visit all of the sites. When this is the case, estimation of a system of visitation equations by ordinary least squares would be inappropriate because of the large number of zero values for the dependent variable. In these circumstances, the logit model can be used to analyze individual site visitation data. The logit model can be interpreted as estimating the probability that an individual will visit a given site as a function of characteristics of the individual and the available sites. A derivation of the logit model and an application to recreation site visit data for the Boston region is presented in Feenberg and Mills [1980].

The logit model provides a straightforward basis for calculating the benefit per visit of an improvement in quality (Q) at a site, at least if a measure of price or travel cost is included in the logit equation. Other things equal, an increase in Q leads to an increase in the probability of visiting the site and a higher level of utility for the individual. Total differentiation of the logit equation makes it possible to calculate the increase in price or travel cost per visit which would leave the probability of visiting unchanged after an increase in Q. This compensating increase in price is the benefit per visit of the higher Q.

The hedonic price method

A & B raised some questions about using HP to estimate the benefits of nonmarginal changes in environmental quality. I have two comments. First, even if the identification problem has not been solved so that inverse demand functions are not known, it is possible to extract some useful information from the data on marginal implicit prices. Each marginal implicit price provides one point on the individual's inverse demand function. It would then be possible to make some assumption about the shape of the inverse demand function through that point in order to derive an ersatz demand function for the purposes of approximating benefit measures. For some discussion of possible assumptions see Freeman [1979, 144–147].

My second comment concerns A & B's suggestion that the hedonic-price function itself would shift rendering inaccurate benefit estimates derived from the original hedonic-price function. I am not convinced that there is a problem here. Assume that the inverse demand functions are known for all individuals. Also assume that individuals rent houses from absentee owners. The relevant area under the individual's inverse demand function measures the value to that individual of an increase in Q, assuming the individual's income and prices do not change. With no changes in housing rental rates, the benefits accrue entirely to occupiers. If housing prices do change, the first order effect is to alter the distribution of benefits between occupiers and owners. There is also a possible second-order effect as changing attribute prices shift the individual's inverse demand function. But without further analysis of the likely direction and magnitude of such shifts, it is not clear that there is any systematic or empirically significant bias involved in failure to take these shifts into account in estimating benefits.

Contingent valuation

I would like to sketch out a line of reasoning that might put the problem of hypothetical bias in a somewhat different light. When we assume an individual has a preference ordering with the usual properties, we are in effect assuming that there is a true value, B^*, of the individual's maximum willingness-to-pay for a specified environmental change. Assume we use some format to ask the individual to reveal B_i, an observed bid, where the subscript i refers to the ith time the instrument is administered to the individual. The individual's response can be modeled as: $B_i = B^* + e_i$, where e_i is the error term. If there are no sources of bias in the instrument, then the mean of the distribution of e_i is zero and the expected value of B_i is equal to B^*. If the hypothetical nature of the survey instrument is one reason to predict systematic errors (that is, a mean value for e_i that is different from zero), then it would be correct to refer to this as a problem of hypothetical bias. I have not yet seen a persuasive line of reasoning leading to a prediction of systematic error due to hypothetical questions. Unless such an argument could be made, we should not be talking about hypothetical *bias*. Furthermore, if survey instruments could be designed to eliminate the other sources of bias (for example, starting-point bias) or if the magnitude of such biases could be estimated, then the hypothetical nature of the instrument leads only to greater variance around the "true" value. Then, if individuals have similar preferences except for the influences of socioeconomic variables which can be controlled for (a standard assumption in empirical economics), then the standard error of the estimate of a group's mean bid can be reduced by increasing sample size. If this line of reasoning has any validity, it may be that while the hypothetical nature of the question may be a serious problem at the individual level, the problem might be reduced to manageable portions through aggregation and the law of large numbers.

Commentary on the Assessment

First I think A & B are correct to caution against the automatic preference for related-market or indirect methods for estimating values. Many of these models or techniques do have problems of model specification, estimation, limited data, etc. Nor should one automatically prefer CV for its theoretical simplicity, ease of application, or whatever. The choice of a method must be made on a case by case basis after examining the nature of the problem and the strengths and limitations of the available techniques.

Second, I think economists practicing in the field of resource valuation must undertake a systematic discussion of the criteria and appropriate framework for making choices about techniques. Some of the issues involved were discussed in the Palo Alto Conference on the State of the Art Assessment of the Contingent Value Method [Cummings, Brookshire, and Schulze 1986]. I would suggest that this discussion focus on the bias and accuracy properties of the various techniques and the costs of implementing them. Ultimately choices among alternative techniques can be made on the basis of comparisons of the costs and benefits of the various techniques. The value of information framework provides a basis for considering the comparative benefits of different techniques in providing information in specific decision-making contexts.

References

Adams, Richard M., Scott A. Hamilton, and Bruce A. McCarl. 1984. "The Economic Effects of Ozone in Agriculture." (Unpublished).

Adams, Richard M., Narongsakdi Thanavibulchai, and Thomas D. Crocker. 1979. *Methods Development for Assessing Air Pollution Damages for Selected Crops Within Southern California*. Washington, DC: U.S. Environmental Protection Agency.

Benedict, H. M., C. J. Miller, and J. S. Smith. 1973. *Assessment of Economic Impact of Air Pollutions on Vegetation in the United States: 1969 and 1971*. Palo Alto: Stanford Research Institute.

Bishop, Richard C. 1982. "Option value: An exposition and extension." *Land Economics* 58:1–15.

Booz, Allen, and Hamilton, Inc. 1970. *Study to Determine Residential Society Costs of Particulate Air Pollution*. Research Triangle Park, North Carolina; National Air Pollution Control Administration.

Brown, G., Jr, and J. H. Goldstein. 1984. "A Model for valuing endangered species." *Journal of Environmental Economics and Management* 11(no. 4):303–309.

Courant, Paul N., and Richard Porter. 1981. "Averting expenditure and the cost of pollution." *Journal of Environmental Economics and Management* 8:321–329.

Cummings, R., D. S. Brookshire, and W. D. Schulze. 1986. *Valuing Environmental Improvements: A State of the Art Assessment of the Contingent Valuation Method*. Rowman and Allenhelo, Totowa, N. J.

Feenberg, Daniel, and Edwin S. Mills. 1980. *Measuring the Benefits of Water Pollution Abatement*. New York: Academic Press.

Fisher, A. C., and W. M. Hanemann. 1986. "Option value and the extinction of species." In *Advances in Applied Mirco-economics*, vol. 4. Ed. V. K. Smith. Greenwich, CT: JAI Press.

Freeman, A. Myrick III. 1979. *The Benefits of Environmental Improvement: Theory and Practice*. Baltimore: John Hopkins University Press.

Freeman, A. Myrick, III. 1984. "The sign and size of option value." *Land Economics* 60:1–13.

Freeman, A. Myrick, III. 1985. "Supply uncertainty, option price, and option value." *Land Economics* 61:176–181.

Gillette, D. G. 1975. "Sulfur dioxide and material damage," *Journal of the Air Pollution Control Association* 25:1238–1243.

Graham, Daniel A., 1981. "Cost-benefit analysis under uncertainty." *American Economic Review* 71:715–725.

Graham, D. A., 1984. "Cost-benefit analysis under uncertainty: Reply." *American Economic Review* 74(no. 5):1100–1102.

Harrington, W., and P. R. Portney. 1983. "Valuing the benefits of improved human health." In *Ambient Ozone and Human Health: An Epidemiological Analysis* P. R. Portney and J. Mullahy. Washington, DC: Resources for the Future, Inc.

Hori, H., 1975. "Revealed preference for public goods." *American Economic Review* 65:978–991.

Liu, B-C, and E. S. Yu. 1976. *Physical and Economic Damage Functions for Air Pollutant by Receptors.* Corvallis: Environmental Protection Agency.

Lynn, G. D., P. Conway, and F. J. Prochaska. 1981. "Economic valuation of marsh areas for marine production processes." *Journal of Environmental Economics and Management* 8(no. 2):175–186.

Mathtech, Inc. 1982. *Benefits Analysis of Alternative Secondary National Ambient Air Quality Standards for Sulfur Dioxide and Total Suspended Particulates.* Princeton, NJ: Mathtech.

Mendelsohn, R., and W. J. Strang. 1984. "Cost-benefit analysis under uncertainty: Comment." *American Economic Review* 74(no. 5):1096–1099.

Michelson, I., and B. Tourin. 1966. "Comparative method for studying costs of air pollution." *Public Health Reports*, 81:505–511.

Norton, B. G. 1982. "Environmental ethics and nonhuman rights." *Environmental Ethics* 4:17–36.

Rescher, N. 1980. *Unpopular Essays on Technical Progress* Pittsburgh: University of Pittsburg Press.

Sagoff, M. 1980. "On the preservation of species." *Columbia Journal of Environmental Law* 7:33–67.

Schmalensee, Richard. 1972. "Option demand and consumer surplus: Valuing price changes under uncertainty." *American Economic Review* 62:813–824.

Smith, V. K. 1983. "Option value: A conceptual overview." *Southern Economic Journal* 49:654–668.

Smith, V. K., and W. Desvousges. 1983. "The Valuation of Risk Reductions Associated with Hazardous Waste Regulations." Presented at the annual meetings of the Southern Economic Association, Washington, DC, November.

Smith, V. K., W. H. Desvousges, and A. M. Freeman, III. 1985. *Valuing Changes in Hazardous Waste Risks: A Contingent Valuation Analysis, Draft Interim Report.* Paper presented to U.S. Environmental Protection Agency.

COMMENT 2

KENNETH E. MCCONNELL

This excellent survey of methods of valuing environmental amenities begins with the idea that the market fails to provide efficient levels of these amenities. Valuing amenities is one component of benefit-cost analysis, part of the public response to market failure. The task of valuing environmental amenities is thus part of the process by which the levels of environmental amenities are determined.

The chapter by Anderson and Bishop (hereafter A & B) deals with the techniques, rather than their role in policy. But in assessing these techniques, it is worthwhile to consider how they are used. To determine how well the various techniques are working, we must have an idea of how good the evidence must be. When benefit-cost analysis is utilized in an administrative context, then the valuation of amenities will be lightly scrutinized. However, when the valuation of amenities is part of a legal or political dispute, then not only must the evidence be robust, but the story that is told about behavior must make sense. In either case valuation of amenities must be communicated to a variety of different interest groups, each of course with its own economist. But the point of this discussion is that methods of valuation must be convincing in an arena other than a strictly scientific one.

Several methodological issues mitigate against the standard scientific approaches of looking for anomalies and comparing predictive abilities in evaluating the tools for valuing amenities. First, the valuation process itself presupposes rational behavior by economic agents, and this in turn imposes some strong requirements on how we organize our evidence with econometric models. Simply looking for models that fit well will not do. Second, the whole process of developing valuation approaches exists because these measures are not directly observed. Hence, the standard test of predictive ability, as applied to measures of value, does not work because we can usually measure only estimates, not actual values of amenities.

Thus the development of techniques for measuring the value of amenities differs in two ways from the stereotypical (but probably nonexistent) scientific process. First, the techniques have a bearing on the outcome of decision processes and must be understood by nonspecialists. Second, goodness-of-fit criteria cannot be used to discriminate among competing approaches.

How, then, do we tell whether we are developing *good* methods of valuing amenities? There are several criteria used in practice for judging the acceptability of methods. Does the model tell a good story? A good story means that the model describes behavior that conforms with utility maximization and is consistent with the particular aspect of the problem. Are the econometric results concerning behavior consistent with utility maximization and econometrically robust? That is, the model must not only tell a good story, the data must support the story. Do the valuation results accord with intuition? Although we do not observe measures of the value of environmental amenities, as a profession we are forming some expectations about the range of variation of the value of amenities. The question of *how* we form our expectation about the value of amenities is an interesting one, because we do not observe transactions that explicitly value such amenities.

The Logic and the Evolution of the Travel-Cost Method

The basic model

The travel-cost method utilizes cross-sectional observations on the cost of access to a recreational site and the frequency of visit to a site in order to estimate the demand for access to the site. The travel-cost model was initially conceived as a tool for valuing the access to sites. A & B chronicle the development of this method to its current state, where it is being used in a variety of different forms to value access to sites as well as the environmental attributes of sites. Current versions of the travel-cost model bear little resemblance to the original model. A & B posit the original model as

$$V_i/N_i = f(TC_i)$$

where V_i = visits, N_i = population, TC_i is travel cost from zone i, and $f(\cdot)$ is the per capita demand function to be estimated. While there is a wide variety of computing models, the simplest statement of the conditions that lead to the estimation of demand parameters comes from the maximization of a utility function $U(x_1 \ldots x_n)$ where x_i is the number of trips to site i, subject to a budget constraint

$$\sum_{j=1}^{n} p_j x_j = y$$

Where some of the x_i are not chosen (sites are not visited) the individual's equilibrium conditions can be written

$$\begin{array}{lll} x_i > 0 \Rightarrow U_i - \lambda p_i = 0 & i = 1, \ldots, n_i & \text{(visited sites)} \\ U_i - \lambda p_i < 0 \Rightarrow x_i = 0 & i = n_i + 1, \ldots, n & \text{(sites not visited)} \\ \sum p_j x_j - y = 0 & & \end{array}$$

Now if the utility function contains a stochastic term that is essentially econometrician's error, and is written $U = V(x) \sum \varepsilon_i X_i$ where ε_i is random, then we can rewrite these conditions as

$$\begin{array}{ll} U_i - \lambda p_i = \varepsilon_i & i = 1, \ldots, n_i \\ U_i - \lambda p_i - \varepsilon_i < 0 & i = n_i + i, \ldots, n \end{array}$$

Under appropriate conditions the parameters of $U(x)$ can be estimated via maximum-likelihood methods. In addition we can recover conditional demand functions which can be linked together to allow prediction or welfare measurement.

The gap between this model and the traditional travel-cost model as conceived by Hotelling is enormous. Yet each need is motivated by the same insight—that the consumer must transport himself to the site in order to enjoy its services. Further, each model has the same goal—the calculation of the benefits of site access or site amenities. The basic differences between the models relate to aggregation over households, the availability of imperfect substitution, and the zero consumption levels of some sites. Concerning aggregation, A & B have contrasted the individual vs. zonal approach to the travel-cost model. The original statement was of course in terms of per capita behavior by zones. But most current applications tend to use individual observations. Brown et al. show that in choosing between individual and zonal observations, one makes certain statistical trade offs. However,

McConnell and Bockstael [1984] show that even beginning with a simple model of behavior by individuals, aggregating across individuals is not a simple matter. Hence there is some reason to doubt whether zonal models estimated on aggregate data can reasonably be thought to represent individual preferences. The second development concerns substitute sites. A & B have charted the progression of treatment of imperfect substitutes. It is an issue that cannot be ignored in the spatial context of the travel-cost model, and it is treated with increasing attention to the details, extending from Burt and Brewer in 1971 to Bockstael, Hanemann, and Strand [1984]. A final apparent difference between the original travel-cost model and the formal statement of equilibrium condition is the corner problem. In many settings, consumers visit more than one but not all sites. For example, an ongoing study of recreational demand for 23 beaches on the Chesapeake Bay in Maryland reveals that many participants visit only two or three beaches. Thus estimation of demand parameters and calculation of benefits must account for the fact that most users visit only a few sites.

Even a casual reading of the volume by Bockstael, Hanemann, and Strand shows that solution to the problem of corner solutions is not simple, and much remains to be done, as A & B suggest. It is interesting to ask why the changes in the travel cost model have occurred. Without surveying the literature, one can safely rule out inadequate predictive ability as a source of change in the travel-cost model. Further, the basic range of results, in terms of estimates of consumer's surplus per day, has not changed much over the development of the method. Probably the biggest source of the development of the travel-cost model is the attempt to tell a good story, and to make sure that the story conforms with data typically available. Consider the problem of substitutes. A & B demonstrate the effect of omitting substitutes econometrically. And there is some evidence that substitutes make a difference in numerical results. But the primary driving force for the inclusion of substitutes is the economist's urge to have a good story in the form of a model.

The treatment of time

A & B discuss the problem of time in estimating the demand for recreation. Their discussion is limited to the problem encountered where visitors from different distances have different travel times. Implicity or explicitly the travel time has a cost, and much statistical effort has gone into the measurement of this cost of travel.

The problem of time in the travel-cost model goes much deeper than the travel time. To begin with, recreational decision making in essence involves the allocation of time. The decisions to go on a two-day hunting trip, to visit a beach for an afternoon, or to go on a weekend's canoeing trip are all decisions about the use of time. Early versions of the travel-cost method implicitly assumed that all users were taking trips of the same length, and further, that the opportunity cost of recreational time was equal for all participants in all zones. Even under these conditions, as A & B have discussed, the problem of travel time remains.

When we relax the assumptions about all trips being of the same length and all opportunity cost being equal, we encounter two sorts of problems. First there is the question of how much time should be valued. That is, should just the travel time be valued, or should it be the total time spent on the trip, travel plus time on site? Second is the issue of how to value time. A & B discuss the conversion of travel time into monetary units by using some fraction of the wage rate. Recent research has investigated the valuation of travel time under circumstances where the individual cannot work extra hours. Clearly in those circumstances time still has an opportunity cost, but as Bockstael, Hanemann, and Strand show, it is then appropriate to use the quantity of time (length of trip in terms of hours, minutes, or other appropriate units). Thus, as is obvious from casual observations, circumstances determine the opportunity cost of one's time, and there is room for substantial variation in opportunity cost of time for a group of recreational users.

Professional opinion about the first question—how much time to value—is slowly recognizing the importance of onsite time. A simple example can illustrate its importance. Suppose two people, a student and a cab driver, visit a beach for an afternoon, say four hours. The student has opportunities that would permit earning $4/hour, while the cabdriver could have earned $10/hour. Then the opportunity cost of the trip, exclusive of travel, will be $12 for the student and $40 for the cab driver. Ignoring these costs may bias the estimated effect of costs on trips.

A natural inclination when discussing people with different opportunity costs of time is to suggest that they spend different lengths of time visiting a site. For example, the student might stay five hours and the cabbie only two. This relaxation of assumptions may cause more trouble than it is worth because it forces the economist to analyze two joint decisions—the number of trips per year and the length of each trip. Such jointness causes serious conceptual and econometric problems by making the budget constraint nonlinear.

Prospects for the travel cost model

The development of the travel-cost model since it was first suggested by Hotelling almost forty years ago illustrates a concern that the model tell a good story. In the context of economist's thinking, a good story means obeying the dictates of logic, given an increasing recognition of diverse circumstances. Thus efforts in modeling the demand for substitute sites and the role of time require increasingly sophisticated methods, and result in a much more complete story. But it remains to be seen whether telling a more complete story makes the analysis more relevant, in terms of its impact on public policy.

The Hedonic Model

A & B provide a traditional analysis of the hedonic method. In the following, I suggest a different way of looking at the identification problem, and offer several reasons for being cautious with the hedonic method.

The basic model

A & B provide an introduction to the hedonic model based on the version that Rosen has proposed; this model has a particularly urban, or housing market, flavor. The hedonic model is more general than that and in fact may work better in settings other than the housing market. The logic of the model involves choice among brands. Goods of different brands have different, measurable attributes. A consumer chooses a brand of a good by choosing the attributes. The attributes provide utility; and, typically, buying more of an attribute costs more.

The hedonic model has some obvious intuitive appeal for valuing environmental amenities when environmental attributes are important in the housing purchase decisions. If people pay more for houses with better air quality, then surely we can learn something about the value of environmental amenities from an analysis of housing prices and environmental attributes.

There are two reasons to be concerned with results from hedonic models. The first is the identification problem—which A & B have discussed in depth, but which I will try to examine differently. A second more serious problem concerns the precise workings of the hedonic model. The hedonic market assumes that while each good has an n-dimensional vector of attributes $(Z_1, \ldots, Z_n)$, any combination of these attributes is available for purchase, and that attributes are not tied in lumpy packages. There is reason to believe that this assumption does not hold in the housing market.

The identification problem

We begin by assuming that the hedonic market works as described. Then we ask, what is the identification problem and how is it solved? A & B characterize the problem as distinguishing between the marginal price function and the demand function. This places the identification problem in its traditional setting of market supply and demand curves. But this is misleading for two reasons. First, there is no interaction between supply and demand in the traditional sense because each consumer (house purchaser) takes the hedonic schedule—the relationships between house prices and attributes—as given. The problems of endogeneity and identification occur because with a nonlinear hedonic-price equation the budget constraint becomes nonlinear, so that prices are not parameters. A second reason why the hedonic problem is different is that when the budget constraint is nonlinear, the consumer no longer has traditional Marshallian demand functions. Instead the object of concern is the marginal value function (or marginal rate of substitution function), and the parameters to be recovered belong to the household's preference function. (This view of the identification problem is spelled out in McConnell and Phipps [1985a].)

What is the relevance of this view of the identification problem? A & B give three basic approaches for identification: (1) assume that all households have identical income and preferences; (2) assume the market is segmented, so that different households face different hedonic price equations; and (3) assume functional form restrictions on the hedonic-price equation. It is clear that regardless of how one views the problem, the assumption of identical preferences and income eliminates the problem of identification. The hedonic-price equation is then simply the household's bid function. In the context of nonlinear budgets, the assumption of segmented markets may provide help in identification, but there is currently no strong evidence of such. Further, tests for market segmentation have come to be accepted as rather weak, and not necessarily providing evidence about different hedonic equations. The third approach, assumption of functional forms appropriate for identification has shown to be useful for solving the identification problem, and it can definitely work in the setting where the problem is viewed as simply a nonlinear budget constraint. The trouble with imposing functional form to achieve identification is that it does not have a good economic story to go along with it. Further, as is shown by McConnell and Phipps [1985b], the hedonic-price equation has all the information about buyers, preferences, and the distribution of attributes embodied in it in no particularly meaningful way. Hence there are no economic guidelines for selecting functional form.

While it is clear that the identification problem emerges from household choice with a nonlinear budget, the solutions look unattractive. Identification by exclusion of variables does not have the same appeal in hedonic markets, when the exclusion typically occurs because of functional form, as it does in a commodity market. For example, for agricultural supply and demand, it is quite intuitive to argue that weather should be excluded from demand, and per capita income from supply. Similar intuitive restrictions are not available for hedonic market, and so the prospect of using the Rosen model to recover parameters of the utility function, the desiderata of hedonic analysis, seems remote.

Does the hedonic work for locational amenities?

A & B suggest that "once the identification problem has been solved and the attribute demand function estimated, it is straightforward to determine the aggregate value of the attribute." Recent work suggests that the hedonic model may not be well suited for valuing locational amenities, and that welfare measurement may be quite troublesome.

There are several reasons why the hedonic model may not work in a residential setting. These are restrictions that prevent the consumer from adjusting continuously at the margin, as assumed by theory. First, many of the attributes of houses are discrete, and thus cannot be adjusted at the margin; one cannot buy part of a view or a fraction of a pool. School quality comes in limited quantities because of the limited number of schools. Thus these attributes cannot be adjusted at the margin so that there is an equilibrium in terms of equality of marginal price and marginal costs. Second, there may be substantial "holes" in the set of available attributes, so that consumers choose from this set, rather than moving along the hedonic-price schedules and choosing their optimum. Using a simulation model, McConnell and Phipps [1985b] show that in most cases the consumer is not in equilibrium at the margin, so that welfare measures assuming this equilibrium would not be valid.

These two criticisms of the hedonic model hold for any commodity with varying attributes. For example, cars have discrete, not continuous, selections of horsepower. But the recent criticism of the Rosen model by Cropper [1985] applies specially to the hedonic model for valuing locational amenities. The essence of the criticism is that when attributes are tied to location, even if they are available in infinite supply, as the model assumes, consumers cannot be in equilibrium with respect to all attributes. A simple example can help explain the Cropper result. Let us imagine a city where all houses are located on the single main street of the city, so that residential choices are made along a line. Further suppose that there all houses are identical, except for two locational amenities: at one end of the town is a hazardous waste site and at the other end a noisy and smelly factory. Now the consumer can choose in one dimension a point along the real line, but has two attributes to choose, distance from the hazardous waste site and distance from the factory. Choice of one implies choice of the other. Clearly the standard equilibrium of marginal-value-equals-marginal-cost cannot be reached for both attributes. As Cropper shows, this argument generalizes to an appropriate number of attributes and the two-dimensional setting for choice of residential location.

Prospects for the hedonic model

My conclusions about the prospects for the hedonic model are more pessimistic than A & B's. But it is easy to criticize existing models. Such criticism is only worthwhile when one has better alternatives. Work on discrete-choice models by Ellickson [1981], Lerman and Kern [1983], Horowitz [1983], and Cropper [1985] suggests that this approach may be a good substitute for the hedonic model. The discrete choice models have several things going for them. First, as Horowitz shows, they need not assume the market is in equilibrium. Second, they allow a description of the consumer's bid which does not requires that the consumer be in equilibrium at the margin. Third, the discrete-choice models assume that the household chooses among a set of available housing bundles, thus telling a story that is probably more intuitive to the representative household than the story told by the hedonic model.

Contingent Valuation

The section on contingent valuation was to my mind the most satisfying discussion of valuing environmental amenities. Further, it is hard to argue with A & B about the appeal of contingent valuation when one considers all the flaws in the travel-cost model and the hedonic model. Contingent valuation appears to offer economists a tool that goes right to the heart of the valuation problem, without any of the econometric or modeling problems created by indirect market methods of valuation.

I have two related concerns about development of contingent methods. First there is the nature of tests of validity. These tests, whether they test cash transactions vs. contingent valuation, as in the work by Bishop and associates, or the comparisons of contingent valuation vs. other techniques, such as the work comparing hedonic methods by Brookshire et al., are useful. They give us confidence that contingent valuation is not too far off the mark. Yet they do not utilize the strength of economics, which is a behavioral science. The best evidence that economics can give is an evidence that people behave the way the economists say they behave. Since any kind of valuation implies behavior, it would seem better to compare models via their implied behavior rather than their results. For example, economists are practiced in assessing the effect of distance on the visits to a recreational site. It would help the economist's case if we attempted to develop ways of assessing the behavioral implications of contingent responses.

A related concern about contingent valuation stems from A & B's comment that they might have entitled their chapter "Contingent Valuation Without Apology." They have good arguments for contingent valuation. But I urge continued and balanced work on all methods. The economist's strength lies in the ability to tell good stories about behavior, and market methods of benefit measurement utilize those strengths. Contingent valuation gets the results without utilizing the economist's strength.

Conclusion

The summing up by A & B is quite able. Rather than comment on the thrust of their work, I would like to offer my own comments about trends. Two trends that appear to change the nature of research in valuation methods are (1) the increased use of discrete-choice models and (2) the movement away from estimating and using the standard Marshallian demand curve. In all these methods, travel-cost, hedonic models, and contingent valuation, the most recent innovations appear to be in the use of discrete-choice models. These models help tell a good story, and they seem to fit the choice settings better. The standard Marshallian demand curve has provided economists with the intuition that they have needed to get into the valuation game, but does not apply to the cases that emerge. Marshallian demand curves have little to say about contingent-value method. In the travel-cost model, whether because the marginal value of time is endogenous or because some sites are not visited, the Marshallian demand curve does not hold. In the hedonic model when the hedonic-price equation is nonlinear, the standard Marshallian demand function has no relevance. To make these trends relevant, economists will have to work especially hard to make the new methods and modes of thinking available to noneconomists.

References

Bockstael, N. E., W. M. Hanemann, and I. E. Strand. 1984. *Measuring the Benefits of Water Quality Improvements Using Recreational Demand Models*. Report to the U.S. Environment Protection Agency.

Cropper, M. 1985. "Can the Rosen model be used to value location-specific amenities? Chapter 7 in *Identification of Preferences in Hedonic Models*. Ed. K. E. McConnell. Report to the U.S. Environmental Protection Agency.

Ellickson, B. 1981. "An alternative test of the hedonic theory of housing markets." *Journal of Urban Economics* 8:56–79.

Horowitz, J. L. 1983. "A Bidding Model of Urban Housing Markets with Disequilibrium and incomplete information." Paper prepared for 30th North American Meeting of the Regional Science Association.

Lerman, S. R., and C. R. Kern. 1983. "Hedonic theory, bid rents and willingness-to-pay: Some Extensions of Ellickson's Results." *Journal of Urban Economics* 10:358–368.

McConnell, K. E., and N. E. Bockstael. 1984. "Aggregation in recreation economics: Issues in estimation and benefit measurement." *Northeast Journal of Agricultural and Resource Economics* 13:187–198.

McConnell, K. E., and T. T. Phipps, 1985a. "Identification of the parameters of the preference function: Consumer demands with nonlinear budgets." Chapter 4 in *Identification of Preferences in Hedonic Models*. Ed. K. E. McConnell. Report to the U.S. Environmental Protection Agency.

McConnell, K. E., and T. T. Phipps, 1985b. "The formation and use of the hedonic price equation." Chapter 6 in *Identification of Preferences in Hedonic Models*. Ed. K. E. McConnell. Report to the U.S. Environmental Protection Agency.

4 VALUATION IN A POLICY CONTEXT

Alan Randall

As the content of this book confirms, the valuation problem ranks as one of the three major research thrusts of contemporary natural resource economics. Resource economists are, for the most part, motivated to make creative use of theoretical and empirical analysis to illuminate contemporary issues in natural resource and environmental policy. They are attracted to issues that combine analytical challenge with policy relevance. In chapter 3 Glen Anderson and Richard Bishop have amply demonstrated the analytical challenges inherent in the valuation problem. My task is to place valuation, and especially nonmarket valuation, in a policy context.

The valuation problem arises whenever one wants to compare the economic productivity of some existing environment with the productivity that could be obtained by implementing a proposal to modify it. The valuation problem is essentially a problem in welfare change measurement, that is, estimation of the benefits and costs of alternative policies. While the domain of the valuation problem is much broader than the enquiries, analyses, and reports mandated by the Flood Control Act of 1936 and Executive Order 12291, it nevertheless makes sense to discuss valuation issues in the context of benefit-cost analysis (BCA), broadly construed.

Benefits arise from the provision of anything that generates positive utility and from the removal of anything that generates disutility. Similarly, costs are associated with decrements in things that are desired and increments in undesirables. In the context of natural resources and environmental amenities, not everything that is desired, nor everything that diminishes utility, is exchanged in value-revealing markets. Thus, nonmarket valuation is essential to ensure that BCA outcomes are not dominated by commercially traded items. If policy decisions were to turn on the results of BCA, nonmarket valuation would be essential to ensure that values associated with nonmarketed goods, services, and amenities are not systematically underrepresented in the decision process.

However, it is by no means obvious that policy decisions do—or should—turn on the results of BCA. Perhaps there are other ways, different and possibly more effective, to ensure that noncommercial goods and amenities are considered in the policy arena. Perhaps nonmarket valuation is a foolish undertaking, in that decisions about the disposition of natural environments are made without any real consideration of benefits and costs, as economists construe these terms. Perhaps, even more damning if it were true, nonmarket valuation is an insupportable basis for public choice. There are two reasons why this might be true. First, it could be argued that the scientific status of nonmarket valuation is weak, providing no basis for confidence in the benefit and cost estimates generated. Second, it could be claimed that the BC rule is itself an ethically unacceptable policy-decision criterion.

The purpose of this essay is to sift through these and related issues. Since I have linked the valuation problem to BCA, and I have argued that valuation issues are policy relevant to the extent that BCA is or should be influential in policy choice, it is necessary to commence by considering the place of BCA in the policy process.

Benefit Cost Analysis in a Policy Context

The roots of BCA are as deep as those of normative economics itself, and the roots of economics can be traced to the social contract theory of political philosophy. Major variants of social contract theory shaped the forms of government in the United States. The social contract notion has itself since been discarded by political philosophers, but the fundamental issues raised by the social contractarians continue to shape contemporary debates in both normative economics and politics. It is no mere accident that normative economics, with its concerns about the size and power of government and the proper scope of collective authority over the individual, addresses (albeit in a peculiarly "economic" way) the great issues of contemporary political philosophy.

The social contractarians, starting with Hobbes, who in turn was obviously influenced by Machiavelli, attempted to overturn the Great Tradition of top-down government by elites and replace it with a bottom-up theory of government. The Great Tradition had placed society in the ascendancy and argued that individuals enjoy privileges to the extent that they earned them by discharging responsibilities and duties to society. Hobbes turned all of this on its head by defining society as a human artifact, and therefore not fundamental, while individuals were fundamental units enjoying at the outset certain natural rights. The central issue in the ethics of government was, then, that of the legitimacy of authority.

Hobbes argued that anarchy was so intolerable that individuals would freely choose to delegate rights (which were theirs at the outset) to a government strong enough to secure and maintain law and order. For later social contract theorists, however, Hobbes' social contract was defective in that it made little provision for citizen control over government subsequent to the initial delegation of rights.

Now, we consider three post-Hobbesian variants of social contract theory, and relate them to BCA. This exercise is very productive in that it allows us to define, and to critique, an ethical justification for the BC criterion as a policy-decision rule and to construct a theory of welfare change measurement consistent with this role for BCA.

The utilitarian, potential Pareto-improvement (PPI) model of BCA

To social contract theorists, the fundamental question was this: Given that where preferences differ among individuals but circumstances require collective action, such action necessarily involving a degree of coercion, under what circumstances is governmental coercion justified? What are the limits to the legitimacy of authority? The roots of modern political and economic approaches to collective choice can be found in three variants of social contract theory.

Individualism, Voluntary Exchange, and Unanimity. Locke's version of the social contract assigned authority to the individual, as did Hobbes'. However, in Locke's version the delegation of authority from individuals to government is always conditional. Government, deriving its authority from the people, must act in the public trust and the citizenry may rise up and overthrow a government that has violated that trust. Some commentators have seen in Locke's social contract not merely a rationale for occasional revolutions against intolerable regimes, but strict limits to the authority of any government. That is, individuals are guaranteed certain rights and a government invading or denying these rights would exceed its rightful authority. Thus, Locke is seen as a founder of philosophical individualism, with its emphases on private property and Bills of Rights.

Modern individualism, as expressed by, for example, the political economist James Buchanan [1977], emphasizes Pareto-safety in economics and in politics. Pareto-safety is the criterion that no change that harms any individual can be considered an improvement. In economic activity, this criterion is satisfied by voluntary exchange among individuals whose expectations are secured by completely specified, enforced, and transferable property rights. Assuming the individual is the best (the only) judge of his/her own well-being, we can be assured that no one would voluntarily enter a trade that would make him/her worse off. To put it another way, trade is individually optimal, ex ante. That things may subsequently work out differently than expected in no way denies the postulate of ex ante optimality.

The fundamental economic measures of value, willingness to pay (WTP) for beneficial changes, and willingness to accept compensation (WTA) for adverse changes—which under ideal conditions converge to market price at the trading margin—are those that emerge from voluntary exchange.

In the political sphere, Pareto-safety means that a proposed change must enjoy unanimous consent if it is to be implemented. The idea of the public interest is explicitly denied. All that matters is the individual, and no individual should be coerced into accepting political change that is not in his/her interest.

In the cases of nonrival and nonexclusive goods, for which some form of collective provision seems essential, individualistic theories of public finance emphasize Wicksellian notions of voluntary taxation. Recent developments include *incentive-compatible mechanisms*, which in concept permit simultaneous determination of the optimal quantities of public (i.e., nonrival and nonexclusive) goods and optimal individual taxes. In principle, these devices solve the conflict between diverse individual preferences and the necessity of collective action: since each person pays his/her individual WTP (but no more) for goods, each would voluntarily consent to the optimal level of collective provision.

The General Will, The Public Interest, and the Social Welfare Function. Rousseau's version of social contract theory starts with the premise that all men are bound to the realization of equality, without which politics and justice are contradictions in terms. Governments expressing the "general will" must legislate only laws that are addressed to the common good of the society's members and extend the same rights to and impose the same duties on each citizen.

Rousseau's philosophy foreshadows the modern emphasis on political equality and constitutional government. While Locke emphasizes sovereignty of the individual, Rousseau stresses the active participation of citizens in the political process as an indispensable condition for government by consent.

Modern public interest theories of government posit that deliberative bodies are capable of identifying and interpreting the general will and of establishing policies and programs to implement it. To promote the general will over the interests of powerful but selfish few, some considerable regulation of individual activities to protect the "public health, welfare, safety, and morals" may be justified. There is no need to minimize the scope of government, so long as government serves the interests of the general public. Thus, programs to promote economic activity, to rectify "market failure" (i.e., to internalize externalities and to provide public goods and "merit" goods), and to promote equality of economic opportunity may all be seen as enhancing the general welfare and thus as within the purview of government. Some conflict between individual aspirations and the general will is inevitable, but public interest theorists hope that individuals will be adequately protected by constitutional procedures and majority institutions.

In mainstream economics, public interest and general will notions are expressed in the concept of the social welfare function [Bergson 1938; Samuelson 1948], which unambiguously quantifies social well-being as some unique function of individual utilities. Thus, assuming individual aspirations sometimes come into conflict, a social welfare function must specify the social consensus as to which kinds of individuals count how much. In practice the social welfare function is empirically elusive, while there is much controversy, at the theoretical level, about the possibility of its existence.

The public-interest/social-welfare-function approach permits a wide range of regulatory initiatives, public investments, and uses of the taxation power to pursue goals beyond mere allocation of revenue. A case can be made that these things are legitimate uses of authority in the public interest. While it is seldom possible to prove or disprove such a case objectively, public interest doctrine does not require this kind of proof. Rather, its premise is that, given a satifactory political environment, those things that are approved through the public decision process will, ipso facto, be in the public interest.

Utilitarianism. Bentham, who was influenced by the social contract theorists and was a contemporary of the early classical economists, popularized the notion that man's motivations were the pursuit of pleasure and the avoidance of pain. It is due to his influence that the word "utility" acquired two meanings: its customary meaning of usefulness and, in technical economics, its association with individual satisfactions and thus preferences. Initially, utility was thought to be, at least in principle, measurable on some cardinal scale.

While the difficulties of the cardinal concept of utility were mostly theoretical in the case of individual choice, they became crucial for political philosophy when the analysis was expanded to collective choice. Bentham thought that the proper criterion for collective choices was "the greatest good for the greatest number." That sounded fair enough, but entailed obvious difficulties in the quite plausible case where very great good for a few might be directly opposed to rather trivial good for many. If cardinal utilities could be summed across individuals, however, that could provide one solution to the problem: choose the alternative that maximizes the algebraic sum of utilities. As it turned out, that avenue proved problematical, because no satisfactory ethical justification could be established for such a procedure.

BCA as a test for potential Pareto-improvements. The notion that activities that were in some important way public should be evaluated by some sort of utilitarian test has a long history. Adam Smith [1776, (bk. IV, ch. 9)] observed that it is a characteristic of public works that their benefits to the individual are smaller than what they would cost the individual should he/she go it alone; however, their aggregate benefits to all members of the community may well exceed their costs. Smith clearly implies a benefit-cost test: public works would be justified if their social benefits exceed their social costs.

In a remarkable paper published in 1844 and titled "On the measurement of the utility of public works," J. Dupuit [1844 (1952)] proposed that benefits be measured in terms of consumers' surplus, a concept that remains central to modern BCA.

In 1908 E. Barone [1908 (1972)] suggested that proposals for change be evaluated by a compensation test, an idea that was popularized by Kaldor [1939] and Hicks [1939] in the late 1930s. *If* the gainers from some proposed change *could* compensate those who would otherwise lose to the full extent of their threatened losses, and still enjoy a net gain, that change could be judged acceptable even if compensation did not actually occur. The compensation test is clearly utilitarian in nature,[1] and resolves the difficulties inherent in interpersonal comparisons of cardinal utility by reformulating the test to require interpersonal aggregation of money-valued gains and losses.

Since consensual changes—those that leave some net beneficiaries and no net losers, and therefore could be implemented without objection—had come to be called Pareto-improvements, it is unsurprising that proposals that passed the test of potential compensation were designated *potential Pareto-improvements (PPIs)*. The Pareto-safety and PPI criteria are related in the following ways:

1. For both criteria, consumer sovereignty reigns; the individual is the judge of what is good for him/herself.
2. For both criteria, the fundamental value measures are WTP for beneficial changes and WTA for adverse changes. Values are determined with the status quo as the reference point; that is, as though each affected party had a right to retain his/her current level of welfare.
3. For both criteria, individual valuations are constrained by individual endowments. Relative endowments determine the relative influence of each individual in Pareto-safe markets and in tests for PPIs.
4. The two criteria diverge sharply when it comes to the implementation rule. Under Pareto-safety, change must be consensual and therefore potential dissenters must be mollified by assurance of compensation to the full extent of their perceived losses. Under the PPI criterion, it is required only that the benefits of change to whomsoever they accrue exceed the costs, where benefits and costs are measured by rules (1) through (3), above. Uncompensated change is permissible when aggregate benefits exceed aggregate costs.

BCA is a test for PPIs. The pragmatic task in BCA is to employ appropriate empirical methods within an economic-theoretic framework consistent with the PPI concept, to determine ex ante whether it is likely that a proposed change would, if implemented, generate a PPI (or, less often, to determine ex post whether a previously implemented change had produced a PPI). In a series of articles published elsewhere, I have been quite explicit about what I believe to be the correct economic-theoretic framework for valuation for BCA purposes [Brookshire, Randall, and Stoll 1980; Randall 1982, 1984]. Rather than repeat the argument here, I simply state the major conclusions.

1. The appropriate value indicators for BCA are the Hicksian compensating measures of welfare change. Thus, beneficial changes are evaluated at WTP and adverse changes at WTA.
2. In the special case where homogeneous and divisible goods are ex-

changed in infinitely large and frictionless markets, WTP and WTA are both equal to $P \Delta Q$, i.e., unit price multiplied by the quantity change. In other cases, $P \Delta Q$ will misevaluate the change, overstating benefits and understating costs. While there are some situations in which serviceable approximations can be identified, benefits and costs must, in principle, be measured as Hicksian compensating measures of economic surplus.

3. Arguments to the effect that Hicksian equivalent measures of economic surplus are proper cardinal indices of individual welfare, while compensating measures are not, do not change the above conclusions. First, only the compensating measures provide (in principle) a perfect filter for PPI; equivalent measures do not. Second, if it is important to rank a menu of competing proposals in order of their net benefits, this can always be accomplished by a sequence of pairwise comparisons using compensating value measures. Third, while the Hicksian equivalent measures provide an unambiguous ranking of many projects for an individual, an interpersonal aggregation problem remains. The ranking of projects for a group, determined by the algebraic sum of equivalent values, depends on base prices, which may be arbitrary. This problem does not occur with compensating measures.

The PPI and public policy. In this section, we examine the status of the PPI in ethics, in law, and in the public-policy-decision process.

Ethical Critiques of the PPI Criterion. Since the PPI criterion evaluates collective (i.e., governmental) initiatives by an explicit set of rules, it is an easy target for critics who object to the ethical premises underlying those rules. Ethical critiques come in considerable variety and are shaped by the ethical perspective of the critic. Here, I pass over the more exotic critiques (e.g., those of the romantics and the mystics) to concentrate on objections from within the social-contract-theory tradition.

Philosophical individualists can scarcely object to the valuation ethics of the PPI, since both approaches share a common valuation framework. The actual and potential Pareto-improvement criteria should ideally agree when evaluating any set of alternative bundles of goods, services, and amenities.

Nevertheless, the PPI criterion provides no security for the individual. If it were to become the universal criterion for collective decisions, individual rights would be completely subordinated to the overall good of the collective. Resource reallocation could then proceed legitimately with government taking from the inefficient and giving to the efficient (as opposed to the exchange process in which the efficient purchase those resources from the less efficient). Thus, philosophical individualists would be implacably opposed to such a collective rule. They favor efficiency, of course, but insist that it emerge spontaneously from individual transactions rather than be deliberately imposed by governments armed with benefit-cost analyses.

Public interest theorists would be little happier with such a decision rule, since it would enshrine a narrow, unidimensional concept of the general will. Similarly, economists of the social-welfare-function school find the PPI criterion unduly restrictive. That criterion can be interpreted as one very specific social welfare function: one in which an index of real consumption is substituted for utility and additional consumption by any individual is evaluated as equally welfare-increasing regardless of the circumstances of that individual. Few who defend the social-welfare-function concept would consider this the only acceptable form for the social welfare function.

Neither the public interest philosophers nor their economist counterparts of the social-welfare-function school can abide a social choice criterion that explicitly denies the relevance of any public interest beyond the algebraic sum of private interests weighted by private endowments.

Immediately above, I have sketched a legitimate critique of the PPI from the public interest perspective. Recently, Mark Sagoff [1981] has attempted a much more sweeping critique, but one that fails to withstand scrutiny. Sagoff outlines a public interest rationale for governmental action, claiming that government exists because citizens in their collective wisdom have chosen to handle some things differently than private property and market institutions would handle them. Government exists, in part (he claims), to give citizens some respite from the rigors of market outcomes. So far, so good. He then associates efficiency with property and markets, and the BC test with efficiency. Thus, he argues, it is a "category mistake" (i.e., a simple logical error) to inquire about the benefits and costs of governmental initiatives: government undertakings are not in the category of things that can be evaluated in terms of economic efficiency.

This argument is itself incorrect, since it is based on a false premise about the nature of the BC test. The BC test is not an attempt to impose on government the alien values of the market. Rather, it is a test for PPIs; and the PPI is a utilitarian criterion, derived from an explicit theory of government. One can argue, and many do, that the PPI is not an especially defensible criterion for governmental decisions. However, one cannot argue correctly that the PPI and hence the BC test are strictly inapplicable, on purely logical grounds, to government.

Regardless of Sagoff's misadventure, the PPI remains unacceptable—as a single and general rule for social choices—to philosophical individualists, adherents of the public interest, social-welfare-function schools, and—for that matter—a good many utilitarians (see note 1).

The PPI and the Law. As indicated earlier, American law and governmental institutions reflect the social-contract-theory influences prevalent at the time of their formation. Individualistic philosophy is institutionalized in the Bill of Rights, the codification of private property rights and the constitutional proscriptions against taking of property without just compensation. Public interest concepts are established in the equal protection clauses, the police power (which regulates private activity to protect the "public health, welfare, safety, and morals") and, for that matter, in the forms of constitutional democracy itself.

The PPI is not so strongly entrenched in law and public institutions, perhaps because it was formally developed much more recently; even its antecedents were not especially prominent in 1776. On the other hand, the relatively unobtrusive position of the PPI in public institutions may be due to the persuasiveness of the individualist and public interest critiques of its ethical foundations.

As I have pointed out elsewhere [Randall 1982], BCA may be used as a ranking device (to array competing alternatives in order of their net benefits), as a filter for PPI, or as an information system that may be influential but not necessarily decisive in policy decisions. I am not aware of any situations in which governments use the BC test as a strict ranking criterion to determine policy choices in order of priority. The BC test is used as a filter for federal water resources projects, and Executive Order 12291 is an attempt (by no means entirely successful) to impose a filter on certain regulatory initiatives. Nevertheless, BCA is most commonly used to generate information that may be weighed, formally or informally, in the decision process without imposing a formal, mechanistic BC decision rule.

Wherever BCA is used in public affairs—be it as a filter for PPI or an information system to be treated as a consideration but not a decision criterion—it is superimposed on the body of existing law, with its individualistic and public interest provisions.

As an example, consider a structural water resources project approved on the basis of the benefit-cost criterion. Assume the project will use structural materials and labor provided by the private sector, some river-bottom land, and a segment of a flowing stream. The structural materials and labor will be obtained through the market. From the sellers' perspective, the exchange will be voluntary and Pareto-safe. The land will be acquired through the power of eminent domain; the farmers will be compensated at the fair market value of their land, but for coerced sales that compensation will be less than Pareto-safe. The funds to purchase structural materials and compensate farmers whose land is taken are gathered through coercive taxation of the general public, few of whom can expect to benefit directly from the project. Recreationists who enjoy the free-flowing stream segment are without property rights and will lose stream amenities without compensation. They, along with any disgruntled taxpayers and farmers whose land has been condemned may, under current institutional arrangements, press their cases in various public forums.[2]

In principle, it would be possible to base the relationships between citizens and government entirely on the PPI concept. However, that has not occurred, in the U.S. or anywhere else. Instead, one observes PPI tests, if they are applied at all, superimposed on a preexisting system of more fundamental laws and institutions.

The PPI and the Public Policy Process. Social contract theory is an endogenous theory of government, one that seeks to derive normative principles. Consider, now, a modern endogenous model of government that is more positivistic in intent.

Drawing on some two decades of public choice literature, I visualize a policy process that is very diffuse, with a wide variety of interests involved, and a large number of different arenas offering themselves as loci for conflict resolution: electoral politics; legislative and administrative institutions at the federal, state, and local levels; quasigovernmental organizations; the judicial system, with its courts and professional advocates; the public information media; and markets, large and small, but all subject to law.

In such a system, no one is entirely above self-interest. Even within government, different agencies may pursue conflicting goals; and individual public servants may pursue individual goals not always congruent with those of their department or the administration as a whole. Individuals within and without government will allocate their endowments—and endowments are broadly defined to include, for example, political contacts and information-media skills, in addition to income, wealth, education, and technical skills—across the various decision loci, to achieve their objectives. They may invest in order to maximize within existing institutions or to maximize via institution-changing behaviors. Different individuals will perceive their best strategies differently and behave accordingly.

The distinction between government and the rest of society becomes blurred. Individuals will seek some things through markets, and other things through a variety of government institutions. Individuals will seek to use the power of government institutions to modify market behavior and market outcomes.

Channels of communication are diffuse, rather than linear. It is not always possible to predict in advance which individual(s) will make the final decision or, for that matter, which of the various arenas will be the locus for the final decision. In fact, few decisions are truly final. Most kinds of decisions—the exceptions including, for example, the irreversible destruction of natural environments—may be later reversed, often at some tolerable cost. This being the case, individuals and coalitions that are disappointed with particular decisions will continue to seek reversal of those decisions in the same arena and in others.

This diffuse public decision process has a voracious and omnivorous appetite for information, which is not merely accepted at face value, but interpreted, criticized, defended, and evaluated. Many divergent kinds and qualities of information—fact oriented and in varying degrees accurate, inaccurate, or intended to mislead; goal oriented, and in varying degrees, conventional or revolutionary—compete for attention. Participants in the policy process continually add to the stock of information: evaluating it; promoting the validity of some of it, while disputing other parts of it; and deleting that which fails to withstand critical examination.[3]

It is not clear that this kind of public policy process, which on superficial examination may look like a mere babble of discordant voices, has any demonstrable optimality properties. Nevertheless, there are persuasive defenses of such a system. Defenders have ranged from Benjamin Franklin (who argued that, if forced to choose, he would have chosen an independent press and no government rather than a government unscrutinized by an independent press) to Karl Popper [1950], with his spirited defense of "The Open Society."

Consider the place of the PPI criterion and BCA in the diffuse policy process. Assume that society is a collection of individuals seeking their own ends through all avaliable avenues, private and public. Assume each attempts to maximize his/her wealth position. One's wealth position can be improved by receiving the economic surplus from productive activities and/or by receiving transfers of wealth from others. The rent-seeking individual is indifferent among these sources of personal benefit. Thus, in the rent-seeking model, PPIs are pure public goods. But, all is not lost. Observation suggests that societies, modern and traditional, develop institutions to provide public goods. Recent developments in the theory of repeated games have established the rationality of cooperative behavior in certain circumstances. The upshot is that public goods do get produced and distributed, although not always in optimal quantities.

So it is with PPIs. We are aware that dead-weight losses due to the success of others in using public institutions to gain transfers for themselves limit our own economic aspirations. Rational rent-seekers seek also to limit the transfers that others obtain, and they do this for both efficiency and distributional reasons. It is impossible for each rent-seeker to police all the activities of other rent-seekers that might diminish the size of the economic pie. However, it is rational to seek establishment of a layer of standing institutions (watchdogs, if you will) to ensure that the rent-seeking activities of others do not get out of hand. It is rational to prefer that such institutions exist in general, even if there are particular instances when they make it difficult for one's own rent-seeking activities. It is also, of course, rational to seek to undermine particular watchdog institutions focused on one's own special domain of rent-seeking, and to undermine particular watchdog activities addressed to exposing the costs of one's own rent-seeking.

BC analysts are paradigm cases of watchdogs. The observation that most others in the policy process seldom speak the language of PPIs, and a few of them address these concerns with undisguised hostility, should not lead BC analysts to doubt the relevance of their own activities. The watchdog institutions in which BC analysts work emerged endogenously in response to a demand for *someone* to address these concerns.

In addition to its public role, BCA also exerts influence in a more immediately private role. While BCA identifies PPIs and is thus directed toward social product (a public good), its information content includes much that is of interest to citizen rent-seekers as they pursue their interests through market and government institutions. Readers of BCA documents often can discern how policy proposals are expected to affect their own interests. This knowledge is useful as they decide what position to take vis-à-vis each proposal. In addition, BCA may well unearth a variety of information helpful in promoting their chosen positions.

Benefit-cost information may be a rather effective form of propaganda,[4] because there is some congruence between the public-good nature of the PPI and the dominant ideology in western societies. The PPI is associated with efficiency and economic growth, which are widely accepted goals of these societies.

If one accepts the argument that open exchange of information is salubrious for public decision making, BCA plays positive public and private roles therein: the public role in reporting about PPIs, and the private role in providing information that individuals may use in identifying and pursing their own advantage.

The PPI: Criterion or Desideratum? The import of the foregoing arguments is that in the real-world policy process, one would expect typically to find BCA exerting some influence but seldom playing a strictly decisive role in public decisions. Ethical objections to the PPI criterion militate against establishment of a general and strict BC criterion for policy decisions. Moreover, the general absence of a single identifiable decision locus and the plethora of individuals and coalitions pursing their own interests through available avenues militate against establishment of *any* formal decision rule.

Nevertheless, one observes, from time to time, attempts to elevate BCA in the decision process. Recall President Carter's directive to tighten the rules for national economic development evaluation of water projects and his attempt to centralize BCA of water projects within the Water Resources Council. More recently, President Reagan issued Executive Order 12291 which mandated BCA for regulatory initiatives.

These attempts to elevate BCA in the decision process can be interpreted as efforts by some participants in the decision process to place constraints upon other participants. (Notice that I characterize the President himself as no more than a participant.) Neither President Carter nor President Reagan had an overriding interest in improved economic analysis for its own sake, one suspects. Rather, President Carter operated upon the premise that too many resources were being devoted to structural modifications in river basins, and at least some of those projects would surely look rather unimpressive in BC terms. President Reagan believes the U.S. is over regulated, and surely some of the plethora of regulations would look bad in BC terms. Both Presidents sought to use BCA for the specific purpose of making it a little harder for others to press the case for things they themselves do not much like. Note, also, that this point was not lost on the above-mentioned "others." Congress knew exactly what was going on, and took much of the bite out of President Carter's initiatives. The role that BCA plays in public decisions can itself become the focus of political in-fighting.

The formal role and the less formal influence of BCA in the policy-decision process may ebb and flow. Nevertheless, most of that ebbing and flowing is within the zone of "influence upon policy choices" rather than the zone of "policy-decision criterion".

Quality control in BCA. There is no doubt that BCA is a research activity. The interesting question, however, concerns the provisions for quality control in BCA. One way to ask this question is: Is BCA, or can it ever be, a science? To address this question we must consider, first, the demarcation of science and nonscience and, second, the possibility of scientific statments about PPI.

The Demarcation of Science and Nonscience. There is a long tradition of attempts to distinguish between (1) those activities that are concerned entirely with reason and fact, and to call them science, and (2) all other intellectual activities such as literature and metaphysics, and to call them nonscience. It is enough to start the present discussion with a relatively recent development, logical positivism. This was the most ambitious of the modern attempts at demarcation and it is not unreasonable to suggest that most of the subsequent writing in philosophy of science was directed toward resolving some of the problems inherent in logical positivism.

The logical positivists set for themselves an ambitious agenda: to unify science and to rid it of all metaphysical elements. They posited four basic tenets.

1. All complex propositions can be derived from atomic propositions and for each atomic proposition there should correspond an atomic fact.
2. Atomic facts are elementary sense observations.
3. The distinction between science and nonscience is identical to the distinction between sense and nonsense, or meaningfulness and meaninglessness.
4. A statement is meaningful if a method for verifying it can be described.

Logical positivism, then, insisted that there is no meaningful distinction between science and reasoned discourse, but at the enormous cost of claiming that reasoned discourse is limited to statements that are constructed entirely from observables and are, at least in principle, verifiable. This claim was, of course, insupportable; but I will spare you the details of the downfall of logical positivism. I cannot resist, however, commenting that the claim, quite common among contemporary economists, to be logical positivists must be based on substantial ignorance about what logical positivism stood for.

Karl Popper in his *Logik* [1934 (1959, 1968)] made not one but two major breaks with the logical positivists. First, he argued that it was not essential that all scientific propositions be derived from simple observable facts. Scientific statements could be based on premises about unobservables, so long as consequences that are observable could be rigorously derived therefrom. Thus, for example, the gene theory of inheritance can be scientific, in principle, even though genes themselves are not observable. It is necessary only that the gene theory generate consequences about observables. Second, Popper demonstrated that verification of empirical propositions was logically impossible. Since there are an infinite number of potential observations, the absence of a refuting event in any finite sequence of observtions cannot be taken as verification; it is always possible that the refuting event is "out there," waiting to be observed.

Together, these two Popperian insights permitted a new demarcation of science. Scientific statements were those from which it was possible to derive refutable consequences. It was acceptable, for example, to base a scientific theory of inheritance upon nonobservables such as genes, so long as certain events were forbidden as rigorously derived consequences. Observation of the forbidden events would constitute a refutation of the theory. Thus, a meaningful test could be described and the theory could be called scientific.

Since scientific theories need no longer be constructed from elementary statements about sensible (i.e., material) objects, Popper's methodology required a new definition of the venerable notion of objectivity.[5] For Popper [1957], scientific objectivity consisted of the freedom and responsibility to (1) pose refutable hypotheses; (2) test them with relevant evidence; and (3) report the hypothesis, the nature of the test, and the results in a manner accessable to all interested persons. Thus, objectivity remained linked to an interpersonal test of the evidence. However, theories were not to be tested directly by examining their component premises; rather, the test was by attempts to refute their consequences.

While Popper's methodology was a clear improvement on that of the logical positivists, it was not without its own problems. First, the Duhem irrefutability thesis held (correctly) that a pure test of a theory by the attempt to refute a derived conjecture was logically impossible [Blaug 1980, 18, 25, 42, 265]. To derive a conjecture refutable by observation, it is necessary to apply a series of auxilliary assumptions (about the conditions under which the theory might be expected to hold, the appropriate domain for observations, the effectiveness of the devices, and instruments used for observation and measurement, etc.); and it is always logically possible to attribute a refutation to a problem with the auxilliary assumptions rather than with the theory itself.

Second, while Popperian refutation remains an excellent way to rid the conventional wisdom of false theories, it is difficult to see how a body of knowledge can grow under a refutationist methodology. Strictly speaking, all that can grow is the list of refuted (i.e., failed) theories; and this list conceivably could grow indefinitely large and still fail to identify a finite residuum of unrefuted theories. Further, the possibility is always present that subsequent events may refute a currently unrefuted theory. Therefore, it makes little sense to claim that the body of knowledge consists, at any time, of currently unrefuted theories.

In his later writings, Popper [1968] attempted to soften his refutationist methodology with the notion that theories that had survived many attempts to refute them could be considered "highly corroborated" and possessing of substantial verisimilitude or "truth-likeness." These attempts are not so convincing, since Popper himself had shown the logical fallacy of verification not only of absolute statements but also of probabilistic statements. Accumulated failures to refute could not, then, make a theory probably true.

Third, Popper's demarcation of science from nonscience must be considered a failure. As Popper himself admits, the history of science contains relatively few crucial experiments that refuted important propositions. Popper's demarcation simply made science too exclusive.

Imre Lakatos [1970] has made important amendments to the Popperian scheme of things, developing a theory of the growth of knowledge that nevertheless retains an important place for attempts to refute conjectures derived from theories. Other modern methodologists go further in dismantling the Popperian scheme. Paul Feyerabend [1975] argues, with some plausibility, that Lakatos' amendments lead logically to the complete abandonment of the essentials of the Popperian scheme. Donald McCloskey [1983], with his concept of a rhetoric of science, and Stephen Toulmin [1972] who finds some scientific merit in the way lawyers approach the notion of evidence, may be interpreted as attempting to lead the philosophy of science back toward the notion of reasoned discourse.

This time, however, reasoned discourse is used as a broadening concept. Rather than insisting that all reasoned discourse must satisfy a narrow definition of science (as the logical positivists had done), McCloskey, Toulmin, and others are arguing that the attempts at a restrictive demarcation of science from nonscience have failed, and the scientific enterprise differs only in degree (if at all) from other learned undertakings such as literary criticism and jurisprudence.

It is possible to read Popper as giving some support to this view. While Popperian scientific objectivity consists of three elements, it is the third that is far and away the most important. Frank and open reporting of the scientific enterprise permits criticism, and it is criticism that provides the interpersonal discipline of science. It is notable that while others have found in Popper support for various kinds of positivist and empiricist philosophies, Popper refers to himself as a critical rationalist. It is notable that criticism is a fundamental element common among all forms of reasoned discourse, and is also essential to the diffuse public decision process and the "open society."

In summary, I conclude that the Popperian refutation test represents a useful ideal for science, and occasionally permits the elimination of false theories from the conventional wisdom. Nevertheless, it provides an unsatisfactory demarcation of science from nonscience, since it would exclude the great majority of the activity that is generally regarded as scientific. Further, modern philosophy of science raises considerable doubts as to whether a strict and a simple demarcation is possible and whether it can ever be helpful or even meaningful to prescribe a few simple rules which, if followed faithfully, will give assurance that one's activities are scientific. Rather, the distinctions between science and reasoned discourse are, if anything, a matter of degree, and criticism appears to be the fundamental element of both science and reasoned discourse.

Reasoned discourse about values and ethics, as well as about relationships among phenomena, is entirely possible. Further, criticism itself is sufficient to ensure that value statements cannot for long masquerade as "is" statements.

On the Possibility of Scientific Statements About PPI. First, there are no interesting questions about whether there is any scientific basis for the idea that it is socially desirable to implement policies that offer PPI opportunities. Of course, this issue is entirely one of ethics and values. Thus, any definition of "scientific" that excludes inquiries into the value realm must necessarily regard such issues as nonscientific. On the other hand, individuals who are not much interested in distinguishing between the realms of science and of values and ethics will not find this question interesting.

The interesting question is: What, if any, scientific status can be accorded to statements about the existence (or nonexistence) of particular PPI opportunities? At the outset, consider the logical structure of the PPI concept. First, it starts with a model of individual choice in which preferences constrained by the initial utility level determine a schedule of Hicksian compensated demands from which WTP (or WTA, as the case may be) can be calculated. Demand theory does have some refutable consequences and, since demand theory itself is considered well established, particular empirical estimates inconsistent with demand theory are likely to be rejected as invalid. Nevertheless, a wide range of magnitudes for WTP (WTA) is permissable. Second, individual WTPs (WTAs) are aggregated according to the logical rules inherent in the PPI construct. Deductive logic and criticism are sufficient to expose conceptual error in applying Hicksian demand theory and aggregating according to the PPI rules.

Consistency with the requirements of the theories of demand and welfare change measurement is, however, only a part of the story. BCA is an attempt, often ex ante, to assemble and interpret a broad array of physical, biological, and economic information in order to identify PPI opportunities. Benefits and costs are magnitudes and BCA requires attempts to measure their quantities. The customary devices for quality control over estimates of magnitudes are, in varying degrees, available. Often, the statistical precision of estimates of mean or expected values can be calculated. Benefit and cost estimates may be replicated by independent researchers. Where two or more alternative estimation procedures are available, cross-checks for consistency of results are possible.

So, various methods exist to exert some quality control over benefit and cost estimates. Nevertheless, quality control may be incomplete. In the event that results of attempts at replication or methodological cross-checks show some lack of convergence among alternative estimates, it is often tempting and sometimes justifiable to take refuge in the Duhemian stratagem of casting suspicion on various auxilliary assumptions and conditions so as to declare the results of the test inconclusive.

It is not always possible to construct genuine Popperian refutable hypotheses in the context of BCA (this point is elaborated in the following section). Nevertheless, as I have argued above, much of what is usually called science is unable to satisfy the Popperian ideal. The devices of criticism and reasoned discourse, upon which most of what is commonly called science depends, are available in BCA. The underlying theory of BCA is precise, and deviations therefrom may readily be detected. Empirical estimates of important quantities and values are often less precise, and less readily validated. Nevertheless, the device of criticism remains. Note that independent replications and methodological cross-checks of empirical results are themselves specialized and rather structured forms of criticism. In addition, criticism of methods used, the data sources, and the plausibility of results can cast additional light on the degree of faith that should be placed in particular benefit and cost estimates.

Therefore, I conclude, BCA is a learned activity with quality controls not unlike those available in many other fields of what is commonly called science. Nevertheless, it is essential to be reminded of one most significant caveat. The devices of criticism and reasoned discourse, upon which we rely, are effective only in an environment where information flows freely. Professional and lay criticism protects the general public from incompetent and misleading BCA. Further, it serves to reveal the degree of precision or imprecision of benefit and cost estimates and the reliability or otherwise of the methods and data upon which they are based. Where BCA documents are treated as internal memoranda within public agencies, and are therefore unavailable to outside professionals and the general public, the assurances provided by criticism and reasoned discourse are no longer available.

Note, in this context, the convergence between scientific methodology and public choice. The processes of criticism and reasoned discourse provide, I argue, the best hope for quality control in science and scholarship and for reasonably satisfactory and tenable outcomes in the diffuse public-decision process.

Alternative models

The utilitarian/PPI model of benefit-cost analysis has a lot going for it: its derivation from a coherent (if, perhaps, not universally acceptable) normative theory of the relationship between citizens and government; its history of theoretical development which, in many respects, parallels that of micro- and welfare economics at large; and its current well-developed conceptual basis in preference theory, demand theory, and the theory of welfare change measurement. In spite of these rather strong advantages, the utilitarian/PPI model does not command the allegiance of all commentators. Here, I consider two alternative models for BCA and examine their shortcomings. For me, the utilitarian/PPI model remains the preferred model.

The run-government-like-a-business model. Some commentators treat BCA as merely an extension to the public sector of the economic feasibility studies long used in the private sector. In this model, the purpose of BCA is to impose upon government, as a matter of conscious policy, some of the discipline that market forces are believed to exert upon the private sector.

This model is readily demolished. It really does not make much sense to run government like a business. On the contrary, it is cogently argued that government exists because citizens understand that there are some important things that business just cannot do and some sociocultural goals that business serves poorly. Government exists, among other reasons, to give citizens some respite from business.

I should note in passing that, had Sagoff [1981] proposed his "category mistake" argument in this context, it would have enjoyed some validity. One could argue that there are many kinds of government policies that are simply not in the category of things that are to be judged by the criteria of business accounting.

The run-government-like-a-business model is not merely inconsistent with any coherent normative model of government. It is also inconsistent with BCA practice. Business accounting concerns itself with only those costs and returns that bear directly upon the firm's "bottom line." On the other hand, BCA identifies all beneficial and adverse effects of policy, to whomsoever they accrue, and values them according to the principles not of profit and loss but of the PPI. BCAs of proposed policies dealing with air and water pollution, environmental hazards, workplace safety, and the like, are specific attempts to determine whether net public benefit might be obtainable from initiatives designed to correct the excesses and negligences of business.

BCA as a rational planning device. Earlier in this chapter, I conceptualized a diffuse public policy process in which rent-seeking individuals and coalitions pursue their self-interests through a variety of market and governmental institutions. While that model has considerable appeal and seems to be gaining adherents, the earlier rational planning model retains some influence. To me, the rational planning model serves as neither an acceptable normative model nor a plausible positive model of public administration. Nevertheless, since its implications for BCA practice are quite different from those of the utilitarian/PPI model, a critical examination of the rational-planning model seems essential.

The rational-planning model is constructed around the concept of a professional civil service, in the venerable British tradition (or myth, if you will), dedicated exclusively to a set of values associated with that particular concept of professionalism. While the upper layers of the civil service constitute an elite, democratic values are preserved (it is believed) by having elected and politically responsive bodies specify goals in broad terms and make the ultimate decisions about the overall direction of policy. While the civil service is responsive to the public as represented by its elected politicians, the internal workings of the civil service are to be completely insulated from political influence.

Within a particular agency of the civil service, communication channels are linear rather than diffuse, and vertical rather than horizontal. The director specifies the policy issues of concern, the policy goals, and the terms of the inquiry. Experts within the agency are then to perform analyses that are positive, objective and scientific, and entirely uninfluenced by whatever values the experts themselves may hold. The experts are then to report the results of the analysis to the director, without recommendations. The director then decides, and experts unhappy with the decision keep their peace.

What does the director decide? The director may be empowered to dispose of relatively minor policy matters. On major issues of policy, the director decides what information will be transmitted to his/her elected overseers who must ultimately make the policy decisions.

As a normative model of public administration, the rational planning model is subject to criticism on the grounds that it places too much power in the hands of a professional elite and justifies this on the basis of an impossible dream: the dream of an objective and scientific basis for policy decisions.

As a positive model of the policy process, the rational planning model is simply inconsistent with the vast body of evidence about how policy is made and implemented.

From the perspective of scientific methodology, the rational planning model has major problems. While the experts are required to perform objective analyses, their role model explicitly violates the first and third conditions for Popperian scientific objectivity [Popper 1957]. The first is violated by the rational planning requirement that the director, not the scientists, identify the issues to be researched, the questions to be asked, and the terms of the inquiry. The third Popperian condition is violated by the linear communication pattern: under rational planning the scientist or expert reports his/her findings only to his/her superior within the agency, while Popperian objectivity requires reporting in a manner accessible to any interested person. There is general agreement among philosophers of science that the integrity of the scientific process is guaranteed not by the impeccable personal ethics of individual scientists but by the institutions of science which serve to identify and expose work that is incomplete, incompetent, or influenced by the values of the researcher. Foremost among these institutions are those that facilitate and encourage rational discourse and scholarly criticism. These things are actively discouraged by the rational planning tradition.

In summary, I claim that the rational planning model is an unacceptable normative model of the relationship between citizens and government, an implausible positive model of governmental processes at variance with observation, and an attempt at "scientific" government that is based upon an unacceptable philosophy of science. Nevertheless, there remain some believers in the rational planning model. Furthermore, some of those believers regard BCA as a tool in the arsenals of rational planners. There are others who reject the rational planning model and claim that, since BCA is obviously a rational planning device, it too should be dismissed out of hand [Shabman 1984].

But, as we have seen, the roots of BCA are much deeper than the early and mid-twentieth-century tradition of rational planning. Further, the place of BCA in an environment of rational discourse and scholarly criticism, and in the diffuse policy process, is quite different from that implied by the rational planning model. Thus, we must reject the idea that BCA must itself be rejected because it is a tool of the discredited rational planning tradition.

We must also reject the rational planning framework as a model for BCA and its application. The utilitarian/PPI model provides rigorous and restraining guidelines as to what is, and what is not, acceptable theory and practice in BCA. If BCA were conceived as merely a rational planning tool, its conceptual basis would be changed from a rigorous test for PPIs to pretty much any kind of structured evaluative system the planners want. What is to defend the conceptual basis and empirical methods of BCA from renegotiation each time the planners perceive that their objectives and/or information needs have changed? How is the citizenry, with resources too limited to allow indepth examination of each case, to interpret brief summary results of BC analyses if BCA itself is conceptually and empirically malleable at the whim of particular planners.

These kinds of problems arise frequently with respect to the use of BCA in government agencies. For example, Perry Brown [1984] and others with influence at the US Forest Service, an agency that has long had a strong rational planning aspect to its internal ideology, have waged a long and tenacious battle to have BCAs of Forest Service policies and programs consider not only benefits and costs as defined by the PPI criterion but also a wide variety of psychological, social, and cultural effects of forest recreation that some people consider real and beneficial.

Attempts to treat BCA as a rational planning tool, and therefore as malleable to the needs of the particular situation, are not confined to non-economists. There is a long tradition among World Bank economists of deviating from the PPI criterion when evaluating benefits that accrue to the impoverished (see Scandizzo and Knudsen [1980]). The fear is that the effective demands of the impoverished are necessarily rather small (on a per capita basis) and, unless some deviation from PPI principles is allowed, the benefits of activities to improve their lot might turn out to be too low. In a similar vein, Mishan [1976] has argued for one specific departure from PPI principles. For evaluating environmental improvements, Mishan would use the Hicksian equivalent measure of value, since that measure would increase the calculated value of such innovations by implicitly assuming that citizens had enjoyed a right to these environmental improvements all along.

One may concede the good intentions of the proponents of each of these deviations from the PPI tradition in benefit-cost analysis. Nevertheless, I am convinced that it is best if BCA is confined to rigorous attempts at implementing the PPI criterion. That way, a firm basis exists for understanding and critiquing any attempt at empirical BCA. Clearly, general adherence to the PPI concept increases the information value of BCAs and reduces the transaction costs of critically evaluating them.

Valuation

The foregoing has presented a wide-ranging argument for the utilitarian/PPI model of BCA. That having been done, much of the work required to place valuation of natural resources and environmental amenities in its policy context is already completed.

Nonmarket valuation and its contribution to policy

The remaining task is to detail how the general arguments just discussed apply to valuation and, especially to valuation in the absence of direct information about market demands.

The PPI and the logic of valuation. The logic of the PPI criterion suggests a complete and unambiguous theoretical framework for valuing the beneficial and adverse effects of proposed policy. Hicksian compensating value measures are to be used; this requires that beneficial effects be evaluated at WTP while adverse effects are evaluated at WTA.

These value measures are seldom directly observed. Where near-perfect markets are in operation, observations adequate for estimating Marshallian demands may well be attainable. If so, it is often possible to calculate approximate [Willig 1976; Randall and Stoll 1980] or exact [Hausman 1981; Bergland and Randall 1984] Hicksian demands from observable data.

Where—for reasons of nonrivalry, nonexclusiveness, or institutional choice—important categories of natural resources and environmental amenities are not directly traded in organized markets, methods for attempting their valuation in PPI terms have been developed. The mainstream methods may be grouped into two broad categories: contingent valuation methods (CVM) where, in experimental or survey situations, sampled citizens use contrived or contingent markets to determine and report their valuations for resources and amenities; and the weak-complementarity/implicit-price (WC/IP) methods in which markets in certain goods and services (e.g., residential land or travel services) are analyzed to extract information about the value of closely related environmental services and amenities. These various methods, and their conceptual underpinnings, have been discussed in chapter 3 of this volume by Anderson and Bishop and, elsewhere, by Freeman [1979] and the present author [Randall 1982, 1984], among others. Below, I concern myself with the scientific status of the nonmarket valuation enterprise, and the role of nonmarket values in the policy process.

The scientific status of nonmarket valuation. Sagoff [1981] has argued that nonmarket valuation is an exercise entirely unconstrained by the disciplines of scientific procedure. Empirical values for certain categories of resource and environmental services are so tenuous, Sagoff claims, that the economist is free to report values consistent with his/her preferred BCA outcome. Thus, he argues, nonmarket valuation (and therefore, all BCAs that have a nonmarket component) reduces to mere storytelling.[6]

Others, including several economists, are less sweeping in their criticisms, but nevertheless worry that nonmarket value estimates are fundamentally irrefutable, presumably because "true" values are strictly unobservable. There are two difficulties with this argument.

First, modern theories of hypothesis testing do not require that economic values themselves be observable in order to enjoy scientific status. The logical positivists required that scientific propositions be constructed only of observables. However, logical positivism is no longer considered a tenable philosophy of science, and the structure of the Popperian hypothesis-testing notion of scientific objectivity is quite different. It is not essential that the antecedents or premises be statements about observables. All that is needed is that observable and refutable consequences can be derived from these premises. It is then possible to attempt to deny the premises by denying the consequence. Thus, nonmarket valuations would be perfectly acceptable scientific statements if it were possible to construct interesting refutation tests about consequences deduced from such valuations.

In principle, such consequences can be deduced. The existence and magnitude of an unrealized PPI suggests that, if appropriate markets could be established, certain predictable patterns of trade would be observed. There are more possibilities for this kind of test than the casual observer might expect. The literature contains interesting examples of such tests. In 1974, Sinden [1974] reported the results of a test constructed in exactly this way. Further, the methodological cross-checks quite common in nonmarket valuation circles (see Bishop and Heberlein [1979] and Brookshire et al. [1982]) may be given this kind of interpretation. For example, CVM results may suggest that, if appropriate markets existed, benefits of a certain magnitude would be revealed in trade. Such direct markets do not exist, but markets in closely related goods and services may exist and it may be possible to deduce the predicted pattern of trade in these markets. Then, the hypothesis that values derived from these markets by WC/IP methods should approximate those obtained with CVM (or should deviate from them in predictable ways [Brookshire et al. 1982]) is a deduced consequence of this chain of logic. Admittedly, such tests are replete with Duhemian loopholes, since it is possible and often reasonable to argue that defects in data and analytical methods account for any empirical anomalies. Nevertheless, with respect to refutability, nonmarket valuation is on the same footing (in principle, if not always in degree) with many other kinds of scientific and scholarly undertakings.

Second, consider the common, and more contentious, case in which estimated nonmarket values are not used to derive refutable consequences. In these cases, the exercise is one of measurement. A magnitude is to be estimated. In this context, is it or is it not crucial that no observable true magnitude exists corresponding to what is to be measured (i.e., WTP or WTA), and thus a comparison of estimated values with true values is impossible? I would argue that there is literally nothing special about this situation. There are no phenomena of nature that come with their true magnitudes stamped upon them and certified by their creator. Measurement is always an exercise in estimation and its reliability is always limited by the precision of measurement instruments, devices, and procedures and the power of the theory upon which the measurement exercise is based.

Measurement exercises seem more firmly grounded in theory in some cases than in others; and some measurement devices and procedures seem more precise than others. For some categories of benefits and costs, estimation procedures are indeed primitive and their precision is uncertain but suspected to be rather loose. There have been considerable advances in benefit estimation, but there is yet room for many more.

Nevertheless, it would be foolish to make too much of the argument that benefit estimation is unscientific because there are no observable true values with which to compare the estimates obtained. That kind of argument is based on a misunderstanding of the nature of estimation, and therefore makes no sense. Even if it did make sense, it would have no special import for benefit estimation, since it would apply also to all other kinds of measurement and estimation exercises.

Finally, I have perhaps granted the critics too much by attempting to rebut these various arguments to the effect that benefit estimation does not meet the standards of science. To engage in this kind of argument requires implicit acceptance of the notion that scientific and nonscientific enterprises can readily be distinguished. Yet, I have argued that attempts to develop a rigid demarcation between science and nonscience have failed. If a rigid demarcation is insupportable—and science is therefore, like other scholarly activities, an exercise in reasoned discourse and, at best, critical rationalism—what is to be gained by arguing that valuation procedures in BCA cannot be called unscientific?

The principles of reasoned discourse and the third (i.e., critical) condition of Popperian scientific objectivity are clearly applicable to BCA, and especially so when BCA is performed in strict accordance with the utilitarian/PPI model. The theory and methods of nonmarket valuation are sufficiently well developed, and in many cases the bodies of reasonably well substantiated or replicated data are sufficiently large, to provide a basis for criticism to ensure quality control in valuation. Where data are dubious, methods overreach the theory, and results are somewhat conjectural, there is no shortage of critics to point out these shortcomings. Thus, in the open society with its diffuse policy decision process, citizens enjoy considerable protection from being misled by shoddy or dishonest BCA work.

It is well to recognize that ex ante BCA is necessarily a speculative enterprise. BCA requires assessment of the physical and biological consequences of change, and evaluation of those consequences in terms of the PPI criterion. In general, as one moves through the array of pertinent values—from raw materials values, to current amenity use values, future use values, option and existence values—assessments of consequences and their economic values becomes less reliable. The difficulties are compounded (on both the supply and demand sides) when one considers that change affects whole systems, not merely isolated components thereof [Hoehn and Randall 1982].

Economists experienced in these kinds of applied BCA problems are well aware of the limitations and shortcomings of their valuation techniques. Nevertheless, many of us have experienced case after case in which the uncertainties associated with economic valuations are dwarfed by the imprecision pertaining to estimates of the physical and biological consequences of policy.

If, for many important classes of policy questions, benefit and cost estimates are necessarily imprecise and the possibility of misevaluating PPI opportunities is real, two questions arise: (1) Is it possible to provide guidance for applied BCA in a limited information environment? (2) What useful purposes are served by necessarily imprecise BCA estimates in the diffuse policy process? The first question is addressed immediately below and the second question in the following section.

Valuation in a limited information environment. One may ask, why should we worry about guidance for the BC analyst operating in a limited information environment? After all, the diffuse policy decision process, in a society with strong scholarly traditions of criticism and reasoned discourse, limits the capacity of incomplete and unreliable BCAs to mislead. That is true, but there remain strong public and private reasons for BCA practitioners to do all in their power to maintain high-quality standards in their work and to seek continuing improvements in BCA techniques. First, consider the public reasons. BC analyses are not inexpensive; nor are the processes of criticism. More reliable BC analyses are clearly preferred to less reliable, because they reduce the transactions costs of public decisions and increase the likelihood that the choices eventually made will be satisfactory and thus politically tenable.[7] The private reasons concern the incentives and rewards that impinge upon BC analysts themselves. The wealth of BC analysts as a group is likely to increase as BCA, generically, enjoys increasing public esteem.

The wealth of individual BC analysts increases as their work comes to enjoy a reputation for high standards of competence and integrity.

A meaningful set of guidelines for BCA in a limited information environment can be reduced to two general rules. (1) Do not let the unattainability of perfection stand in the way of the attainable good. Where information is relevant and reasonably reliable insofar as it goes, but insufficient for unambiguous interpretation in terms of the PPI criterion, it is better to display that information, warts and all, than to omit all reference to the beneficial or adverse effects addressed by that information. In BCA, omitted effects are treated as though they make no contribution, positive or negative, to a PPI. (2) Never claim more precision than is reasonable for any benefit or cost estimate. Display is encouraged not only for point estimates of benefits and costs, but also for statistical confidence intervals, less formal indicators of completeness and reliability, and sensitivity analyses.

Typically, certain resources and amenities susceptible to influence by proposed policies routinely enter the channels of commerce. For them, records of market transactions lead routinely to the accumulation of rather complete secondary data sets that are informative about physical productivity and market valuations. Other natural resources are managed by public agencies that provide services to citizens and routinely record the utilization of these services. For still other environmental services and amenities, no organized market generates evidence about use and value and no government agency records public use. If these latter services and amenities are to be adequately represented in BCA, the burden of gathering relevant information rests upon the BC analyst and other subject matter specialists whose skills can be directed to the task.

Valuation of NonMarketed Goods and Services. Given the inherently richer data base for valuation of marketed goods, effort should be channeled specifically toward economic evaluation of nonmarketed goods and services, to redress the imbalance. Values associated with expected future use, options for future use, and existence deserve special attention. Continuing development and refinement of theory and empirical methods can be expected to accompany a trend toward more routine application. Again, it often turns out to be the case that the errors introduced in economic valuation are smaller than those pertaining to estimates of fundamental physical and biological relationships.

It must be expected that benefit and cost value data, comparable in completeness and reliability with that available for commercially marketed goods and services, will remain unavailable for some nonmarketed services which, nevertheless, are vitally important considerations in the selection of appropriate policies. In such cases, it is essential that whatever information is obtained be documented. This implies the careful assembly and display of information that falls short of identifying contributions, positive or negative, to PPIs.

Documentation of Positive Value. It is often possible to document that environmental services are being provided and are of unambiguously positive value. Recently, the present author was involved in research (see Tolley et al. [1984]) demonstrating that people in aggregate make the kinds of choices that necessarily imply that they place positive value on atmospheric visibility. Careful documentation that certain environmental values are real and positive serves effectively to counter the erroneous implication that those things that cannot readily be valued in PPI terms are without value.

Documentation of Positive Production of Services. As a last resort, it may be possible to document that certain kinds of environmental goods and services are being provided in positive quantities. This information also serves to correct the tendency to ignore those things that cannot easily be incorporated in a single-valued BC ratio or net present value.

Sensitivity Analysis. Where there is uncertainty about technical coefficients and value estimates, sensitivity analysis is appropriate. Benefit and cost estimates are based on the best estimates of technical relationships and Hicksian compensating surpluses, but the range of magnitudes these items might take is recognized. The arithmetic is reiterated, using various alternative magnitudes within this range, to determine whether final conclusions are sensitive to assumptions about technical and economic magnitudes. When uncertainty is unequally distributed across the vector of environmental services and amenities, special attention should be addressed to sensitivity analysis where the uncertainty is greatest. Clearly, the outcome of BCA in PPI terms is inconclusive if sensitivity analysis shows that benefits of a proposed policy exceed its costs under some plausible technical and economic assumptions but not under others.

Inverse Sensitivity Analysis. There may be environmental services that are recognized as significant, but for which it is impossible to make plausible estimates of crucial technical or economic magnitudes. In such cases, inverse sensitivity analysis should be used. Inverse sensitivity analysis answers the question: How large would an unquantified benefit or cost item need to be, in order to reverse the end result of a BCA that omits that item? Inverse sensitivity analysis is a useful indicator of the robustness of BC conclusions in cases where particular beneficial and adverse effects are admittedly unmeasurable in PPI terms.

Valuation, limited information, and public policy. What useful policy purposes are served by necessarily imprecise BCA estimates? Before attempting to answer this question, I will dispose of two interrelated arguments to the effect that BCA estimates are of little policy relevance in general, and especially when environmental quality, human health, etc. (i.e., the very kinds of things for which benefit and cost estimates are most tenuous) are involved.

First, it is often argued (e.g., by Shabman [1984]) that BCA is irrelevant to policy because there are many participants in the process whose goals and concerns are not entirely consistent with the PPI criterion. Of course, many participants have objectives that are inconsistent with, and sometimes directly opposed to, the PPI. However, that observation does no damage to the position I have developed in this chapter. I have argued neither that PPI considerations should for ethical reasons dominate policy decisions, nor that a broad-based consensus would be expected (on the basis of some predictive model of public choice) to converge upon the policy option that looked best, ex ante, in PPI terms.

The import of my argument is that the PPI status of policy proposals is of some public concern, and has some implications for the self-interest of certain groups of affected citizens. Further, the value matrix of Western society includes (but is not necessarily dominated by) a positive respect for economic efficiency and growth objectives closely related to the PPI. Under these conditions, one could expect BCAs to have some influence on the conduct of policy debate and the outcome of policy processes; one would not, however, predict BCA to be dominant. Given that BCA is influential, one would expect to observe, among the mosaic of established organizations involved in the policy process, some dedicated to performing BCAs and disseminating the findings. Given the public-good nature of the PPI and the fact that the PPI may well be influential but seldom is decisive in policy choice, one would expect the size and influence of these organizations to be limited.

Second, it is sometimes argued [Shabman 1984] that to evaluate, say, environmental improvements in PPI terms is to miss the entire point of the environmental movement.[8] The environmental movement is dedicated to bringing about some fundamental changes in the society's value system and the laws that transform a system of values into a structure of authority. Thus, it is argued, it is entirely irrelevant to evaluate these kinds of changes in terms of the PPI, with its status-quo-based valuation rules. Conflicts about whether society will produce relatively more environmental amenities and fewer commercial goods and services should, and will, be resolved in other ways and without reference to the PPI.

Again, this argument does not invalidate my position. Surely, some participants in the policy process are seeking a fundamental reassignment of rights. But there are also others seeking to defend and further entrench the status quo. Still others (maybe a majority) see neither environmental quality nor commercial goods and services as unmitigated "good things" to be enjoyed in infinite quantities to the exclusion of all else, if only that were possible. They may well be willing to readjust their consumption bundles to include a little more in the way of amenities if the cost in goods and services was not too great, or vice versa. BCA can speak effectively to and for these people, even if few of them really believe the PPI should always decide these kinds of issues. Since I argue only that the PPI status of policies is of some limited interest, arguments that it is not (or should not be) decisive do not threaten my position.

Now to the main issue: what useful policy purposes are served by necessarily imprecise BCA estimates and, especially, estimated values of nonmarketed goods and amenities?

Earlier in this chapter, it was argued that there were public and private reasons for participants in the diffuse policy process to have some interest in the information provided by BCA: Public reasons because PPIs are public goods in a rent-seeking society, and private reasons because BCAs typically include information useful to individuals in discerning how proposed policy would effect their own interests. Further, it was argued that BCA served a potentially effective propaganda function, since the PPI is associated with economic efficiency and growth, concerns that are well embedded in Western value systems.

These arguments pertaining to BCA in general have clear application to nonmarket valuation. With a competent and unassailable BCA available, the various interests must confront the choice in terms of, among other things, benefits *and* costs. With benefits documented it is no longer plausible to argue in terms of costs alone; with costs documented it is not so easy to argue that proposals offer unmitigated social benefits. With unpriced and nonmarketed benefits and costs evaluated and documented, it is implausible to conduct the economic debate in purely commercial terms. No longer can it plausibly be claimed that there are overwhelming economic arguments for the "development option," while the benefits of the "preservation option" are confined to sentiments and emotions existing only in the woolly heads of environmentalists. To the extent that PPIs matter, it is important to know that at least some proposed policies to increase the output of environmental services even at the expense of commercial goods would generate PPIs. To the extent that BC analyses are useful forms of propaganda, it is important that the commercial is not overrepresented and the nonmarketed not underrepresented in BCA. In these ways, then, a major function of BCA and nonmarket valuation in the diffuse decision process is to define, or perhaps redefine, the terms of the debate.

Given the imprecision that sometimes afflicts estimated benefits and costs of environmental policies, the final results of empirical evaluation in terms of PPIs may often be inconclusive. In these cases, too, BCA and nonmarket valuation serve useful roles in the policy process. To show that the economic and PPI arguments with respect to some proposal are inconclusive, undermines claims (often emanating from commercial interests) to the contrary. Further, when the PPI status of policy is inconclusive, there is a meaningful sense in which participants in the policy process are freed to focus upon the other issues involved; often, that is, upon the issues that really matter.

Conclusions

Since this has been a long chapter, and one that has addressed a variety of issues concerning BCA and nonmarket valuation in a policy context, it may be useful to summarize the major conclusions in a list of succinct statements.

1. Benefit-cost analysis (BCA) is an empirical test for potential Pareto-improvements (PPIs).
2. The PPI criterion is one solution to the aggregation problem in utilitarian philosophy. Hence:
    a. The PPI criterion is derived from a coherent theory of the relationship between citizens and government.
    b. It is not a logical error to enquire as to whether the benefits might exceed the costs for some proposed action of government.
3. The value system of the PPI may be summarized as follows:
    a. The individual is the best judge of what is good for him/herself.
    b. Individual values are determined with the status quo as a reference point; i.e., as though each affected party had a right to retain his/her current level of welfare.
    c. Some persons are indeed better off than others, and relative wealth determines the relative influence of each person's preferences in tests for PPIs.
    d. Given that individual valuations are determined according to the above principles, aggregate values are determined by algebraic summation of individual values.

   e. If and only if a proposed policy generates a positive net aggregate value it is judged to be a PPI.
4. Ethical objections may be raised, from both individualistic and public interest perspectives, to establishment of the PPI as a universal policy decision rule.
5. In relatively few cases does the law require a BCA filter for public investments and/or policies. Even in these cases, the PPI criterion is superimposed on the preexisting structure of laws which, in the United States, serve individualistic and public interest ideals.
6. In a diffuse public policy process, information about the PPI status of proposals serves public and private roles: a public role because PPIs are public goods in a rent-seeking society; and a private role because individuals and coalitions can often discern from BCA documents how proposals are likely to affect their own interests. Further, BCA information may have a significant propaganda function in the process through which public opinions are formed.
7. In the diffuse public decision process, PPI information is often of some influence but is seldom strictly decisive in policy choice.
8. The PPI criterion imposes a rigorous conceptual structure on BCA. Benefits amount to the sum of Hicksian compensating value measures (WTP) across beneficiaries; costs are the sum of like measures (WTA) across losers.
   a. Hicksian compensating value measures often are not directly observable. However, economists have identified the special conditions under which unit price is an acceptable value indicator; and, for the cases where these conditions do not hold, they have developed methods of calculating approximate and exact Hicksian value measures from observable data.
9. While the PPI model of BCA is clearly to be preferred, two alternative models are sometimes suggested.
   a. The run-government-like-a-business model is easily rejected since (i) there is no convincing reason to impose on government the values of business and (ii) BCA practice clearly departs from this model, and for good reasons.
   b. The rational planning model is a two-edged sword, since those who favor it have attempted to undermine the rigorous PPI conceptual basis of BCA while some who reject it have insisted that BCA should likewise be rejected since it is "obviously a rational planning tool." In this chapter the rational planning model is rejected, as is the idea that BCA is a rational planning tool.
10. The PPI conceptual structure of BCA both requires that nonmarket

valuation be performed where markets generate inadequate value information and establishes the theoretical framework for nonmarket valuation.

11. With regard to the scientific status of nonmarket value estimates in BCA:
    a. Attempts at a rigid demarcation of science and nonscience have failed. Even the Popperian scheme, based on refutation of consequences deduced from theories, is not an acceptable demarcation.
    b. Science is now seen as an enterprise based on criticism and reasoned discourse, not unlike other scholarly activities. In this enterprise, theoretical constructs, measurement, and estimation procedures, and attempts at replication of results and refutation of deduced conjectures, all have their places and are all subject to criticism. That which withstands criticism is tentatively accorded credibility.
    c. BCA and nonmarket valuation are enterprises of this type. If it is meaningful to call any kind of enterprise scientific, these too are scientific enterprises.
12. For some classes of (e.g., environmental) amenities nonmarket valuation is a somewhat speculative exercise and the value estimates obtained are of uncertain validity.
    a. The critical processes in science and in the diffuse public policy process ensure that few are misled for long, about the precision and validity of these estimates.
    b. Tenuous as they are, these estimates may play a useful (but, surely, not decisive) role in the choice among policy alternatives.
13. In this diffuse public policy process, the fundamental role of nonmarket valuation is to change the terms of the debate. Participants are forced to recognize that the environmental costs of development are real and comparable with its commercial benefits; and the commercial costs of preservation are real and comparable with its environmental benefits. The question becomes one of society's product mix: What mix of commercial goods and environmental amenities do we want?

Notes

[1] Note that, while the compensation test is clearly a welfare criterion of the utilitarian kind, several other utilitarian concepts of the good have been proposed and examined in the literature. The PPI is *a* (not *the*) utilitarian welfare criterion, and there are many utilitarians who

have strong objections to the PPI.

[2]This paragraph is reprinted, with minor editing, from Randall [1984, 69], with permission from Westview Press.

[3]This paragraph and the four that preceded it are reprinted, with minor editing, from Randall [1982, 86–87] with permission from the editor, *Southern Journal of Agricultural Economics*.

[4]Propaganda is defined as material disseminated purposefully to bolster one's own cause or damage the cause of another. The distinguishing feature of propaganda is its purpose, rather than its content. Propaganda may be factual material, rumor, innuendo, or blatant falsehood. However, material that is not only supportive of one's cause but also of sufficient veracity to withstand critical scrutiny is the most effective propaganda of all.

[5]The origins of the term "objectivity" lie in the idea that sense observations about material objects provide a basis for science as distinguished from theology and metaphysics. In that context, objectivist, materialist, and positivist were near-synonymous terms. Popper's scientific objectivity is a process in which sense observations are crucial for testing, but not necessarily for constructing, theories. In scientific methodology, objectivity has never had connotations of impartiality with respect to the effects of research results on subsequent allocation or distribution.

[6]Sagoff clearly intends the term "storytelling" to suggest a procedure in which scenarios are created and tales are spun without any meaningful tests of verisimilitude. The storyteller is essentially without external restraint, in Sagoff's rendition.

However, Benjamin Ward [1972] and Charles Wilber [1978] have proposed that a methodology—variously called storytelling, pattern modeling, and holism—be taken seriously. This methodology, they claim, characterizes much of what economists do—including enterprises as diverse as comparative statics, computer simulation, and institutional economic analysis—and has its own system of checks and tests for verisimilitude.

[7]The rational planners would also value accurate and reliable BCAs: if BCA is a tool that permits planners to make scientific policy decisions, it is obviously important that BCAs be as scientific as possible. However, as we have seen, the rational planning model does not hold BCA to the PPI construct. Rather, beneficial and adverse effects can be evaluated (scientifically, of course) within whatever conceptual guidelines the planner deems appropriate.

[8]Similar arguments may be addressed to the economists' habit of proposing Pigovian charges be levied on polluters [Shabman 1984].

References

Barone, E. 1908 (translated 1972). "The ministry of production in the collectivist state." *Penguin Modern Economic Readings: Socialist Economics*. Ed. A. Nove and D. M. Muti. London: Penguin Books.

Bergland, O., and A. Randall. 1984. "A method of calculating exact consumer's surplus from observable data." Paper prepared for presentation at annual meeting, Association of Environmental and Resource Economists, Dallas TX, December 28–30.

Bergson, A. 1938. "A reformulation of certain aspects of welfare economics." *Quarterly Journal of Economics* 52: 311–334.

Bishop, R. C., and T. A. Heberlein. 1979. "Measuring values of extramarket goods:

Are indirect measures biassed? *American Journal of Agricultural Economics* 61: 926–930.

Blaug, M. 1980. *The Methodology of Economics: Or How Economists Explain*. Cambridge: Cambridge University Press.

Brookshire, D. S., A. Randall, and J. R. Stoll. 1980. "Valuing increments and decrements in natural resource service flows." *American Journal of Agricultural Economics* 62: 478–488.

Brookshire, D. S., M. A. Thayer, W. D. Schulze, and R. C. d'Arge. 1982. "Valuing public goods: A comparison of survey and hedonic approaches." *American Economic Review* 72: 165–177.

Brown, P. J., 1984. "Benefits of outdoor recreation and some ideas for valuing recreation opportunities." In Peterson and Randall [1984], 209–220.

Buchanan, J. M. 1977. *Freedom in Constitutional Contract*. College Station: Texas A and M University Press.

Chipman, J. S., and J. C. Moore. 1980. "Compensating variation, consumer's surplus, and welfare." *American Economic Review* 70: 933–949.

Dupuit, J. 1844 (translated 1952). "On the measurement of utility of public works." *International Economic Papers* 2: 83–110.

Feyerabend, P. K. 1975. *Against Method: Outline of an Anarchistic Theory of Knowledge*. London: NLB.

Freeman, A. M., III. 1979. *The Benefits of Environmental Improvement: Theory and Practice*. Baltimore: Johns Hopkins University Press.

Hausman, J. A. 1981. "Exact consumer's surplus and deadweight loss." *American Economic Review* 71: 662–676.

Hicks, J. R. 1939. "The foundations of welfare economics." *Economic Journal* 49: 696–712.

Hoehn, J. P., and A. Randall. 1982. "Aggregation and disaggregation of program benefits in a complex policy environment." *American Journal of Agricultural Economics* 64:1079 (abstract).

Kaldor, N. 1939. "Welfare propositions in economics." *Economic Journal* 49: 549–552.

Lakatos, I. 1970. "Falsification and the methodology of scientific research programmes." *Criticism and the Growth of Knowledge*. Ed. I. Lakatos and A. Musgrave. Cambridge: Cambridge University Press.

McCloskey, D. N. 1983. "The rhetoric of economics." *Journal of Economic Literature* 21: 481–517.

Mishan, E. J. 1976. *Cost Benefit Analysis*. London: George Allen and Unwin. 2nd edition.

Peterson, G., and A. Randall (eds.). 1984. *Valuation of Wildland Resource Benefits*. Boulder, CO: Westview Press.

Popper, K. R. 1934 (translated 1959, 1968). *The Logic of Scientific Discovery*. New York: Harper of Row, Torchbooks.

Popper, K. R. 1957. "Philosophy of science: A personal report." *British Philosophy in Mid-Century*. Ed. C. A. Mace. London: George Allen and Unwin, 155–191.

Popper, K. R. 1950. *The Open Society and its Enemies*. London: Routledge and Kegan Paul. (4th edition, 1962).

Popper, K. R. 1968. *Conjectures and Refutations: The Growth of Scientific Knowledge*. New York: Harper and Row (Torchbooks).

Randall, A. 1982. "Economic surplus concepts and their use in benefit cost analysis." *Review of Marketing and Agricultural Economics* 50: 135–164.

Randall, A. 1982. "Policy science in the land-grant complex: A perspective on natural resource economics." *Southern Journal of Agricultural Economics* 14: 85–92.

Randall, A. 1984. "Benefit cost analysis as an information system." In Peterson and Randall [1984], 65–75.

Randall, A. 1984. "The conceptual basis of benefit cost analysis." In Peterson and Randall [1984], 53–63.

Randall, A. 1984. "Theoretical bases for nonmarket benefit estimation." In Peterson and Randall [1984], 77–88.

Randall, A. and J. R. Stoll. 1980. "Consumer's surplus in commodity space." *American Economic Review* 70: 449–455.

Sagoff, M. 1981. "Economic theory and environmental law." *Michigan Law Review* 79: 1393–1419.

Samuelson, P. A. 1948. *Foundations of Economic Analysis*. Cambridge: Harvard University Press.

Scandizzo, P., and O. K. Knudsen. 1980. "The evaluation of the benefits of basic needs policies." *American Journal of Agricultural Economics* 62:46–57.

Shabman, L. A. 1984. "Water resources management: Policy economics in an era of transitions." *Southern Journal of Agricultural Economics* 16: 53–66.

Silberberg, E. 1978. *The Structure of Economics—A Mathematical Analysis*. New York: McGraw-Hill.

Sinden, J. A. 1974. "A utility approach to the valuation of recreational and aesthetic experiences." *American Journal of Agricultural Economics* 56: 61–72.

Smith, A. 1776 (reprinted 1970). *The Wealth of Nations*. Ed. A. S. Skinner. London: Penguin Books.

Tolley, G. S., A. Randall, and 7 others. 1984. *Establishing and Valuing the Effects of Improved Visibility in Eastern United States*. Washington, DC. Final Report, U.S. Environmental Protection Agency.

Toulmin, S. 1972. *Human Understanding*. Oxford: Clarendon Press.

Ward, B. 1972. *What's Wrong with Economics*? London: Macmillan.

Wilber, C. K. (with R. S. Harrison). 1978. "The methodological basis of institutional economics: Pattern model, storytelling and holism." *Journal of Economic Issues* 12: 61–89.

Willig, R. D. 1976. "Consumer's surplus without apology." *American Economic Review* 66: 587–597.

COMMENT 1

ANN FISHER

Alan Randall makes a case for using benefit-cost analysis (BCA) to support public policy decisions. Even though potential Pareto improvement (PPI) is not universally accepted as a decision rule, he argues that the PPI information in a BCA serves several useful public and private roles that may influence—but seldom determine—policy choice. With this background, along with that on the valuation problem itself provided by Anderson and Bishop, we can turn to some pragmatic questions about where resource economics stands in terms of using BCA now, and what needs to be done to make this tool more useful in the future.

BCA's Role in Resource Policy

There is considerable resistance to using BCA in making policy decisions. Randall covered three basic reasons for this: (1) society's political philosophy; (2) BCA's scientific basis; and (3) the sheer expense of conducting a

The views presented here are the author's alone and should not be considered to represent those of the U.S. Environmental Protection Agency.

complex BCA. While these reasons apply to any public policy choice, they tend to be more severe for decisions about natural resources. This is because resource policy effects on complex ecosystems are difficult to predict, and the categories of effects ordinarily are not traded in markets, so estimates of their values are not readily available.

Reduced flexibility

Resistance also comes from decision makers' reluctance to accept any framework that might restrict them from exercising their discretion, and from recognition of BCA's past abuses (particularly for projects under the Flood Control Act of 1936). Randall states that public and private interests ultimately are protected from such abuse by critical review of BCAs, which can occur except under the rational planning model. Simple availability of a BCA may be insufficient, however, if it is written in very technical terms (as is common), and if interested parties are so scattered that transaction costs prevent them from enlisting the aid of an expert who can interpret the document. Thus availability of a BCA for critical review might be defined to require that it be written so the layman can understand its contents.

Using the right baseline

Another reason for the reluctance to accept BCA in evaluating resource and environmental policy is disagreement about an appropriate reference point for individuals' initial endowments. This occurs because some property rights are not defined clearly. This is particularly important when the proposed policy involves a loss of entitlement because of persistent differences between empirical estimates of maximum willingness to pay (WTP) to prevent an adverse change, and minimum compensation (i.e., willingness to accept (WTA)) required to agree to the change.[1]

The economic theories behind BCA imply that so long as income effects are small, WTP and WTA should be approximately the same.[2] While this condition may not hold for some resource policy decisions, it does hold for most of the studies where substantial divergences have been estimated. Since there may be shortcomings in the WTA questions used in these studies, it has been recommended that the smaller WTP estimates be used in BCA.[3] Until this issue is resolved, it appears that property rights must be assigned carefully for a reliable BCA.

For example, the loss of benefits estimated for a development project that will eliminate some wilderness recreation (or hunting, fishing, etc.) opportunities will depend on how much of these opportunities people are assumed to have rights to without the project. Similarly, the benefits estimated for programs to reduce air or water pollution depend on how clean is the air or water to which they have property rights. If the status quo is better (or worse) than what is perceived as the appropriate initial endowment baseline, this should be accounted for in the BCA.

Legal limitations and requirements

Randall discusses the broad legal foundations that could support reliance upon a PPI criterion. However, another reason BCA is not used more widely as one basis for policy decisions is that several laws prohibit its use. For example, the Clean Air Act requires the U.S. Environmental Protection Agency (EPA) to set primary standards for national ambient air quality with adequate margins of safety for protecting public health, without considering the costs of achieving those standards.[4] (Of course, once a standard is set, EPA can examine the cost effectiveness of alternative ways of reaching it.) Similarly, Congress's recent reauthorization of the Resource Conservation and Recovery Act appears to preclude use of BCA in deciding whether to prohibit specific hazardous wastes from land disposal.[5] Instead, the legislation requires that each of a long list of hazardous wastes be banned from land disposal unless EPA can show that such disposal will not harm human health or the environment. This completely overlooks the possibility that alternative disposal methods might be both more dangerous and more costly to construct, operate, and eventually close.

Such legal restrictions apply to relatively few types of natural resource policy decisions, but their existence for some programs often seems to have spillover effects for others. For instance, an agency's legal staff seems more comfortable with consistent decision criteria across as many programs as possible. The lawyers sometimes argue that it will be difficult to defend a BCA criterion in one program when it is proscribed in another.[6] Such behavior by an agency's legal counsel can be viewed as consistent with Randall's conceptualization of the diffuse public policy process in which individuals and coalitions pursue their self-interests through a variety of market and governmental institutions. Unless the agency's lawyers have a strong preference for the outcome they expect to be indicated by a BCA, they may opt for keeping their work load smaller by encouraging consistency across the agency's programs.

On the other hand, Executive Order 12291 requires BCA as part of a regulatory impact analysis (RIA) for each major regulation, regardless of whether its results can be used in the decision process. When the law precludes the use of BCA in the decision, the RIA must include a statement to that effect. The Office of Management and Budget (OMB) issued guidance to amplify the executive order, indicating that the Reagan administration's intent was to have agencies identify laws that force inefficient regulations so that the legislation could be changed. I am not aware of any instances where the law has changed as a result of such a finding.

In the diffuse policy process he described, Randall interprets Executive Order 12291 as President Reagan's attempt to place constraints on other participants. The likelihood that proposed and existing regulations might not pass a PPI test means the executive order would move agencies toward the president's goal of less regulation. Conducting the required RIA undoubtedly has kept some inefficient regulations from being submitted to OMB. At the same time, it is interesting to note how many regulations have been proposed where the RIA shows positive net benefits. This may have come as a surprise to the administration, and may help explain why OMB takes so long to review an RIA.[7]

Potential for BCA in Upcoming Decisions

As Randall points out, BCA has not been, and perhaps should not be, the primary decision criterion in the public policy arena. Factors related to data availability and the technical implementation of a BCA, along with considerations aside from efficiency, support the need for flexibility in the decision process, rather than a rigid BCA rule.

In line with this flexible approach, it may be that a policy proposal will not require a full-fledged BCA in order to provide the efficiency information of interest to the decision maker. In some cases, cursory examination will show that a proposal's benefits clearly outweigh its cost to society, so that it can be justified on efficiency grounds.[8] In others, a quick look will reveal that benefits are few and relatively small compared with the costs of implementing the proposal. Such information suggests abandoning the proposal, given society's multiple needs and scarce resources. In these cases, more information is not worth gathering since it would be unlikely to lead to a different recommendation on PPI grounds.

The third possibility is that preliminary examination will show substantial benefits but will not make clear whether they exceed the costs of implementing the proposal. In this case, a more detailed BCA is required if the efficiency aspects of the policy are to be determined. However, the extent and detail of the BCA should depend on the potential magnitude of making the wrong decision from an efficiency perspective (i.e., the costs of being wrong) and the potential to influence that decision. Thus, a proposal that might turn out to be mildly inefficient but expensive merits a less exhaustive BCA than another that might be inefficient and very costly. Since analytical resources are scarce, the efficient natural resource economist will conduct a "mini" BCA on how extensive his/her BCA should be for a particular policy proposal.

Differing precision in BCAs

Regardless of the degree of detail desired to match the magnitude of the decision, differences in data availability and in the sophistication of our valuation methodologies lead to four levels of BCA, with decreasing precision:

1. All benefits and costs can be identified, quantified, and monetized.
2. All benefits and costs can be identified and quantified, but some cannot be monetized satisfactorily (either because their inherent nature makes valuing them controversial—as with morbidity and mortality—or because our present valuation methodologies are limited—as for valuing ecosystem changes).
3. All benefits and costs can be identified, but some cannot be quantified and thus cannot be monetized. (For example, the analyst may be able to say that strip mining in an area will affect species X, Y, and Z, but shortcomings in measurement techniques may prevent him from saying how much each species is affected.) Others can be quantified, but not monetized, as in (2).
4. Some benefits or costs cannot be identified, perhaps because of limitations in our basic understanding about ecosystem structures and functions. For those that can be identified, (3) may apply.

The monetization of benefits and costs relies on prices for those commodities traded in markets, and on estimates of Hicksian compensating values for the remaining ones. These values may be estimated through direct methods (what Randall calls contingent valuation, broadly defined) or through indirect methods (his weak complementarity/implicit price approaches).

To accommodate the fact that the degree of precision will vary across different benefit-cost analyses, I have for some time recommended the following approach for the policy decision process. The first step is to consider the available benefit-cost information (keeping in mind that the extent of BCA should be keyed to the magnitude of the policy decision, and to the likelihood that new information will affect the decision):

1′. If information is available for (1), is the net benefit estimate positive?
2′. If information is insufficient for (1) but adequate for (2), list and describe the nonmonetized benefits and costs. For plausible ranges for values of the nonmonetized benefits, is it likely that they are large enough to change the sign of the net benefit estimate?
3′. For a BCA in level (3), calculate the net benefits on the basis of available information. List and describe the measures of the quantified but nonmonetized benefits and costs; list and describe the unquantified benefits and costs. On balance, are the values and magnitudes of these categories likely to reverse the sign of the net benefits estimate?
4′. Conduct an analysis as close to (3′) as possible. Use any available information to describe potential but unidentified benefits and costs. Given the expected reliability of this information, is it likely to be important enough to reverse the recommendation based on the (3′) analysis?

This organization of benefit and cost information makes a complex, multidimensional decision more manageable by combining information into a smaller number of categories. It focuses attention on the nonmonetized and/or unquantified benefits and costs, so that explicit decisions must be made about their importance relative to the monetized benefits and costs. In each case, the decision maker should consider the uncertainties in the estimate, perhaps through the sensitivity and inverse sensitivity analyses suggested by Randall.[9]

Equity considerations

The information provided to this point in a BCA shows whether a particular policy proposal would lead to a PPI. By its very nature, the efficiency conditions of a PPI ignore equity aspects. Since society may be unwilling to support a policy that is viewed as particularly unfair, it may be worth recognizing that the BCA is only one component in the diffuse decision process. In particular, the PPI information may stand a better chance of being a real component of the decision process if it is accompanied by explicit statements about the proposal's expected equity effects. In a broadly defined benefit-cost *assessment*, the analyst provides information about the distribution of benefits and costs in addition to the PPI information.[10] This allows a more informed response to the question: Are the equity impacts important enough to either negate the recommendation based on the net benefit estimate or lead to a recommendation for some other mitigating action?

What next?

Examination of the steps in (1′) through (4′) emphasizes that BCA essentially relies on a damage-function approach—values are applied to changes in quantities of physical and biological measures. As Randall points out, the scientific measures of these changes often have substantially more uncertainty than the imprecise valuation methods economists use. This illustrates the most important needs for improving the applications of BCA: namely, a better understanding of underlying physical and biological processes, and more reliable data for predicting the outcome of a policy option.

When the data problem is particularly serious (i.e., when the BCA is closer to that in levels (3) and (4)), it may be desirable to consider valuing the policy action directly, rather than its expected outcomes. For example, it may be difficult to predict the precise ecological (and other) effects of a 50 percent reduction in sulfur dioxide (which is a contributor to acid rain). Similarly, it may be difficult to predict the ecological effects of energy development adjacent to a unique wilderness area, or the specific reduction in health risks from more stringent hazardous waste regulations. In such cases, a description of the policy proposal could be developed, along with explicit recognition of the uncertainties in identifying and measuring the types, quantities, and values of outcomes. Citizens, experts, and/or decision makers then would be asked to assign values to the policy action itself.[11] As more scientific information becomes available and narrows the uncertainties about the outcomes of a proposed policy, then the valuation of benefits and costs can be assigned to the outcomes rather than to the policy action itself.

Over time, current and future research will improve not only the methods we have for predicting the types and amounts of outcomes that will occur as a result of a policy decision, but also those for estimating the values for each type. Then some BCAs that today are in level (4) will move up to level (3), or even (2). Some of these prediction problems, such as measuring the impact on ecosystems and determining option and existence values, may be difficult to solve. At the same time, new problems will arise in the natural and environmental resources arena, so that there still will be some BCAs in the less-satisfactory levels (3) and (4). Unfortunately, not to decide is to decide. To make sure efficiency considerations are included in policy decisions that cannot wait for perfect information, natural resource economists have an incentive to provide the best BCA information possible while pointing out its strengths and weaknesses.

Notes

[1] Studies by Hammack and Brown [1974]; Sinclair [1976]; Brookshire and Randall [1978]; Bishop and Heberlein [1979]; Rowe, d'Arge, and Brookshire [1980]; Banford, Knetsch, and Mauser [1980]; and Knetsch [1984] found WTA to be 2.5 to 16 times as large as WTP.

[2] Willig [1976] showed this for price changes, while Randall and Stoll [1980] showed it for quantity changes.

[3] Cummings et al. [1984] make this recommendation. Others (e.g., Gregory, [1984]) are concerned that the divergences can be explained only by modifying the theories behind BCA. Tversky and Kahneman [1981] suggest that insights from psychology may explain why the payments people demand for giving up an entitlement seem to be larger than the maximum they would agree to pay to keep the same rights.

[4] Sections 109(a) and 109(b), 42 U.S.C. 7409.

[5] *Congressional Record*, October 3, 1984, H 11104-H 11144.

[6] This is made difficult when some of the agency's laws require an approach that is similar to BCA. For example, the Federal Insecticide, Fungicide, and Rodenticide Act (FIFRA), Section 2(bb), 7 U.S.C. 136(bb), requires EPA to examine both the benefits of using a pesticide to increase agricultural and forestry yields and the risks associated with its use. FIFRA does not require monetization of the risks in order to get a net benefit number. Similarly, to receive EPA funding, states must show that combined-sewer-overflow projects will "substantially restore" impaired shellfishing and swimming, and a reasonable relationship between these benefits and the project's costs (Construction Grants Regulation §35.2024(b)).

[7] For the effect of the executive order on environmental policy, see Smith [1984].

[8] This ignores the possibility that a more refined BCA could point to the specific size of the policy proposal that would maximize net benefits, giving the largest PPI.

[9] As is typical of other authors, Randall emphasizes the need to focus on the uncertainties in valuing nonmarket natural and environmental resources. Usually, these are on the benefits side of the ledger. At the same time, the cost side should not be neglected. In many instances cost analyses have concentrated on their distributional impacts, rather than on the overall costs to society.

[10] See, for example, Desvousges and Smith [1983].

[11] In a pioneering attempt, Schulze et al. [1983] asked households to value a hazardous waste regulation directly. Smith and Desvousges (1985) asked households to value changes in risk from hypothetical hazardous waste regulations of varying stringency. A next step would be to tie their valuations to changes in risk actually expected from a proposed policy.

References

Banford, N., J. Knetsch, and G. Mauser. 1980. "Feasibility judgments and alternative measures of benefits and costs." *Journal of Business Administration* 11:25–35.

Bishop, R., and T. Heberlein. 1979. "Measuring values of extramarket goods: Are indirect measures biased?" *American Journal of Agricultural Economics* 61:926–930.

Brookshire, D., and A. Randall. 1978. "Public Policy, Public Goods and Contingent Valuation Mechanisms." Staff paper 68, Department of Agricultural Economics,

University of Kentucky.

Cummings, R., D. Brookshire, W. Schulze, and D. Coursey. 1984. "Valuing Environmental Goods: A State of the Arts Assessment of the Contingent Valuation Methods." Washington, DC: U.S. Environmental Protection Agency. Draft.

Desvousges, W. H., and V. K. Smith. 1983. "Benefit Cost Assessment Handbook for Water Programs." Research Triangle Park, North Carolina: Research Triangle Institute. Draft.

Gregory R. 1984. "Interpreting Measures of Economic Loss: Evidence from Contingent Valuation Studies." Eugene, OR: Decision Research. Unpublished.

Hammack, J., and G. M. Brown. Jr. 1974. *Waterfowl and Wetlands: Toward Bioeconomic Analysis*. Baltimore: Johns Hopkins University Press.

Knetsch, J. 1984. "Legal rules and the basis for evaluating economic losses." *International Review of Law and Economics* 4:5–13.

Randall, A., and J. Stoll. 1980. "Consumer's surplus in commodity space." *American Economic Review* 70:132–149.

Rowe, R., R. d'Arge, and D. Brookshire. 1980. "An experiment on the economic value of visibility." *Journal of Environmental Economics and Management* 7:1–19.

Schulze, W., et al. 1983. "Experimental Approaches for Valuing Environmental Commodities." Washington, DC: U.S. Environmental Protection Agency. Draft.

Sinclair, W. 1976. "The Economic and Social Impact of the Kemano II Hydroelectric Project on British Columbia's Fisheries Resources." Vancouver: Fisheries and Marine Service, Department of the Environment.

Smith, V. K., ed. 1984. *Environmental Policy under Reagan's Executive Order*. Chapel Hill: University of North Carolina Press.

Smith, V. K. and W. H. Desvouges. 1985. "An Empirical Analysis of the Economic value of risk changes." Working paper, Vanderbilt University (December).

Tversky, A., and D. Kahneman. 1981. "The framing of decisions and the psychology of choice." *Science* 211:453–458.

Willig, R. 1976. "Consumer's surplus without apology." *American Economic Review* 66:589–597.

COMMENT 2

V. Kerry Smith

Decisions *always* imply valuation. A rejection of the principles underlying benefit-cost analysis does not free any decision on a public project from assigning values to the outputs provided by that project. If, for example, the Environmental Protection Agency (EPA) chooses not to modify the existing primary ambient air quality standard for ozone (a regulatory impact analysis was working its way through EPA at the time this paper was written), this decision can be interpreted as a judgment by the policy makers within EPA that what would be delivered by the revision (whether it is more or less stringent) is not worth the cost.[1]

Graham and Vaupel [1981] offered a striking example of this point in their comparison of 35 analyses of lifesaving programs. Their approach calculates the value of the risk change[2] that was implied by each of the analyses. These implicit values were estimated using the net additional cost of the policy per life saved. The results imply values that range from 0 (for a group of transportation safety policies, such as mandatory air bags or compulsory seat-belt usage) to the $169 million implied by OSHA's analyses

Partial support for this research was provided by the centennial chair research funds provided by Vanderbilt University.

of the acrytonitrile standard for workplace concentrations (at 0.2 parts per million). Decisions on any of these actions place the implied value for a statistical life on one side or the other of these estimated costs or shadow values.

What is really at issue in discussions of the role for benefit-cost analysis in the policy-making process is how *private individuals' values* for the goods and services involved should be reflected in that process.

As Alan Randall has suggested, the definition of a conceptual role for private individuals' values and the task of measuring those values for specific natural and environmental resources are among the major research challenges of contemporary natural resource economics. His essay provides a thoughtful assessment of the alternative rationales for using benefit-cost analysis within a society's decision calculus. It deals explicitly with some of the current philosophical criticisms of the use of benefit-cost analysis for decisions involving natural and environmental resources; and leads the reader through many of the difficult conceptual issues associated with describing individuals' values for nonmarketed goods and services. It is, therefore, an excellent starting point for the research that will confront resource economists for the next decade. However, having recognized the merits of his work, every author knows agreement makes dull reading. Consequently, the balance of my comments will be directed to the areas that have been omitted from Randall's essay and to conclusions that one might not wish to accept without a fuller exposition of opposing positions.

My discussion is presented in five parts. The first of these describes some alternative philosophical arguments against benefit-cost analysis and relates them to Randall's critique of Sagoff's [1981] work. The next describes the actual, as opposed to the theoretical role, of benefit-cost analyses in the policy-making process. In the third part, this discussion is extended to an explicit consideration of the nonutilitarian factors that influence the range of choices evaluated in the benefit-cost studies actually done in formulating environmental policies, and the corresponding implications of these factors for the practice of policy decisions based on such analyses. Fourth is a discussion of the measurement of nonmarket values, since these values are the means for reflecting consumer sovereignty—the theoretical linchpin for benefit-cost analysis; and the last part considers whether the imperfections in the implementation process overwhelm all hopes for modest improvements in the allocation of resources by using the information provided in a benefit-cost assessment.

Is Sagoff's Argument Randall's Straw Man?

Randall has provided a clear and convincing (certainly to most economists) argument that benefit-cost analysis is a method for organizing information so that the results of that organization can be used to judge whether the action under study represents a potential Pareto-improvement (PPI) in the status-quo resource allocation. That is, if the action yields aggregate benefits exceeding costs then it is a movement toward efficiency even though some individuals may lose. With positive aggregate net benefits, it would be possible for those who gain to compensate the losers and still realize a positive residual. This is the accepted position of applied welfare economics. With this argument developed, Randall then asks how does it square with philosophical descriptions of the rationale for and the criteria to judge government intervention in order to influence individual behavior, as well as with the existing practice of such interventions in the United States.[3]

On both of these counts, the discussion is interesting but incomplete. For example, Randall uses Sagoff's critique of benefit-cost analysis as a counterpoint in his development of the rationale for adopting a PPI criterion and, with it, benefit-cost analysis. Without agreeing here with Sagoff, it is nonetheless possible to argue that Sagoff's position must be placed within a broader set of philosophical critiques of benefit-cost (BC) analysis. Clearly, as Randall observes, the use of a benefit-cost test is not an attempt to require that market institutions be used for allocating all resources. Indeed, it is the very absence of markets that motivates much of public-sector involvement for environmental resources. Rather, it is the desire to allocate resources to their highest valued uses that lies behind the use of the BC test. Nonetheless, to define procedures that yield decisions responsive to this goal requires assumptions. And it is with these assumptions that many philosophical arguments legitimately quarrel.

For example, an alternative source of criticism can be found in the work of Alastaire MacIntyre. MacIntyre[1983] uses philosophical critiques of utilitarianism to question the logical antecedants of the BC methodology. He identified five questions that he contended both address incompletely:[4]

1. Utilitarian analysis, in MacIntyre's view, maintains that decisions are based on searching for the best (i.e., highest-satisfaction outcome). Yet, there must, by definition, be some principle to limit the range of choices, otherwise there would be an infinity of possibilities and a corresponding paralysis of choice. This limitation is also, in his view, shared a benefit-cost analyses.

2. There do not exist scales of measurement for comparing many alternative sources of pleasure. MacIntyre observed that:

> It is clear that the pleasure-of-climbing-a-mountain, the pleasure-of-listening-to-Bartok and the pleasure-of-drinking-Guiness stout are three very disputable things. *There is not some one state to production of which the climbing, the listening, and the drinking are merely alternative means*. Nor is there any scale on which they can be weighed against each other. [MacIntyre 1983, 142] (emphasis added)

3. As Randall acknowledged, benefit-cost analysis accepts a Kaldor-Hicks criteria and thereby treats everyone equally. Some philosophers (and economists, notably Sen [1973]) would contend that relief of pain or suffering should always be a more important goal than the promotion of pleasure.
4. How does one define unambiguously the consequences of a given action?
5. What is the time scale relevant to assessing the consequences of a given action?

Benefit-cost analysis is not invalidated by the answers to any of these questions. Detailed answers can be developed for each. Thus, while they do not reverse Randall's overall assessment, the answers serve to identify some of the implicit assumptions of the BC test and with them, areas for further research. Consequently, a few comments will be offered on each.

Consider the first question. It has at least two implications. First, at a general level the BC test does not require an examination of all possibilities. It is not a judgment that the action is best, but simply that is preferred to the status quo. Thus, at one level MacIntyre's argument might be judged irrelevant to BC analysis. At another level, however, considering that the values entering the BC calculations are based on individual choices, it is relevant to the interpretation of these values. That is, the critique of utilitarianism might be important to values derived from the microeconomic description of individual behavior that underlies BC analysis. Conventional models of individual behavior recognize this possibility and limit the choice set. They accomplish the limitation on choices by strategies that often combine a variety of different types of assumptions. A separability restriction implying that individuals consider sets of commodities or sevices as groups in their utility-maximizing decisions is one type of assumption. Such assumptions are based on observing behavior and forming judgments.

Most economists have little difficulty in accepting this approach, given the wide range of empirical evidence supporting the general conclusions of demand theory. Nonetheless, what this question does serve to highlight is the fact that the judgments used to construct these frameworks affect their relevance for applications of different benefit-cost analysis. For example, while one might readily accept an estimate of the loss in consumer surplus (measured as a price change) for damage to a single recreation site, it would not be reasonable to simply scale this value by the number of sites involved in an action that led to the loss of all facilities in a region. In fact, it is these types of problems that lie on the outer boundary of current research in benefit analysis. How do we systematically model the processes through which individuals limit their choice set of decisions involving environmental resources? Is it possible to develop theoretically consistent models of these choices that allow for zero consumption levels of some commodities, and yet describe how this decision might change? How sensitive are the benefit estimates derived from models that ignore these problems by aggregating commodities to avoid the corner solutions to these simplifying assumptions? Each is an important question that indirectly relates to the practical implications of this criticism of utilitarianism. (See Bockstael, Hanemann, and Kling [1985] for discussion of some of these issues.)

MacIntyre's second question strikes at the assumed existence of utility functions. Here again, economists would have little difficulty in maintaining this assumption and, therefore, in conditioning BC analyses on it. Yet, at the same time in many respects some of the most challenging aspects of benefit analyses—the estimation of nonuse values, for example—find their origins in a concern over conventional economic models of the consumption. A sympathetic reading of MacIntyre can find such concerns in his examples. Of course, the nature of the issues involved are different. Benefits research seeks to answer: How do nonuse values relate to the consumption and *use* of resources?

The third question is simply a reflection of the relevance of equity to BC analysis. That is not at variance with the BC literature. The BC test does not, however, seek to respond to equity goals. As Randall observes, our estimates are conditioned upon an existing distribution of income and wealth. While it is possible to gauge the sensitivity of BC analysis to distributional assumptions, this is not the same as responding to an equity objective. Indeed, distributional objectives will be argued later in this paper to be central to understanding the limitations imposed on the role BC analysis plays in the policy making process.

The last two questions should not, contrary to MacIntyre, be viewed as criticisms of BC analysis. Rather, they are part of the structure of any specific analysis. Identification and treatment of direct and indirect effects, as well as the time horizon and discount rate used for analysis are concerns to the implementation of the benefit-cost method. However, their importance will depend on the problem at hand.

Once again, as with any procedure to organize information, BC analysis will require specific assumptions to deal with these questions. The presence of the questions does not invalidate the method, it highlights the importance of knowing the sensitivity of the information presented to how they are answered. Thus, while Randall's summary of the philosophical foundation of benefit-cost analysis is likely to become a standard reference on how the principles of applied welfare economics can be related to theory of government, it should not be regarded as a comprehensive analysis of the practical implications of philosophical criticisms of the benefit-cost methodology. Consequently, the next two sections of this paper attempt to provide a discussion that complements his conceptual overview by identifying some of these practical issues.

The Statutory Role of Benefit-Cost Analysis in Policy

To my knowledge, there are no cases where the results of benefit-cost analyses provide the exclusive information set on which policy decisions are based. Since virtually all of the concerns of noneconomists over the application of BC analysis to policy issues have assumed such exclusivity, their arguments are frequently *irrelevant* to the actual circumstances.[5] While Randall's discussion recognizes this point, it does not develop its implications in sufficient detail.

The factors determining the information used in the decision-making process follow from the legislation establishing the policy mandates; the rule-making process that translates these mandates into operating procedures; and, often, the courts through judicial review of decisions based on these operating procedures.[6] Thus, the most frequent actual role for the BC test is within a framework where multiple factors contribute to the ultimate decisions.

In environmental policy design, distributional considerations have played a large role. Distribution in this case is usually not concerned with interpersonal equity in conventional terms. More often than not, the distributional concerns found in the design of legislation and in its requirements for information focus on the gains and losses arising from a policy in a way that reflects the impacts on the various interest groups involved in the compromises needed to assure its adoption.[7] Thus, distributional objectives are reflected in how policies share the benefits and costs of their outputs. Navarro's [1981] summary of the factors influencing the major provisions to the 1977 Clean Air Act Amendments is a good example.

Taken together, the changes substantially reduced the economic benefits received by the Sunbelt under the original provisions of the Clean Air Act. In some cases, the costs of meeting such objectives can be substantial. Portney [1982], for example, estimated that the jobs in coal mining saved as a result of two coal-related amendments cost as much as $750,000 a year for each job.

Similar restrictions have found their way into the procedures for preparing the information used in regulatory policy. For the "criteria air pollutants," costs cannot be considered. In principle, the standard is to be defined only on the basis of its implications for the health of groups of individuals judged to be sensitive to the pollutant.

In regulating emissions from point sources into the water, concern must be directed to the economic feasibility of any proposed standard for the industry to be subject to the controls. Moreover, regulations in both areas must respond to the Regulatory Flexibility Act of 1981 by assessing the effects of new or modified regulations for small businesses. Many more examples of sources of a multiplicity of objectives could be offered. These are sufficient to make the point that the BC test is one of a set of information that is before policy makers.

Of course, it is also important to recognize that there is not *one* policy maker who is responsible for the decisions. Final decisions on any particular action are the result of a complex interaction of decision makers. White's [1981] account of the process leading to revision to the ozone standard during the Carter administration is a good example of this interaction. Another can be found in the effluent guidelines for the iron and steel industry. The process has involved a couple of decades of decisions, decision makers, lawyers, and judges.

Executive Order 12291 issued by President Reagan in 1981 required that benefit-cost analyses be conducted for all new major regulations, except where the law explicitly prohibits one or more aspects of the analysis in support of the decision process. Randall argues this order is simply an attempt to reduce regulatory activity by placing constraints on the participants in the decision-making process. These constraints could take a number of forms. The one Randall emphasizes would assign a role to benefit-cost analysis. An alternative view might suggest the intent was to increase the cost of a regulation to a point where agencies would not undertake one. Under this view, the findings of the benefit-cost test are then irrelevant to the decisions.

By contrast, a more sympathetic view of the Order would imply that the BC test is imposed precisely because of the multiple objectives resulting from the compromises required for passage of any important legislation. Under this perspective, the imposition of a BC test is not an attempt to have benefit-cost criteria rule over all decisions, but to evaluate systematically the opportunity costs of meeting these other objectives in terms of their efficiency costs. As Brandt [1985] recently argued, this concept of opportunity cost is one of the most influential contributions the economist can make to the process of policy formulation.

Where does this leave us on the statutory role of the BC test? It is unlikely that decision processes will ever resemble pictures offered by those describing the philosophical role of government. Consequently, the criticism that benefit-cost analysis is an inappropriate exclusive basis for public-sector decisions is the wrong issue to address.

What is relevant is whether a benefit-cost test, as part of a set of information, can contribute to improving the decision process—forcing an evaluation of the opportunity costs of other objectives, in terms of their impacts on efficiency. This is, in part, an empirical question. It is not, however, independent of the quality of the analyses undertaken in assembling the information for the BC test. Moreover, there is always the potential for political manipulation. Randall appears optimistic on both issues, though he is cautious in arguing for the protection provided by the incentives that are part of scholarly activity when benefit-cost analyses are treated as internal memoranda. In such cases they are unavailable to outside professionals and the general public, and are often not subjected to a professional review.

As we will discuss in more detail, it is clear that imposition of a BC test alone will not assure that the information is assembled correctly and used appropriately. If a system that recognizes each objective's opportunity cost (i.e., where other objectives are recognized as potentially important to decision making but considered in a common metric) is to work, it is essential that there be internal to the government, but external to the agency or department of government, guidelines and explicit evaluations of the analyses prepared. Without these constraints, the benefit-cost requirement becomes one more procedural detail, contributing to the cost of decisions in the public sector, but not necessarily contributing to the quality of those decisions.

Discretion in Policy Design and the Benefit-Cost Test

Our arguments to this point have considered, at a progressively specialized level, the role for a benefit-cost test in policy. In the previous section, it was argued that a benefit-cost analysis is one of many sets of information used in decision making. This is not where the limits imposed upon benefit-cost analysis by the political process stop. They find their way into the process of doing the analysis itself. It should be noted that the influence I have in mind is again not the often suspected political manipulation of the figures to achieve a particular objective. Rather, it is the intervention into the logical process of performing a benefit-cost analysis that results from statutory requirements. Perhaps the most direct way to distinguish this intervention from political manipulation is with examples.

Under the Clean Air Act, the EPA administrator is charged with the responsibility to propose and, after public review, to promulgate national ambient air quality standards for the criteria pollutants to protect public health with an adequate margin of safety. As we noted earlier, costs are, in principle, not to be considered. Yet, at the same time, the Office of Management and Budget has required that the regulatory review materials for such standards include a benefit-cost analysis. The result is a decision structure that separates the process of defining the standard from the activities associated with performing the benefit-cost analysis.

This has a number of implications. First, it provides an example of how nonutilitarian criteria can influence the definition of the alternative standards that are evaluated within a benefit-cost framework. In the revised particulates standard, for example, the alternative definitions of the standard did not include cases that appeared to be superior from an efficiency perspective.

Second, the separation can introduce unnecessary complexity into the benefit-cost analyses. Again, the particulates standard can be used as an example. The proposed revision to the standard involved changing the units of measurement used to define the earlier standard. The original standard was specified in terms of total suspended particulates, while the revision was in terms of particles of 10 microns or less.[8] The change resulted from health science research suggesting that these may be the greatest source of health effects. However, it imposed an increased level of uncertainty on the estimates of the benefits and the costs of the standard because none of the available information was measured in these terms. All the monitoring information had measures of ambient air quality in terms of the old system of measurement. Thus, some conversion from actual measures to implied ambient concentrations was necessary.[9]

Finally, the definition of the extent of compliance for counties around the United States and the associated estimates of the impacts of a standard can be different for the different groups involved in the development and evaluation of that standard. Those groups defining the standard want to reflect the intent of the law, while those preparing the benefit-cost analysis wish to reflect what is likely to happen. Here again, what is at issue is neither political manipulation nor inadvertent error. it is interpretation of the statutes.

When the law requires protection, the analysis of air standards as part of a risk assessment have often assumed full compliance to gauge whether the effects *at the standard* represent protection of human health. At the same time, it may be recognized that full compliance is unlikely and thus the population experiencing improved air quality would be substantially less than envisioned in the risk analysis.

This is a complicated way of suggesting that the protection implied by the standard may not in fact be realized; and, in terms of information for the decision maker, may not be what is evaluated in the benefit-cost analysis.

The analyses conducted for the criteria air pollutants are not isolated cases. If we consider the effluent guidelines for waterborne residuals, it is clear that definitions of standards are based on an interpretation of *best practical technology* (BPT) or *best available technology* (BAT) by engineers judging what is feasible for firms within an industry. Indeed, the benefit-cost analysis for the iron and steel effluent guidelines was conducted for a predefined set of changes in the effluent streams that was designated as options for the BAT standards. In some cases, there was no change from the current BPT standard. However, in no case was a cost-effectiveness analysis (or indeed a full benefit-cost analysis) conducted for all the feasible standards.[10]

Indeed, careful review of the benefit-cost analyses conducted for any of the environmental regulations would reveal that they reflect the scientific, legal, and practical realities of the decision process.

Given the myriad forces that shape benefit-cost analyses prepared in resource agencies today, especially those associated with environmental policy, it is not surprising that there is a diversity of opinion as to their net contribution to improved decision making. Crandall [1984], for example, argues that a benefit-cost requirement for policies involving air pollution is unlikely to improve the current system. It does not, in his view,

> ... address the other serious flaws in the current air pollution program because these flaws are either legislated or are the product of federal-state inertia in devising sensible approaches to enforcement and setting priorities. [Crandall 1984, 224]

It is a program requiring radical surgery and the process of introducing benefit-cost analysis to remedy these problems is akin to applying a Band-Aid instead of surgery. By contrast, Portney [1984] has also recently acknowledged the weaknesses in the present system, but suggests that even small margins for improvement can imply large efficiency gains, more than sufficient to offset the costs of the activities required to prepare benefit-cost analyses.

While not an optimist by nature, my own view of the prognosis is closer to Portney's assessment than Crandall's. However, it is conditioned upon an important qualifying assumption. A commitment to developing benefit-cost information that can be a part of the decision process *must* require consistency in what is evaluated. It is impossible to use alternative types of information developed with inconsistent assumptions. At present, this is a common occurrence in the benefit-cost analyses prepared under the requirements of EO 12291. To eliminate the practice requires reorganization of the activities associated with developing the benefit-cost analyses, so that the maintained assumptions, measurement practices, definition of standards, time horizon, compliance assumptions, etc. are mutually consistent.

While such requirements appear to be so basic as to seem trivial in a volume focused on the contemporary problems in resource and environmental economics, they actually lie at the heart of converting a BC test from appealing rhetoric to relevant policy analysis.

Valuing Nonmarketed Commodities

The feasibility of implementing the benefit-cost test for most decisions involving environmental resources rests with whether or not it is possible to measure consumer's values for nonmarketed commodities. Randall's answer is clearly in the affirmative, noting (in his concluding statements) that while the estimation of these values can be a speculative exercise— "The critical processes in science and in the diffuse public policy process ensure that few are misled for long, about the precision and validity of these estimates."

Anderson and Bishop (chapter 3) offer a similarly optimistic conclusion, noting that where indirect market methods do not provide a basis for valuation, all available evidence indicates that properly designed contingent valuation (or direct survey) methods can successfully elicit these values.

Unlike many areas of economics, the estimation of consumers' values for changes in their conditions of access to most natural and environmental resources never faces a predictive test. That is, we will *never* know the true values for any nonmarketed commodity. This contrasts with a model of a market (or an economy) that can be used to forecast price or quantity movements (or the time paths for macroeconomic variables) and these forecasts compared with what actually happened.

Valuation exercises never impose the discipline of a forecast test on its participants.[11] Consequently, the critical processes leading to the redirection of research and the associated revisions in the common understandings of the values for nonmarketed commodities are, at best, more indirect and vague in the guidance offered, and, at worst, downright slippery and potentially useless to the policy maker. Judgment plays an extremely important role in what each researcher treats as acceptable for the particular task at hand. Moreover, these judgments are often conditioned by what each analyst perceives will be the profession's willingness to accept his or her estimates of these values.

Recently, we [Smith, Desvousges, and Fisher 1984] undertook reevaluation of a comparative analysis of a travel cost model and a contingent valuation survey for valuing water quality improvements originally reported in Desvousges, Smith, and McGivney [1983]. The process involved revising a varying parameter, travel cost demand model for water-based recreation sites to improve the estimator, so that it more accurately took account of limitations in the measure of site usage.[12] Table 4–1 summarizes the results. The revised model led to large differences in the indirect method's valuation

Table 4–1 A Comparison of Benefit estimates for water quality improvements (1981 dollars)

	Water Quality Change		
Approach	*Loss of Area*	*Boatable to Game Fishing*	*Boatable to Swimming*
Contingent valuation[a]	20.14	11.48	28.00
First-generation generalized travel cost[b]	82.65	7.01	14.71
Second-generation generalized travel cost[c]	1113.46	209.17	463.30
Revised "simple" travel cost[d]	3.53	7.16	28.86
Contingent valuation 50%	10.07–30.21	5.74–17.22	14.00–42.00
Revised travel cost 50%	1.77– 5.30	3.58–10.74	14.43–43.29

[a] These estimates are slightly different from those reported in Cummings et al. 1986. They reflect the different number of observations associated with the two iterative bidding estimates used by these authors in their appraisal of the best estimates, and compute the grand mean taking these differences into account.

[b] These estimates are taken from Desvousges, Smith, and McGivney [1983].

[c] These estimates are derived using the revised generalized travel cost model described in Smith and Desvousges [1985]. The revised comparison is discussed in more detail in Smith, Desvousges, and Fisher [1984].

[d] These estimates are taken from Smith, Desvousges, and Fisher [1984]. They are based on a simple travel cost model estimated using the responses of survey respondents who used the sites along the Monogahela River.

of a water quality change. These differences were so great as to lead to rejection of the plausibility of the model and, in turn, a search for an alternative framework. The results in the table suggest that, with the exception of the valuation of a water-quality-induced loss of a recreation site, the conclusions of a comparison with the contingent valuation estimates were unchanged.

Does this mean that simple travel cost models are remarkably robust or that contingent valuation estimates are closer to the true values of the benefits individuals received from a water quality improvement? I would suggest that it does not. Rather, it highlights the role of judgment in model selection and evaluation. Vernon Smith [1985] recently made a similar point in responding to comments on the role of experimental economics. He observed that an important weakness in the way economists exert judgment was their tendency to be verificationist rather than falsificationist in their approach to the development of economic science.[13] A forecast test disciplines judgment. Without it the critical assessments inherent in the scientific process are exceptionally difficult. Both Randall and Anderson and Bishop give limited attention to the potential importance of this issue to progress in benefit measurement.

Genuine progress in the development of valuation methods requires that more attention be given to procedures for assessing the authenticity of the approaches for benefit estimation. Three research tasks seem well suited to this objective:

1. Contingent valuation with behavioral tests

Survey methods have tended to focus exclusively on attempts to elicit household values for changes in nonmarketed commodities, and an evaluation of the performance of these efforts using comparisons with estimates from indirect market approaches such as the hedonic and travel cost models. Since these comparisons involve two estimates of an unknown "true" valuation it is unreasonable to expect that they will advance our understanding of the factors influencing the performance of either method. The operating conditions of Cummings et al. [1986] probably offer the best overall summary of what can be learned from these comparisons.

What is needed is a model of how individuals answer such questions in a format consistent with conventional microtheory. Such a framework would offer the opportunity for developing testable hypotheses and, with them, provide an indirect basis for judging the consistency of the CV approach to benefit measurement.

2. Laboratory and field experiments

Bishop and Heberlein [1979] provided the first field experiment to compare contingent and real markets for environmental resources that were more easily accommodated within a private market. They, together with their coauthors (see Bishop et al. [1983; 1985]), have continued this important work in understanding the relationship between the performance of actual and contingent markets. Coursey, Schulze, and Hovis [1983] have adapted the laboratory methods of Vernon Smith to evaluate the performance of contingent and actual markets with public goods.

Both lines of research demonstrate the potential for experimental methods for understanding the performance of survey methods for valuing nonmarketed goods. It should be possible to turn these methods to more direct evaluation of other methods for benefit estimation. While it should be acknowledged that experiments can never fully mimic real-world decision processes, they do offer one potentially important source of critical input for evaluating benefit estimation methods.

3. Focus groups

The last approach is probably the most controversial from the perspective of most economists and yet, in many respects, it is the most direct. It involves an effort to communicate with the individuals we wish to model—discussing with them the factors influencing their decisions. Such sessions represent opportunities to understand, albeit in an informal framework, the relationship between our economic models of decision making and the actual decision processes.[14]

All three of these tasks are prospective sources of the critical information necessary to learn and advance the process of estimating values for nonmarketed commodities. However, this advancement will require redirection of the methods away from their present exclusive task of valuation to the testing of hypotheses implied by each of the approaches for estimating consumer values.

Prospects

In the final analysis, the extent to which benefit-cost analysis can be expected to play a constructive role in decision making associated with resource and environmental issues will depend on:

a. the development of guidelines and a coordinated, detailed review (external to the agency) of benefit-cost analyses conducted for the purpose of providing input to policy decisions;
b. the reorganization of the activities associated with defining the set of actions to be evaluated with benefit-cost analysis; and the establishment of its informational needs as an *equal partner* with those for other dimensions of the information set provided to environmental policy-makers; and
c. a conscious recognition of the need to invest in the development of methods and measures for valuing nonmarketed environmental resources.

It is not unusual to call for improvement and further research as a part of the continuing development of benefit-cost analysis as a component to a program to improve the quality of the decision making on aspects of environmental policy (especially from individuals participating in doing that research). However, more than the routine call for improved methods is involved. Without an explicit recognition of the paucity of information as well as a basic understanding of the requirements of the valuation task of benefit-cost analysis, the prospects for a BC test are not especially good.

There has already been a tendency to rely to a great extent on "off the shelf" research findings with involved efforts to adapt them to suit the requirements of a particular benefit-cost analysis. These activities must rely on professional judgment, and often have little basis for disciplining the speculation involved in developing these estimates. They are justified as the best that could be done within the time and resource constraints of each decision. Yet there is little by way of systematic research developed to improve what is available "on the shelf" for the future.

Tasks must be completed and a benefit-cost document prepared. Such procedural responses ultimately limit the prospects for benefit-cost information serving as one important constituent of the decision makers' repertoire.

As both the Randall and the Anderson-Bishop chapters acknowledge, progress in valuation estimation has been great in the past decade and a half. However, without the organizational, procedural, and research commitment that has not been forthcoming, the prognosis for the future must be regarded as highly uncertain.

Notes

[1] A regulatory impact analysis is the document prepared within the EPA describing the proposed standard, its economic impacts, a benefit-cost analysis, an analysis consistent with the Regulatory Flexibility Act of 1981, and a detailed statement of the rationale for the proposed action.

[2] This risk measure is often referred to as comparable to the value of a "statistical life." This value is simply the aggregate of individuals' payments for risk reductions for a group of individuals sufficient to reduce the expected deaths by one. See Viscusi [1984] for a more detailed discussion.

[3] Ann Fisher's comments on this chapter deal specifically with several important aspects of existing practices in relationship to Randall's argument.

[4] A more complete and detailed discussion of his position as well as other philosophical arguments relating to benefit-cost analysis is available in a recent book by Shrader-Freschette [1985], (see especially chapter 2).

[5] A comparison of the discussion in MacIntyre [1983] with that in Zeckhauser [1981] illustrates the substantial differences in perspectives on the process of decision making.

[6] For a discussion of the process in the context of implementing the multiple use and sustained yield legislation, see Krutilla and Haigh [1980]. Huber's recent papers [1983a, 1983b, 1986] on the new-old risk dichotomy also illustrate how the three components of the process can influence the development of policy.

[7] Zeckhauser [1981] has argued that policy makers' attention to the distribution of net benefits is central, in a democratic society, to the adoption decisions for policy. He observed that:

> The political process recoils from the "let the chips fall where they may" nature of traditional efficiency maximization. In particular, it attempts conscientiously to redistribute resources so that cost impositions are reduced, even if this can only be achieved at the expense of substantially greater reduction in benefits.
>
> . . .
>
> This pattern of choice is in sharp contrast with the dictates of benefit-cost analysis which focuses exclusively on efficiency and considers not at all the distribution of chips." [Zeckhauser 1981, 218]

[8] The current and proposed particulate matter standards are given as follows (in micrograms per cubic meter):

Format	*Primary*	*Secondary*
CURRENT STANDARDS		
Annual (geometric) mean TSP concentration	75	—
24-hour TSP concentration	260	150
PROPOSED STANDARDS (range)		
Annual (arithmetic) PM 10 concentration	50–65	—
24-hour PM 10 concentration	150–250	—
Annual (arithmetic) mean TSP concentration		70–90

[9]To develop these conversions, EPA has proposed functions that relate TSP measures to the probability of exceeding a given level of particulate matter measured in terms of particles of 10 microns or less (PM 10). For example, if a probability of zero is assumed for exceeding a 150 μg/m³ 24-hour PM 10 standard is required, the corresponding maximum 24-hour concentration of TSP must not exceed 150 μg/m³. If the probability is increased to 0.05, then the 24-hour TSP concentration can be increased to 215 μg/m³.

[10]See Ferland [1983] for a detailed critique of the regulatory impact analysis.

[11]Bishop and Heberlein's [1979] experiments introducing simulated markets for hunting permits come the closest to this type of test. In their case, however, one is evaluating a hypothetical versus actual institution—the market for permits. It is not a comparison of true and estimated valuations.

[12]The dependent variable was subject to both truncation and censoring. In the original analysis, a diagnostic index was used to gauge the effect of these problems on ordinary least squares estimators and only those sites with the smallest impacts were included in the sample for analysis.

[13]Smith observed that

> ... I think it has become pretty obvious where our professional weaknesses are concentrated. Economists, while spouting the rhetoric of the falsificationist, are in fact verificationist to the core. We all do it. We take a proposition, conjecture, or theory, then search for supportive historical or empirical examples [Smith 1985, 265n.]

[14]See chapter 8 in Smith, Desvousges, and Freeman [1985] for a discussion of the results of using focus groups with a study attempting to estimate individuals' valuations for reductions in the risk of exposure to hazardous wastes.

References

Bishop, Richard C., and Thomas A. Heberlein. 1979. "Measuring values of extra-market goods: Are indirect measures biased?" *American Journal of Agricultural Economics* 61:926–930.

Bishop, Richard C., Thomas A. Heberlein, and Mary J. Kealy. 1983. "Contingent valuation of environmental assets: Comparisons with a simulated market." *Natural Resources Journal* 23:619–633.

Bishop, Richard C., Thomas A. Heberlein, D. W. McCollum, and M. P. Welsh. 1985. "A Validation Experiment for Valuation Techniques." Draft report to the Electric Power Research Institute. Department of Agricultural Economics, University of Wisconsin-Madison.

Bockstael, Nancy E., W. Michael Hanemann, and Catherine L. Kling. 1985. "Modeling Recreational Demand in a Multiple Site Framework." Paper presented at AERE Workshop on Recreation Demand Modeling, Boulder, Colorado, May 17–18.

Brandt, John E. 1985. "Distilling frenzy from academic scribbling: How economics influences politicians." *Journal of Policy Analysis and Management* 4(3):344–353.

Coursey, Donald, William D. Schulze, and John Hovis. 1983. "A Comparison of Alternative Valuation Mechanisms for Non-Market Commodities." Unpublished paper, University of Wyoming.

Crandall, Robert W. 1984. "The political economy of clean air: Practical constraints on White House review." In *Environmental Policy Under Reagan's Executive Order*. Ed. V. Kerry Smith. Chapel Hill: University of North Carolina Press.

Cummings, Ronald G., David S. Brookshire, and William D. Schulze. 1986. *Valuing Public Goods: The Contingent Valuation Method*. Totowa, NJ: Rowman & Allanheld.

Desvousges, William H., V. Kerry Smith, and Metthew P. McGivney. 1983. *A Comparison of Alternative Approaches for Estimating Recreation and Related Benefits of Water Quality Improvements*. Environmental Benefits Analysis Series. Washington, DC: U.S. Environmental Protection Agency.

Ferland, Kathey A. 1983. *Benefit Cost Analysis in Environmental Decision Making: A Case Study of the Implementation of EO 12291 in the Environmental Protection Agency*. Unpublished Masters Essay, Department of City and Regional Planning, University of North Carolina at Chapel Hill.

Graham, John D., and James W. Vaupel. 1981. "Value of life: What difference does it make?" *Risk Analysis* 1(1):89–95.

Huber, Peter. 1983a. "The old-new division in risk regulation." *Virginia Law Review* 69.

Huber, Peter. 1983b. "Exorcists vs. gatekeepers in risk regulation." *Regulation* 7 (November–December):23–32.

Huber, Peter. 1986. "The old-new risk dichotomy and environmental policy: A case study of electric power in the courts." In Advances in Applied Micro-Economics.

Vol. 4. Ed. V. Kerry Smith. Greenwich, CT: JAI Press.

Krutilla, John V., and John A. Haigh. 1980. "Clarifying policy directives: The case of national forest management." *Policy Analysis* (fall).

MacIntyre, Alastair. 1983. "Utilitarianism and cost-benefit analysis: An essay on the relevance of moral philosophy to bureaucratic theory." In *Ethics and the Environment*. Ed. D. Scherer and T. Attig. Englewood Cliffs, NJ: Prentice Hall.

Navarro, Peter. 1981. "Clean Air Act Amendment: Energy, environment, economic and distributional impacts." *Public Policy* 29:121–146.

Portney, Paul R. 1982. "How *not* to create a job." *Regulation* 6 (November–December):35–38.

Portney, Paul R. 1984. "The benefits and costs of regulatory analysis." In *Environmental Policy Under Reagan's Executive Order*. Ed. V. Kerry Smith. Chapel Hill: University of North Carolina Press.

Sagoff, Mark. 1981. "Economic theory and environmental law." *Michigan Law Review* 79:1393–1419.

Sen, A. K. 1973. "Behavior and the concept of preference." *Economica* 40(August):241–259.

Shrader-Freschette, K. S. 1985. *Science Policy, Ethics and Economic Methodology*. Boston: Reidel.

Smith, Vernon L. 1985. "Experimental economics: Comment." *American Economic Review* 75(March):265–272.

Smith, V. Kerry, and William H. Desvousges. 1985. "The generalized travel cost model and water quality benefits: A reconsideration." *Southern Economic Journal* 52(October):371–81.

Smith, V. Kerry, William H. Desvousges, and Ann Fisher. 1984. "A Comparison of Direct and Indirect Methods for Estimating Environmental Benefits." discussion paper #83–W32 (revised), Vanderbilt University.

Smith, V. Kerry, William H. Desvousges, and A. Myrick Freeman, III. 1985. *Valuing Changes in Hazardous Waste Risks: A Contingent Valuation Analysis*, vol. I. Draft Interim Report to U.S. Environmental Protection Agency, Vanderbilt University, February.

Viscusi, W. Kip. 1984. "The valuation of risks to life and health: Guidelines for policy analysis." In *Evaluation of the State of the Art in Benefits Assessment Methods for Public Policy Purposes*. Arthur D. Little, report to National Science Foundation, December.

White, Lawrence J. 1981. *Reforming Regulation: Processes and Problems*. Englewood Cliffs, NJ: Prentice Hall.

Zeckhauser, Richard. 1981. "Preferred policies when there is a concern for probability of adoption." *Journal of Environmental Economics and Management* 8(September):215–237.

INDEX